Langoa

The Tipperary Gentry

Volume 1

William Hayes & Art Kavanagh

2003

i

The Tipperary Gentry

Published by Irish Family Names
C/O Eneclann, Unit 1, The Trinity Enterprise Centre, Pearse St., Dublin 2,
11 Emerald Cottages, Grand Canal St., Dublin 4
and Market Square, Bunclody, Co. Wexford, Ireland.

ISBN   0 9538485 2 3

Coat of Arms by Tomas O'Baoill, Heraldic Artist, The Towers I.D.A.
Centre.

Set in Times New Roman 12 pt.

Authors' Acknowledgements

The Authors are deeply grateful to the following – Gilbey's Wine Importers for the funding which helped finance this project, Mr. Arthur Carden, Senator Martin Mansergh, Miss Mabel Langley of Brittas Castle, Diana Langley of Archerstown, Mr. & Mrs. Ponsonby of Grove, Mr. Anthony Barton of Chateau Langoa, Mr.& Mrs. Nicholas Grubb of Castle Grace, Mr. & Mrs. Louis Grubb, Mr. J. McTiernan, our subscribers, the various authors mentioned whose works have been acknowledged in the book and The National Library for its assistance in making data available.

Subscribers

Mr. Nicholas Grubb
Miss. A.M. Langley
Mr. J.G. Ryan
Mr. M.R. O'Connell
Mrs. J. Ryan
Mr. L. Murphy
Miss O. Mathews
Mr. G. M. Barton
Mr. B. Caldwell
Mrs. R. Richardson

Contents

Preface

What matter that at different times
Our fathers won the sod
What matter if at different shrincs
We pray to the one God
In fortune and in fame we're bound
By links as strong as steel
And neither shall be safe or sound
But in the other's weal
(*Thomas Davis*)

William Smyth writing in *Tipperary History & Society* said of the Cromwellian adventurers and soldiers who got lands in Tipperary 'They came with notions of exploitation and of gaining wealth; they belonged to a growing commercial nation and they were to leave a deep impression on the landscapes and societies into which they intruded....the great phase of their rule was to last only one hundred and fifty years, but within that period they were to direct the transformation of the landscape and social structures of at least half the parishes in Co. Tipperary.'

The gentry were part of what came to be called in the late 18th century, The Ascendancy, a name coined by the editor of the *Dublin Journal*. Membership of this elite was not confined to people of noble birth or inheritors of landed estates. The gentry revitalized itself by recruiting from talented professionals such as John Hely-Hutchinson, a gifted lawyer, or from the ranks of the successful business families such as the Bartons, Grubbs and Scullys of Tipperary.

It is a fact that the vast majority of landlords did their utmost to try to cope with the Famine. They remitted rents, they sold their personal chattels and they gave unstintingly of their time on committees and boards.

There were good and bad landlords but as can be ascertained from the pages of this book, the good, fortunately, well outnumbered the bad. The legacy of beautiful houses and well maintained demesnes has all but been lost. Fortunately enough remain to ensure the continuity of settlement so vital to our understanding of history.

List of Illustrations

Armstrong

The Farneybridge Branch

The Cromwellian soldier, Hulett, whose Christian name does not appear in available documents, must have looked out over the battlements of Farney Castle with some satisfaction. He would have been able to trace the course of the tree-fringed Farney River which went southwards beneath the castle to join the Suir, and the line of the old pilgrim road to Holy Cross Abbey that came westwards over the Rock Hill to cross the stone bridge near the foot of the castle. The battlements presented a fine view of the good country reaching away eastwards towards the Abbey, and of the hill country to the west rising up to the Drombane hills. The castle was now his, together with some 60 acres in its vicinity—his allotment for his role in soldiering in the successful Cromwellian campaign in Ireland. The allotment of castle plus land was named Farneybridge, after the old stone bridge across the little Farney River.

He would have looked down on the five or six old thatched houses which had survived, despite the military campaigns, on the castle lands, and with particular satisfaction on the inn he had built to provide an extra enterprise for his new home. The castle had been damaged, and in 1654 it was recorded that it "wanted repair". But he had attended to those repairs and had done them well.[1]

Whatever plans he had for his future here were shattered sometime in October 1660 by the arrival of the County Sheriff armed with an official letter authorizing him to take possession of the castle in the name of King

---

[1] Civil Survey 1654, County of Tipperary, Vol. 2, p. 118

Charles II, who had recently been restored to the English throne. The king had issued letters patent allowing James Butler, whom he had created Marquis (and later to be Ist Duke) of Ormonde, to regain possession, "without obstruction", of all the lands that had belonged to him and his ancestors, which had been confiscated in the Cromwellian invasion.

When the representatives of the marquis arrived at Farney Castle they found the sheriff in possession, and he handed over to them the key of the castle door. They had much business to do on behalf of Lord Ormonde, so they lost little time in leasing parcels of the castle lands and the inn Hulett had built. The repairs Hulett had done to the castle were noted by them—the castle had been "well repaired", they reported.[2] What became of Hulett, and what compensation he got, if any, is not on record.

The lands between Farney Castle and Holy Cross Abbey was part of the lands belonging to the then dissolved Cistercian monastery. At its dissolution the marquis' ancestor, Black Tom Butler, the 10th Earl, had been granted those lands, and the lands of a number of other religious houses in Tipperary, thus augmenting his already vast estates. These new lands needed to be fortified, and Farney Castle and other stone fortresses such as Golden Castle, were ordered to be built in the 1580s in strategic places along the western boundary facing the hill country which was part of the old Gaelic chiefdoms of the O' Dwyers and the Ryans. Farney Castle also guarded the old river crossing at Farney Bridge.[3]

Shortly after the departure of Hulett from Farney a new tenant arrived to take up possession. This was Captain William Armstrong who founded a family which became one of the new elite families then entering the main stream of life in Tipperary, and which was to be associated with Farneybridge and Holycross up to the 19th century, and nearby Moyaliffe up to the 20th century. William took up a 21 year lease of Farneybridge on 3 November 1660, and by 1666 he was well settled down in the castle and paying six shillings as hearth tax on his three fireplaces.[4]

---

[2] Historical Mss Commission, Ormond New Series, iii, London, 1904, p. 8
[3] Carte, Thomas, Life of the Great Duke of Ormonde, Introduction lxv, 1735-6; Calendar of Ormond Deeds, ed. Curtis, Edmund, Vol. V, No. 342, p. 311, 1937
[4] Pedigrees, Vol XXV, Ms 179, p. 149, Genealogical Office, Dublin; Thomas Laffan, Tipperary's Families, the Hearth Money Records, 1665-6-7, 1911, p. 163

William Armstrong belonged to a militaristic family which had held sway in the Scottish border country around Westmoreland, Cumberland and Northumberland, and which was staunchly royalist. His father, Sir Thomas, had served in Ireland as colonel of the Horse in support of Charles 1 in the course of the Civil War of the 1640s and the Commonwealth rule. Because of his support for Charles II Sir Thomas was twice imprisoned in the Tower of London by Cromwell. After the restoration of Charles II his son William was thus in a favoured position to obtain a grant of land in Ireland under the acts of settlement and explanation, as well as leases of land. Besides securing the lease of Farney Castle and its lands, he obtained a grant of the lands of Bohercarron, Co Limerick in 1666.[5] He married Alice, daughter of Sir Thomas Deane, and was around thirty when he settled in Farney.

Farney Castle (courtesy Mr.& Mrs. Cullen)

William Armstrong was obviously a man on the make. By 1669 he had become a Commissioner for Payroll Tax, and by 1677 he had a lease of sizeable estates in the area, mainly consisting of the former lands of Holy

---

[5] Burke's Irish Family Records, p. 36

Cross Abbey, (including the then partially ruinous buildings of the abbey itself), and the lands of Ballycahill. He died in 1695, and in that year his eldest son, John, who inherited William's possessions, married Juliana, daughter of Robert Carew of Balliboro, Co Wexford.[6]   William's other son, Thomas, became the founder of the Moyaliffe (earlier spelt Mealiffe) branch of the family.

MOYALIFFE, BALLYCAHILL, THURLES, CO. TIPPERARY.

The 2nd Duke of Ormonde, who took over in 1688, was something of a rake, and was adding considerably to the sizeable debts he inherited from his father, so much so that acts of parliament were passed in the 1690s enabling him to raise money by granting leases of his lands for lives renewable for ever, reserving for himself at least two thirds of the rents. On foot of those parliamentary acts, John Armstrong, like many other principal tenants of the time, availed of the opportunity to obtain a lease for lives of the lands bequeathed to him. Besides the yearly rent John was obliged to pay annually "one fatt beef or two fat weathers" to the Manor House and Castle of Kilkenny, and the "best and principal beast" was to likewise paid

---

[6] Hywell Colman, Farney Castle, Typescript Ms, 1970, p. 43

on the occasion of his own death and that of subsequent principal tenants. John was also obliged by the lease to fence in "or distinguish by good marks all the outbounds of the premises and one in every three years at least in the presence of many of the neighbourhood publicly, justly and duly perambulate the same".[7] This reveals that the hedgerow fences around the fields, so familiar today, were as yet not in place. A further act of 1700 gave Ormonde the power to enlarge the leases in perpetuity into fee-farm grants. Following this enactment an agreement was drawn up through which the lands of Farneybridge were sold absolutely to John Armstrong for an advance sum of £335, but he was still obliged to pay an annual fee-farm rent of £80.[8]

This enabled him to establish himself as a landed proprietor for the first time. He exemplified the new landed Protestant gentry then emerging in the wake of the Williamite War, at a time when the Penal Code, enacted at the beginning of the 18th century, was particularly effective in ensuring that the Catholic landowners, then greatly reduced in number, would not be able to build up a power base again.

John died in 1707 and was succeeded by the eldest of his four sons, Colonel William Armstrong, who later became an MP. He was allowed to purchase all the Ormonde rights to the Farney lands in 1754 for a sum of £1974, thereby bringing the Butler connection with Farney Castle to an end.[9] He also purchased the lands of Holycross, around 3,500 acres from the Hamilton family who had purchased them around 1708. Thus in the course of three generations the Armstrongs of Farney Castle rose from tenants to large-scale landowners.

Heaton-Armstrong Line

In 1731 William married Mary, third daughter and co-heiress of Francis Heaton and his wife Elizabeth Curtis of Mount Heaton, near Roscrea. Mary inherited Mount Heaton, and the considerable estates going with it, and she and William lived there, making it their principal residence.

---

[7] National Archives, D23,377, 9th October 1697, No.i. "Duke of Ormond—John Armstrong Esq. Copy Lease".
[8] NA., D.23,378, 4th September 1702.
[9] NA., D.25426; D.23427, no 14, 3rd October 1724; NLI, D5281

The old name of Mount Heaton was Ballyskenagh, a placename still popularly used, although the official name of the townland is still Mount Heaton, named after the Heaton family who lived there for three generations. Mary's father had built the Georgian mansion there, which is now the guesthouse of the Cistercian Abbey of Mount St Joseph.

William and Mary Armstrong founded the Heaton-Armstrong line, and that branch of the family was associated with Mount Heaton until 1818. William was a colonel of the Tipperary Militia and High Sheriff of Tipperary in 1738. He was also an MP. He leased Farney to his younger brother, John, who had been a merchant in Cork. William had only one son, John, born in 1732, who like his father became an MP, representing the borough of Killmallock, and later the borough of Fore. He became a member of the King's Privy Council in 1789. He raised and kept a troop of horse in the King's service, and was twice offered a baronetcy, which he declined. He was about to be created a Peer under the title of Baron Dunamace, but he died in 1791 before the Patent was issued.[10]

John of Mount Heaton was succeeded by his only son, William Henry, born in Toulouse in France in1774, who married Bridget, (Biddy), only daughter and heiress of Col Charles Macdonnell, MP, of New Hall, Co Clare. He was given the title of Lord of the Manor of Roscrea, although he refused the Peerage destined for his father. He voted against the Act of Union of England and Ireland.

Some years before his marriage in 1809, and although living in Mount Heaton, William Henry became was particularly interested in the old village of Holycross which had the well preserved ruins of the abbey at its core. It was his property although still leased to his uncle John's family. He got two sets of plans drawn up for a new town of Holycross, one undated, and the second one dated 1800 and signed by James Miller, "Artizan of Survey and Architecture". These plans are preserved in the National Archives.[11]

---

[10] Burke's Irish Family Records, p. 37
[11] NA, M5256(9) and (2)

Mount St. Joseph Abbey (adjacent to former Mount Heaton House)

Plan one seems to the older version, and shows the "intended roads" into the village, one from the Thurles-Beakstown Road, and the other from the Farney Bridge Road. It also shows the "intended houses" along where the present-day national school and former Catholic church now stand, an inn with stables, and a market place at the south-east corner of the abbey site. The second plan is much more detailed, and ambitious, and shows rows of paired, semi-detached houses, sharing common chimneys. The houses, 120 in all, were to be slated, and each to have a rood (quarter acre) of ground, and intended for tradesmen. The layout of streets included a roughly semi-circular roadway surrounding the old abbey, with houses on the north side of the abbey. Up on the Fair Green, where the first national school was built in the 1830s, was to be the site for a three-storey barracks to accommodate 350 soldiers and their officers. The comment on the map relating to the barracks reads: "do think it as proper a place as any in the kingdom, as to its cheap quarters and handyness to any part of Ireland". A market house is also shown on the Green.

It would appear that William Henry Armstrong was deeply influenced by the new town the Cardens had already created in Templemore, with its wide main street and market house, its other straight streets and lanes, its great military barracks, and its tradesmen's houses, all aimed at development and the introduction of a new Protestant tenantry of craftmen and their families. The tradesmen's houses in Holycoss's new town were to have a length of 22 feet, "as the tradesmen's houses of Templemore". Another revealing comment on the map is, "The whole would form a complete colony of manufactury".

But William Henry's new town of Holycross was not to get beyond the mapping stage. What he did succeed in achieving, however, was building of the very pleasing additions to Farney Castle, which consist of a Tudor styled central block with an octagonal tower on its east side to balance the old 16th century round tower house. It was probably after the design by William Vitruvius Morrison, who was involved in the design of the great castle Langley was building in Brittas, near Thurles. Morrison's name is mentioned in connection with the plans for the new town of Holycross, and the extensions to Farney Castle were in hand around 1800, the time the new town plans were drawn up.

William Henry ended the family's link with Mount Heaton, which he sold in 1817,[12] and he and his wife retired to the Continent. Not intending to return he later sold almost all his estates in Fermanagh, Limerick, Tipperary and England, amounting altogether to about 133,000 acres. In 1834, when living in Lausanne, Switzerland, he granted to Rev Charles William Wall, DD, Senior Fellow of Trinity College, "all that and those manors, towns, lands, tenements, and hereditaments of Holycross and all duties, tolls, customs and advantages thereunto belonging". [13] The lands involved amounted to 1495 acres, and the selling price for the entire property was £18,200. Included was Farney Castle, which from that date became the property of Dr Wall. The Armstrongs (descendants of John)

---

[12] In 1878 Mount Heaton became the property of the Cistercians and was renamed Mount St Joseph. The monks first used the Heaton residence as their monastery before they built their traditional style abbey.
[13] NA, D23402 Armstrong to Wall.

continued to live in Farney as occupiers, and having a leasing arrangement with the new owner of the castle with its fine extension.

William Henry's eldest son, John Heaton-Armstrong, born in Mount Heaton in 1815, retained the title Lord of the Manor of Roscrea, as did his succeesors for two more generations, although they were born on the Continent and lived there. John followed a military career in the Austrian army, but declined the honours of Count of the Austrian Empire and of Imperial Chamberlain. He assumed the additional surname of Heaton by Royal Licence. In later life he became notable as a traveler in South America and Australia, in which latter country he made some valuable discoveries.

The present representatives of this Heaton-Armstrong line live in Aberfoyle, Perth, in Scotland, the current head of the family being Christopher John Heaton-Armstrong, who was born in 1959.

To return to the Farney Armstrong line, the John Armstrong who leased the lands of Farney, as well as the lands of Lisnagrough and Raheen in Holycross parish, from his brother William of Mount Heaton, married Anne, only daughter of Anthony Blunt, Alderman of Kilkenny, in 1740. They had four sons and three daughters. The eldest son, Captain William Armstrong, established a company of Grattan's Volunteers known as the Farney Bridge Cavalry. Its officers were Thomas Pennefather, Ballynira, Thomas Lanigan, Castlefogarty, Simon Hanly, Annfield, and William O'Meara, Booladuff. Captain William was the occupier of Farney Castle when the extensions to it, already described, were carried out. He died in 1827 and was succeeded by his son, yet another William, who was born around 1800. Like his father he became an army captain, and later a major.

Major William continued to live in Farney as occupier, and had only around 156 acres of the former estate for his own use, the Holycross lands having been sold to Rev Charles William Wall. Rev Wall appears to have remained at Trinity, where he was professor of Hebrew, but he did take good interest in his Holycross property, which he showed by getting some important conservation work done on the roofless Abbey church, which helped to ensure its good state of preservation. His Holycross property passed on to his nephew, Rev Garrett Wall, who was the first of the family to come and live in Holycross House in the village, which house is now the residence of the parish priest of the Catholic parish of Holycross-Ballycahill.

Major William Armstrong's death in 1873 marked the end of the Armstrong connection with Farney Castle. Around 1890 the property was purchased by the Molloy family, descendants of a land steward at Castlefogarty, who then had well established business enterprise in Thurles, and the Molloy family had Farney Castle as their residence up to the late 1950s. It is now in the ownership of Cyril Cullen, who lives there with his family, and where he has established a visitor's centre.

The Moyaliffe Branch

The other important branch of the Tipperary Armstrongs became known as the Kemmis-Armstrongs of Moyaliffe. The founder of this branch was, as mentioned earlier, Thomas Armstrong, the younger son of Captain William Armstrong, the first of the Armstorngs to settle in Farney Castle. He acquired the lands of Moyaliffe, (formerly spelt Mealiffe), sometime in the 1690s. Moyaliffe already had much history attached to it, having been established by Geoffrey de Marisco as an Anglo-Norman manor with a sizeable township settlement in the early 13th century. The first fortification erected there was a motte and bailey, and sometime later a stone keep was built on top of the lower motte. The manor also had the status of a parish. In the Irish resurgence of the following century it was regained by local Irish septs of Kilnamanagh, but eventually the Butlers got it back. Before the Cromwellian invasion it was owned by Thomas Butler, and contained 207 plantation acres, which included twenty acres of woodland. Through the Cromwellian settlement it became the property of Bartholomew Fowkes, and it was probably from him that Thomas Armstrong purchased it.

When Thomas came to Moyaliffe he would have found a rather small stone house built fairly close to the foot of the old motte which still had a remnant of its tumbled castle on top. Nearby was the Clodiagh River, called the Kearane River in the Civil Survey of 1654, on which there was an eel weir.[14]   About a quarter of a mile to the north of the old motte was the ruinous parish church and its graveyard.

Thomas and his wife Mary (nee Carew) had fourteen children, seven sons and seven daughters, two of whom, Peter and Juliana, died as infants. The first extension of the small stone house would have been required for such a large family, and this was commenced on a site across the enclosed yard which contained a sunken well. The eldest son William (1704-1768) succeeded after the death of his father in 1751. But he died unmarried and was succeed by his brother, Rev. John Armstrong, MA, (1708-1782), who was educated in Trinity College, and who was vicar and later rector of Tipperary parish. The Moyaliffe line of the Armstrongs were to provide a number of clergy for the Church of Ireland.   John's younger brother, Robert Carew (1709-1790), was ordained and became rector of Shinrone, Co Offaly, and two of John's sons, William and Robert Carew, also became clergymen.

Rev John got some publicity due to an extraordinary service held in St Mary's Church in Tipperary on 6th June 1753. He was the vicar at the time as well as headmaster of the local Erasmus Smith Grammar School on the site of the medieval Augustinian Friary. As he was conducting the divine service that day he was suddenly interrupted by Henry Grady, "a young blade" from Limerick, who with some companions burst into the church to abduct Susannah Grove. Grady swore that he would shoot anyone who stirred in their seat, but the vicar is said to have courageously left his lectern to plead with Grady to desist, but to no avail. The young lady was dragged out of the church and the doors of the church barricaded to prevent pursuit. By coincidence among the congregation that day was the Viceroy of Ireland, Lord Townsend. He was so impressed by the action of the vicar that he promoted Thomas, the vicar's eldest son, who was in the army, to the rank of captain.[15] Some of Rev John's sermons have survived in ms. form among the Moyaliffe Papers.

Rev John's second eldest son, William Carew(Billy), 1752-1839, succeeded to Moyaiffe. As mentioned he was a clergyman too, and he

[14] The Civil Survey 1654, County Tipperary, Vol. 2, p. 105.
[15] Burke's Irish Family Records, p. 661; Denis G. Murnane, The Excel Guide to the Heritage of Tipperary Town, 2002, p. 20

graduated from Trinity College with an MA in 1778. In 1789 he married the Hon Catherine Eleanor Beresford, eldest daughter of Rev William, Ist Baron Decies, Archbishop of Tuam. William's first ecclesiastical appointment was as vicar of Moyaliffe parish, of which he became rector from 1789 to 1797. He later secured the rectorship of Moylough, in the diocese of Tuam, as well as the chancellorship of the diocese of Cashel. It was in his time as proprietor of Moyaliffe that the church was built on the ancient site of Kilvalure, on the opposite side of the Clodiagh River and near Drombane village, to serve as the Protestant parish church of Moyaliffe. He also may have been the proprietor who engaged in the programme of planting the estate with oaks and beeches, including the laying out of a beech walk overlooking the riverbank. Among the oldest trees on the grounds are the sixteen Irish yews in groups of four, decorating the pleasure garden on the west side of the house.

The Chaffpool Branch

The next proprietor of Moyaliffe was John Armstrong, 1791-1846, the eldest son of Rev William Carew. He was educated at Caius College, Cambridge. Two of John's brothers, Marcus Beresford and Alfred Thomas, continued the family's clerical tradition and became clergymen. In 1816 John married Catherine, daughter and heiress of Thomas Somers of Chaffpool, Co Sligo, and thus started the Armstrong-Chaffpool branch of the family. After his marriage to Catherine, distinguished for her beauty and accomplishments, John took up residence in Chaffpool, and set about improving the estate. He built a mansion complete with an extensive range of out-offices, and attended to the landscaping of the surrounds.

He became involved in local politics, becoming a JP and Deputy Lieutenant of County Sligo, and being an ardent Tory acted as agent for the parliamentary election of the Tory candidate in the 1830s. As a landed proprietor and magistrate for both Sligo and Tipperary he was invited in 1845 to give evidence before the Devon Commission. When the Great Famine began to impact heavily in Sligo, John with his reputation as "a most active magistrate and country gentleman" was the unanimous choice as chairman of the Upper Leyny Relief Committee, and later the

Tuppercurry Relief Committee. In late November 1846, while riding from Chaffpool to Tubbercurry to attend a committee meeting, he was caught in a downpour of rain, but insisted on sitting at the meeting in half-dried clothes, and then went home in a jaunting car. He caught a fever as a result and died within days on 2 December. The Sligo Journal, in paying tribute to him, recorded that he "fell a victim of his sense of devotion to the cause of charity."[16] He was survived by his widow and a family of seven sons and two daughters.

Two of his sons, including his eldest son, William, went in for army careers, serving in India. Another son, George (1826-1864) of Chaffpool and Moyaliffe did not marry, and the fifth son, James Wood, (1827-1889), who was a captain in the Royal Navy, succeeded to Chaffpool after his brother George's death. He became a JP, a Grand Juror, and chairman of the Tubbercurry Board of Guardians. He held the office of High Sheriff of Sligo in 1873. He was regarded as a kind and considerate landlord, and after his burial in the family plot in Achonry Cathedral in 1889 the select vestry of Tubbercurry parish church decided to name the chancel of the church "The Armstrong Memorial Chancel".

It was in James Wood's time that the front block of Moyaliffe which provided the pleasing Victorian façade, was built. The plans were drawn up in 1864, the year of George's death. The walled garden containing enclosing about two acres may date from a slightly earlier period.

The last two Armstrong proprietors of Chaffpool were Edward Marcus, James' younger brother, who participated in the Crimean War as Lieutenant in the 55th Regiment, and who died without issue in 1899, and his cousin Marcus Beresford (1861-1923). In 1904 the Armstrong Chaffpool estate, consisting of 4,159 acres, was purchased by the Congested Districts Board for £39,864.

The Ending of the Moyaliffe Connection

These last two proprietors of Chaffpool were also the proprietors of Moyaliffe. Edward Marcus was a JP, and Deputy Lieutenant of Tipperary,

---

[16] John C. McTiernan, Armstrongs of Chaffpool, Typescript Ms.

and served as High Sheriff of the county in 1884. He was responsible for the building of the gate lodges on the estate, and may have been the one who planted the long avenue with its lines of limes. The last mentioned, Marcus Beresford, was the son of William Armstrong of Ballydavid, Co Waterford, who in turn was the son of Rev Marcus Beresford, referred to earlier. He became fully involved in Moyaliffe after the sale of Chaffpool, and in 1905 was appointed High Sheriff of Tipperary. He also followed a military career, and was captain in the 8th Brigade of the Northern Ireland Division of the Royal Artillery. He married Rosalie Cornelia, daughter of Maurice Ceely Maude, Enniskillen, and they had one son, William Maurice, and three daughters, Cornelia Ione Kathleen (1890-1967), Winona Rosalie, and Lisalie Maude born in 1897.

William Maurice, JP, was educated at Eton and Sandhurst, and became a captain in the 10th Royal Hussars. He served in World War 1 on the staff of Major-General Sir Beauvoir de Lisle at Mons, and at the landing and evacuation of Gallipoli in 1916. He was popularly known as Pat among his soldier comrades. He was killed in action in Arras in France on 23 May 1917. He was mentioned in dispatches four times and was awarded the Military Cross. He was buried in Fambourg d'Amiens Cemetery, in Arras. The oak cross made by his comrades and placed on his grave was brought home by his mother and placed on the north wall of the chancel of Kilvalure church, then serving as the parish church of Moyaliffe. All his letters home from the war front were carefully kept at Moyaliffe House, and now form a very important section of the Moyaliffe papers, preserved in the Library of Limerick University. Also brought home was the 'Brodie' helmet he was wearing when killed, showing the entry and exit hole of the 7.92 Mauser round that killed him. Both the oak cross and the helmet are now on display in the War Memorial Section of St Mary's Famine Museum in Thurles.

William Maurice was unmarried. After his father's death in 1923, his sister Winona (1893-1982), popularly called Jess, succeeded to Moyaliffe, and in 1927 she married Captain William Daryl Beresford Kemmis of Ballinacor, Co Wicklow. He was descended from William Kemmis (1777-1864) of Ballinacor and Ballinerin, Crown Solicitor for Dublin and Leinster, and who was married to Ellen, second daughter of Nicholas Southcote Mansergh of Greenane, Tipperary. Like William

Maurice Armstrong, Captain Kemmis was educated in Sandhurst and served in World War 1 with the Inniskilling Dragoons. He retired from the army in 1923. He and Winona had no family and divided their time between Moyaliffe and Ballinacor.

Moyaliffe estate was bought by the Land Commission in the late 1950s and divided mainly among local farmers. Captain Kemmis, who died in 1965, bequeathed Ballincor to his maternal cousin, Major Richard Lomer. Sometime after her husband's death Winona re-purchased Moyaliffe House and about 12 acres of surrounding land, which included the walled garden and a small amount of the yard houses. She lived there until her death in 1982. Some years before that she bequeathed her Moyaliffe property and its contents to a distant relative, Robert George Carew Armstrong, of Natal, South Africa. He was the great-great-grandson of Rev Robert Carew Armstrong, who was born in 1758, and who was the son of Rev John Armstrong, inheritor of Moyaliffe in 1768.

The property was eventually put up for sale by auction in July 1999 and purchased by John Stakelum of Thurles as his family residence. The 300-year link between the Armstrongs and Moyaliffe was finally broken. Sue Armstrong, wife of Graham, son of Robert George of Natal, related to me the significant and emotional moment on 30th September 1999 when she, the last of the family to stay in Moyaliffe House, closed the gate into the property as she left it for the last time. Her closing of the gate symbolically marked the ending of the 300 year Armstrong connection with that ancient and lovely place by the Clodiagh River.

Bagwell

The John Bagwell, who was the scion of the family in the mid 1700s, had so far deviated from his Quaker roots that he bloodied his hands fighting duels. He was known to have fought at least three.[17] He also became the cutting edge of the militant and extreme right wing Protestantism that peaked during that period with the extraordinary trial and execution of Fr. Nicholas Sheehy, Parish Priest of Clogheen.

W.P. Burke in his excellent history of Clonmel states rather quaintly that the history of the Bagwell family previous to 1730 is, like the origin of the Amazon, obscure. We do know that originally the Bagwells were a Quaker merchant family. John of Clonmel had two brothers, William, who was a merchant in Dublin and Phineas. He had one sister, Mrs. Airy. Burke goes on to say that the earlier ancestors, given in Burke's Landed Gentry, are imaginary.

In 1729 John Bagwell,[18] a merchant, of Clonmel, bought 900 acres of the ancestral lands of Lord Dunboyne[19] in Middlethird barony, for under £6,000. This purchase marked the entry of the family into the landed class. In addition to his business activities John Bagwell was a Munster

---

[17] W.P. Burke - History of Clonmel

[18] He was married to a Miss Shaw and he had two sons, John and William. William went on to become an M.P. in 1756.

[19] The Dunboynes were Butlers and close relatives of the Ormondes. In the early decades of the 18th century they had incurred huge debts. In order to alleviate the debts Lord Dunboyne was forced to sell the lands in Middlethird Barony. T. Power in *Land, Politics and Society in 18th century Tipperary.*

correspondent for the Dublin banking firm of La Touche and Kane. At a later stage Bagwell purchased 1500 acres centred on Kilmore near Clonmel, the estate of John Slattery, a Catholic lawyer and agent of Lord Cahir. He also acquired an additional 413 acres so that before the end of the third decade of the century he had a substantial rural estate of 2,730 acres.[20]

A residence was established at Kilmore for the eldest son, John, when he got married in 1736 to a daughter of Hamilton Lowe. John died in 1738 and left two sons. It was his eldest son, John, who attained the notoriety during the Fr. Sheehy affair.

In 1747 in company with the Rialls[21] a banking family, they contrived to have a mayor of Clonmel (Jeremiah Morgan) elected in opposition to the Moore interest. Hitherto the town of Clonmel was almost completely controlled by the Moores. During Morgan's tenure an important set of by-laws was enacted in an attempt by the Bagwells and Rialls to ensure perpetual influence over the corporation and the return of members to Parliament. This led to a victory for William Bagwell in a by-election of 1754, but he died shortly afterwards and the seat went to his opponent Guy Moore. The Bagwells had to wait until 1799 to gain control over the borough when they bought it from Stephen Moore, the second Earl of Mount Cashell.[22]

John Bagwell, MP for Tulsk, was Sheriff of the county in 1763. He was the grandson of John, the Quaker, who founded the Bagwell dynasty. He was associated with the extreme right of Protestantism. Insofar as he was head tenant on the O'Callaghan and Cahir estates he was in the forefront of the confrontations with the Whiteboys. He was involved in the sentencing of two Whiteboys at Borrisoleigh. The two were hanged and six more were publicly whipped through the town on a market day in 1763. He was involved in a Parliamentary enquiry into the causes of disturbances and "the Popish insurrection in Munster" the following year.

This John Bagwell was deeply involved in the case of Fr. Sheehy and his antagonism to priests became evident when he endorsed a grand

---

[20] T. Power in *Land, Politics and Society in 18th century Tipperary.*
[21] John Bagwell's sister, Mary, was married to William Riall
[22] Stephen Moore grandfather of the second Earl was made Viscount Mount Cashell in 1764.

jury statement of 1763, made by the magistrates, linking priests to agrarian crimes. At the time he was High Sheriff of the county.

In 1765, Fr. Sheehy of Clogheen was proclaimed on a charge of treason, with a price of £300 on his head. Prior to that he was presented as an unregistered priest in 1762 and was accused of tendering oaths in 1763. In 1764 he was indicted for intending to 'raise and levy open war and insurrection and rebellion' and for assaulting one John Bridge at Shanbally. At that time he went into hiding with relatives in Limerick. Later he voluntarily surrendered himself in 1765 to Cornelius O'Callaghan[23] on condition he would be tried in Dublin where there might be more impartiality.

He was acquitted of the charge of rebellion in Dublin in 1766 but promptly re arrested and charged with the murder of John Bridge at Shanbally[24] and with plotting to kill Rev. John Hewetson[25], John Bagwell and his son William.[26] Several others were charged also.

It was alleged that the murdered man was a Whiteboy informer who was murdered because he had given information against Fr. Sheehy and his friends.

The prosecution witnesses were said to be most unreliable and the first was described as 'a lady of easy virtue, well known to the common soldiers' who had been denounced as such by Fr. Sheehy. The other two had been members of the Whiteboy movement and were said to have been induced to testify with offers of immunity and rewards.

---

[23] When Fr. Sheehy met Cornelius (whose father and grandfather were Catholics) the latter offered him one hundred guineas and told him to make his way out of the country at once. O'Callaghan knew the feeling of the Tipperary gentlemen and that going to Dublin would not protect him from their vengeance, but he declined. – W.P. Burke *Clonmel*

[24] According to some sources John Bridge, a kind of vagabond or harmless individual had been informing on the Whiteboys. He was given a beating on the day of the assault. According to witnesses Fr. Sheehy was not in the vicinity at all. At some time during the next year Bridge became a missing person, presumed murdered.

[25] Hewetson, from Kilkenny was such an avid prosecutor of Whiteboys that he became known as Whiteboy Hewetson.

[26] There was hostility between the Sheehys and the Bagwells. Edmund Sheehy, a young man in his thirties in 1765 was a successful middleman and he had outbid the Bagwells for an outfarm at Clogheen. Sheehy, described as 'minor Catholic gentry' had an income of about £400 per annum.

In addition, on the day of the trial, the streets outside were patrolled by a party of horse, led by Thomas Maude of Dundrum, who was said to have 'menaced Sheehy's friends and encouraged his enemies'. Fr. Sheehy's defence witnesses were discredited and one of them, Robert Keating of Knockagh was himself arrested on suspicion of being involved in the 'battle of Newmarket'.[27]

This led to further accusations against leading Catholics in the county and several were arraigned and some charged with conspiracy.[28] Three leading Catholics were found guilty of treason on trumped up charges. They were Edmund Sheehy, James Buxton (said to be Fr. Sheehy's second in command) and James Farrell. They were found guilty and executed in Clogheen in May 1766.

Fr. Sheehy and his co-defendant Edward Meehan were found guilty and sentenced to death. They were executed on the 15th. March 1766. Fr. Sheehy was buried in Shanrahan and his grave became a place of pilgrimage where many claimed to have been cured of diseases and other ailments.

Consequent to the executions houses on Bagwell's estate at Shanbally were attacked in 1765 and threats were made on the lives of Bagwell and Maude. Fr. Sheehy's executioner was stoned to death in Kilkenny.

John Bagwell received approbation from the Grand Jury of Co. Dublin for his public service in the matter, along with Thomas Maude and others. Outside the county the affair received much attention and as a result of the 'purge' militant Protestantism was discredited.[29]

---

[27] This referred to a confrontation between Whiteboys and the military in Newmarket, Co. Kilkenny in 1764. Three hundred people attacked a party of Lord Drogheda's Light Dragoons as they escorted nine Whiteboys through the Walsh Mountains from Carrick to Kilkenny jail. Several people were either killed or injured. – Bric in *Tipperary History & Society*

[28] The conspiracy theory included practically all the leading Catholics of the county, including the Bishop, who were said to be preparing for a French invasion.

[29] Lord Charlemont when appraised of the affair reacted by declaring 'The furious and bigoted zeal with which some Protestants were activated was shocking to humanity and a disgrace to our mild religion'- The celebrated Edmund Burke was equally upset and castigated the self-interest of the gentry who promoted the violence and expressed his

In the election of 1768 both Bagwell and Maude were defeated by the pro Catholic or liberal Francis Mathew and Henry Prittie.

The murder of Ambrose Power[30] in 1775 was not premeditated but the assault on his house was an affair of revenge. It was during the attack that Power was killed. That murder sent shock waves through the Tipperary gentry as it was accompanied by threats 'to involve Mr. Bagwell and other Gentlemen of high Character in the same fate.' The following year, 1776, John Bagwell and his family were besieged in their home at Kilmore.

The turmoil in his life carried through into his financial affairs as he had incurred debts totalling almost £20,000 by 1778. In order to part satisfy his banker, Riall of Clonmel, he had to sell his Dunboyne property to Riall for £12,000.[31]

Following the bankruptcy of Stephen Moore in 1781, Bagwell acquired the substantial property of Marlfield. The mansion at Marlfield was located on the river Suir 'in front with the Waterford Mountains and the Galtees to the west.'[32] John Bagwell did not enjoy his Marlfield property for long as he died in 1785.

In advance of the election of 1783 a body known as 'The Constitutional Associating Freeholders' was formed in Clonmel to promote parliamentary reform. Their main aims were to reduce the influence of the crown on parliament, to make representatives more responsive to the views of their constituents and to make voting more equitable by a reduction in the influence of the great interests. The main Tipperary promoters of the association were Edward Moore, Sir William Barker, John Bagwell, Robert Nicholson, John Bloomfield, John Congreve, Richard Biggs and Samuel Jacob.

Those conspicuous by their absence were people who controlled 'pocket boroughs'. These included Cornelius O'Callaghan, Henry Prittie, Thomas Barton, the Moores of Clonmel, Peter Holmes and the

---

incredulity at the charges advanced by them. - T. Power in *Land, Politics and Society in 18th century Tipperary*

[30] He was a magistrate and a landlord. His brother Richard, a Baron, had heard some Whiteboy trials in Clonmel. Ambrose had arrested a Wm. Mackey, a Whiteboy from Fethard.

[31] T. Power Land *History & Society in 18th century Tipperary*

[32] E. Wakefield – *An Account of Ireland* -

Pennefathers of Cashel. Yet surprisingly enough, when matters of reform were debated in the Parliament, in the form of the Volunteer Bill,[33] Prittie and Toler, the standing M.P.s, voted with the minority seeking reform.

Francis James Mathew, the eldest son of Lord Llandaff was elected as an M.P. for the county in 1790. However on petition the seat went to John Bagwell, who had been sponsored by Henry Prittie who did not stand. The other M.P. who topped the poll was Daniel Toler.

Marlfield House 2003
(Photo courtesy Mr. English)

In the last decade of the 18th century there was a nation-wide movement, in the form of the Catholic Committee, in which Tipperary played a significant role. There were representatives from Carrick, Clonmel, Cashel, Nenagh and Thurles on the county committee. The

---

[33] The Bill was defeated by a large majority.

county delegates were Laurence Smith, a merchant from Carrick, James Scully of Kilfeacle and John Lalor of Long Orchard.

In direct response to this and only a day after the delegates were selected the Protestant diaspora of the county held a meeting of gentry, freeholders and clergy which was very well attended. The meeting formulated an address to the two county M.P.s, John Bagwell and Daniel Toler, instructing them to 'vigorously oppose all attempts at innovation or alteration in Church and State' and to support the constitution.

Interestingly when the matter of Catholic Relief was being debated in the parliament John Bagwell the M.P. spoke in favour of the measures. A major Catholic Relief Act was passed in 1793, which gave very many concessions to the Catholics. The passage of the Act was marked by celebrations in Tipperary and by expressions of thanks from local delegates and towns.

From the Bagwell point of view this move towards advancing the cause of Catholic Relief was a dramatic shift in family policy and constituted a total reversal of the political and bigoted thinking of John, of Fr. Sheehy infamy, who had died in 1785.

On the recommendation of John Bagwell of Kilmore, the sheriff in 1793, James Scully was chosen as a Justice of the Peace, the first Catholic ever in the county since the start of the century. He was also made a magistrate

Further concessions for Catholics were sought with a major drive being made in 1795. Grattan's Bill to give complete Emancipation to Catholics was defeated in Parliament but the delegates from Tipperary who voted in favour of the Bill were John Bagwell, John and Francis Hely-Hutchinson, Thomas Barton and Sir Thomas Osborne.

In 1796, Francis Mathew, who had lost his seat, on petition, to John Bagwell, was elected M.P. without opposition when Daniel Toler died in that year. In the election of the following year John Bagwell and Mathew were returned unopposed.

William Bagwell was appointed to the prestigious post of colonel of the new county militia in 1793, much to the chagrin of the Mathew family who sought the post.

The Bagwells wavered during the debate about the Act of Union. Richard Bagwell,[34] M.P. for Cashel from 1799-1801, spoke in favour of the Union in January 1800 but within a short time John Bagwell had been convinced to oppose it and he persuaded his two sons to take the same line.

In the general election of 1802 the two sitting members, John Bagwell and Francis Mathew were returned unopposed.

However when the first Lord Llandaff died in 1806, Francis Mathew was elevated to the peerage and a vacancy arose. There was a general election also held in the same year. Due to clerical manipulation the Catholic vote secured the election of Montague Mathew and Francis A. Prittie. Under the circumstances John Bagwell did not stand.

The fact that John Bagwell had at first espoused the Catholic cause in 1792 improved his chances in the polls dramatically but following his decision to oppose the Union (which held out the prospect of further concessions to Catholics) his popularity declined.

After 1800 when they bought the borough of Clonmel from Lord Mount Cashell the Bagwells became the major political family of the area as they controlled the pocket borough with one representative to go to Westminster.

John Bagwell, who was married to Mary Hare, the eldest daughter of the 1st Earl of Listowel, died in 1816 and left two sons and four daughters. His daughters were Margaret, Jane, Catherine and Mary who married respectively, John Keily of Strancally Castle, Lt. Gen. Sir Eyre Coote, John Croker J.P., of Co. Limerick and Henry Grace Langley of Brittas, Co. Tipperary. His second son was Very Rev. Richard, Dean of Clogher. His descendants are too numerous to detail here. The eldest son, William, was Muster Master General for Ireland.

Colonel William Bagwell represented Clonmel for most of the early decades of the 19th century. He died, unmarried, in 1825 and was succeeded by his nephew John Bagwell.

---

[34] Richard Bagwell, a second cousin of John of Marlfield was elected an M.P. for Cashel in 1799. Cashel was a pocket borough controlled by the Pennefathers and the sale of the seat to Richard Bagwell was an exception. Again in 1809 they sold the seat to Sir Robert Peel who later became the British P.M.

After the 1832 Reform Act, which extended the franchise, the Bagwell hold on Clonmel was broken. They were replaced by distinguished Dublin barristers, such as Nicholas Ball and D.R. Pigot. In 1847 the representative for Clonmel was the Hon. J.C. Lawless the youngest son of Lord Cloncurry of Lyons House, Co. Kildare.

However after nearly a quarter of a century had passed the Bagwells returned to power in the person of John Bagwell, a grandson of the duelist, but a liberal like his father. He represented Clonmel, unchallenged, from 1857 until 1874. John was educated at Winchester and he married the Hon. Frances Eliza Prittie, sister of the 3rd Baron Dunalley.

In the prelude to the election of 1874, John Bagwell's popularity waned. He would not support Home Rule or the demand for denominational education, which was part of the Home Rule policy. He was opposed by A.J. Moore,[35] a scion of that illustrious Clonmel family and lost the election to Moore by a large margin. He died in 1883.

In the 1880s Mrs. Richard Bagwell of Marlfield, like others of the gentry ladies, organised home industries as a means of improving the conditions of the country people. Her husband, Richard, was a noted historian who wrote several books on Irish history. He went to school at Harrow and Oxford and became a distinguished barrister. The books he wrote include *Ireland under the Tudors* and *Ireland under the Stuarts*.

Sometime in the nineties Marlfield was burned. It contained among many other items of great value, a priceless leather-bound library. None of the books were saved. The house was rebuilt by Richard Bagwell. Richard died in 1918. His only son John, who was the Manager of the Great Northern Railway, also had a house on the Hill of Howth. John was a Senator of the Irish Free State. Like his father John was educated at Harrow and Oxford.

Lord and Lady Donoughmore hosted the Annual Flower Show and Fete at Knocklofty and to mark the occasion they always held a house party as did their neighbours, the Bagwells of Marlfield and the Duchess of St. Albans.

---

[35] Moore was supported by the clergy and was created a papal count in 1879. He was also helped by the fact that the secret ballot was used for the first time, in Clonmel, in this election. Comerford in *Tipperary History & Society*

The Fete at Marlfield (courtesy Irish Architectural Archive)

On the Tuesday of Easter week, 1916, Mrs. Bagwell was shot in Harcourt Street in Dublin.

It would appear that Lord and Lady Donoughmore who had spent Easter at Knocklofty were travelling back to Dublin on Easter Monday, with the intention of crossing over to England, when the train was stopped at Thurles and they were informed that it would go no farther as there was a rebellion in Dublin. They decided to try to get to Rosslare but no train arrived to take them south. Instead they went to Clonmel and on to

Marlfield where the Bagwells gave them lodgings for the night. It would seem that the Bagwells decided to travel back with the Donoughmores, to the home they owned on the Hill of Howth.

They were driving by car and as they came down Harcourt Street they were stopped and informed that Stephen's Green was in rebel hands. They turned around and as they went back up Harcourt Street they heard rifle fire. A bullet came through the hood of the car, went through Mrs. Bagwell's shoulder, through the upper part of her husband's arm and through Lord Donoughmore's great coat, giving him a flesh wound, and out through the windscreen. They were driven to the home of Sir Frederick Shaw at Bushy Park in Terenure and were treated for their wounds by a Dr. Albert Crolly.

Lord and Lady Donoughmore left the next day and went back to Knocklofty, hoping to be able to get to England via Rosslare. The Bagwell's stayed on a couple of days in the Shaw's house and the rector of Howth walked from there to Terenure to visit them.[36] The Bagwells took ship to London on the Wednesday of the following week.

In January 1923 the Civil War was in full swing and the threat to burn Senators' houses was put into practice. One of the first to suffer was Marlfield. As if that were not enough John Bagwell was kidnapped three week later, though he did manage to escape within a couple of days.

John, the Senator, who died in 1948, had two sons, Richard[37], who died unmarried, and William, and one daughter Lilla Cecily. William joined the Royal Navy and retired injured as a Lieutenant Commander. He later served in World War II and was again invalided home. He married a widow, Evelyn Watson, and they had one son Hugh William and one daughter Pamela. Hugh William, an old boy of Harrow, is now living in New Zealand, is married and has five daughters. Pamela also married and had two children, Alexander and Carolyn Bush of Somerset.

---

[36] He reported that Sackville Street was in a shambles and all the shops were being looted.

[37] Richard, who was educated at Harrow and Oxford, held the post of Assistant Commercial Manager of the Midland Region Railways.

Miss Frances Bagwell[38] of Jamesbrook in County Cork once said to her neighbour, Mrs. Bell of Fota, who was visiting her at Jamesbrook, 'we will now have luncheon' and proceeded to cook potatoes over the drawing room fire. [39]

---

[38] She was the 2nd daughter of William Bagwell of Eastgrove, Co. Cork. William was the 2nd son of John Bagwell (son of Very Rev. Richard, Dean of Clogher) who inherited Marlfield when his uncle William died unmarried in 1825.

[39] *Twilight of the Ascendancy* – Bence Jones.

Barton

Thomas Barton, originally from Fermanagh, invested some of the profits amassed through the wine trade in Bordeaux in the purchase of the estate of Grove near Fethard in 1751.[40]

This is what the historians at Barton & Guestier had to say about Thomas Barton and the start of the wine business: 'In 1725, Thomas Barton of Curraghmore, Fermanagh, Ireland established his wine négociant business in Bordeaux.[41] Canny, charming and with tremendous business savvy, Thomas quickly earned the respect of French growers. Spotting the foreign thirst for French wines, Barton exported 2,700 barrels of wine in 1728. His was considered to be the premier export business by 1745 and by 1785 Barton's company was shipping 125,000 barrels of wine abroad annually. Nicknamed "French Tom", Barton soon realized two important keys to the enduring success of the company. He understood that business growth relied on the goodwill of an extensive network of growers and that

---

[40] The Grove estate was originally part of the Everard estate. The Everards were Catholics and Sir John was outlawed in 1691 and his estates confiscated. He was restored to his lands in 1702 on payment of a £2,000 fine with the proviso that his son, Redmond, convert to Protestantism. He did that but was elected M.P. for Fethard in the Catholic interest in 1713. During the next three decades his debts grew enormously and in order to control these Everard had to dispose of much of his lands. When he and Lady Everard died in 1742 what was left of the estates passed to his cousin James Long, a Catholic, who had to convert in order to inherit. In order to clear the Everard's debt, Long had to sell the Grove estate to Barton. – T. Power in *Land, Politics & Society in 18th century Tipperary.*

[41] He was thirty-three years old at the time. He went to France in 1722 and worked with his uncles Thomas and William Dickson who had considerable trade with France.

by purchasing his own vineyards to augment fruit from his suppliers, he could ensure quality and consistency.'[42]

He is said to have paid £30,000 for the Grove estate and he also purchased lands in Fermanagh and Leitrim.[43] In addition to the Grove estate in Fethard he also bought houses and lands in the area from James Butcher.[44]

Grove 2003 (Courtesy Mr. & Mrs. H. Ponsonby)

---

[42] There is an error here, as according to the family records Thomas never owned any land in France. A French law known as ' Le Droit d'Aubaine' stated that land in France owned by any foreigner would pass to the French Crown after his death. Though he applied for French citizenship he never received it.

[43] Tony Newport *Fethard & Killusty Newsletter*

[44] Thomas himself spent very little time in Ireland, if any, and lived in a rented accommodation, Château Le Boscq in Saint - Estèphe

Thomas had married his cousin and they had only one son, William. William was the first of the family to live at Grove. Thomas did not leave his lands to William.[45] He left his estates in Tipperary to William's son, Tom, in 1780 when he died.[46] William was given a right of residence there and use of the estate for his lifetime. William was married to Grace Massey a sister of Sir Hugh Dillon Massey. William died in 1792, and Thomas Barton, his eldest son became the sole owner and resident.

Thomas Barton Snr.

---

[45] There was serious acrimony between Thomas and William.

[46] According to Power the purchase of the Grove estate was motivated by Thomas Barton's concern to provide for or compensate his son William on his marriage and for other reasons. T. Power in *Land, Politics & Society in 18th century Tipperary.*

William had five other sons and three daughters. The daughters were Grace, Elizabeth and Margaret who married respectively John Palliser of Derryluskan, Lt. Gen. Sir Augustine Fitzgerald of Newmarket-on-Fergus and the 3rd. Baron Massy.

French Hugh Barton (courtesy Anthony Barton)

The most interesting of the five sons was Hugh Barton or 'French Hugh' as he was called. Hugh inherited the Bordeaux wine business and during the course of his long career invested his money in further properties, notably Straffan, in Co. Kildare, Cootehall, Co. Roscommon, and property in the parish of St. Julien Médoc near Bordeaux.

The Barton & Guestier historians continue the legendary tale of how the company was born: 'As Thomas was passing the reins of the business over to his son William and grandson Hugh, a young Frenchman named Daniel Guestier was making a name for himself by providing supplies to the American rebels during the war of independence. In a series of fast ships developed to run the British blockade, it was Guestier who provided Thomas Jefferson with the Bordeaux wines he loved. In 1787, Jefferson, a discerning collector, developed a list of "first quality growths". He showed this list to the two men whose opinion he valued - Hugh Barton and Daniel Guestier. In 1885 this list was confirmed in the famous 1855 "classification".

When the French Revolution threatened the business interests of his friend Hugh, Guestier ran Barton's wine company during Hugh's forced wartime banishment to Ireland. On a handshake deal with no written agreement, for seven years Daniel Guestier handled Barton's business affairs. In 1802, reunited in Bordeaux, the two friends joined forces and the company became Barton & Guestier.'

Hugh married a Bordeaux lady, Anna Weld Johnston, a naturalized Frenchwoman of Scotch origin. This was to prove vital when he was imprisoned as an alien in 1793-4, as by her efforts he made good his escape to Ireland.[47] Hugh's descendants remained at Straffan and were practically all involved with the Bordeaux Wine trade and Army careers until the early decades of the 20th century. One of his sons, Thomas Johnston Barton, became head of the Glendalough Bartons, a very important family, who were married into such families as the Childers, from whom descended President Erskine Childers.

---

[47] Hugh must have spent some considerable time in Tipperary also, as he was elected Sovereign of Fethard in 1799.

Hugh's younger brothers went into the Army with the exception of the youngest, Dunbar, a High Sheriff, who married an heiress to the Rochestown estate, Elizabeth the daughter of Samuel Riall.

One of Dunbar's grandsons became a very eminent person, Rt. Hon. Sir Dunbar Plunket, Solicitor General for Ireland 1897-1900, High Court Judge 1900-1904, Judge in Chancery 1904-18, Senator of the National University of Ireland and a Trustee of the National Library of Ireland in 1920.

Thomas, who inherited Grove from his grandfather, was married to Mary Ponsonby. They had six children, three sons and three daughters. The eldest son was called William after Sir William Barker. She called her second son Chambre Brabazon after her brother.

Tom, a member of the Whig Club formed by Grattan and Charlemont, was elected M.P. for Fethard and was sovereign of the town on three occasions in 1788, 1792 and 1813.

He founded the Grove Hounds, a very famous hunting coterie, and Mary was an avid participant being a fine horsewoman.

During the bad period of agrarian unrest in the mid 1770s the gentry of Clonmel resolved on making a greater effort to combat the Whiteboys. Rewards were offered to anyone who could inform of Whiteboy meetings or the hiding place of Whiteboy arms. Protection from prosecution and secrecy were promised to anyone who would inform. As the level of violence increased in late 1774 and 1775 there were calls for greater resolution. Candidates intending to stand in the forthcoming general election were told pointedly to be in the forefront of such efforts. Strong action did not come until August 1775 when the gentry in Clonmel resolved on greater effort. Committees were to be established in each barony to receive subscriptions for a central fund out of which payments of £50 were to be made to anyone who would inform on Whiteboy meetings in advance, and a payment of £20 was offered for information on the location of stolen firearms. A promise of protection and a pardon were offered to those who would inform on their colleagues, and in all cases an assurance was given that the names of the informers would be kept secret.

William Barton Junior, (Thomas's son), Matthew Jacob and Ambrose Power (who was murdered in 1775) were very much to the fore in attempting to track down the offenders but despite some success the level of violence was not depleted to any extent.[48] Thomas himself, an M.P. for Fethard in 1785 and a supporter for reform, was Sheriff of the county

Phineas Riall the Clonmel merchant banker and Edward Collins were given the management of the Barton estate in the 1780s.[49]

The Bartons found it difficult initially to achieve any solid influence in the borough. The final agreement on the division of the corporation and the borough representation came only in 1787. By it an equal division was agreed on whereby the nomination of one of the M.P.s was to lie with O'Callaghan, the other with Barton. To complement this it was proposed to reduce the number of freemen so that the influence of both parties could be exercised more effectively. Thus the 900 freemen of 1783 had by 1790 been reduced to 300, and by the 1830s to a nominal 13 or 14. This pattern of a reduction in the number of freemen, once a dominant interest had become established, accords with that at Cashel and Clonmel.

A Volunteer Bill in the House of Commons in favour of parliamentary reform was defeated but three Tipperary men voted for the bill. They were Prittie, Toler and Thomas Barton. As the passing of the bill would have meant the end of the boroughs it was opposed by O'Callaghan of Fethard, Moore of Clonmel and Pennefather of Cashel.

Further concessions for Catholics were sought with a major drive being made in 1795. Grattan's Bill to give complete Emancipation to Catholics was defeated in Parliament but the delegates from Tipperary who voted in favour of the Bill were John Bagwell, John and Francis Hely-Hutchinson, Thomas Barton and Sir Thomas Osborne.[50]

Thomas of Grove, as already mentioned, had three sons and three daughters. The daughters Mary, Grace and Catherine married respectively George Fitzgerald, Lt. Col. Kingsmill Pennefather and Edmund Staples of Dunmore, Co. Laois.

His three sons were William, the eldest, Chambre Brabazon, a Lieutenant in the Army who fought at Waterloo, and Charles Robert, a Major in the Light Dragoons.

---

[48] T. Power in *Land, Politics & Society in 18th century Tipperary*
[49] Ibid.
[50] *Tipperary History & Society*

William, who inherited Grove on the death of his father in 1820, married Catherine Perry of Woodrooff, Clonmel, in 1815. He was a Deputy Lieutenant, a Justice of the Peace and High Sheriff in 1825. He was Sovereign on six different occasions between 1816 and 1830. It was William who gave the site for the present Catholic parish church and erected the public pump[51] on the square, which was in use up to the 1930s. During his period of occupancy Grove House was rebuilt under the directions of the famous architect William Tinsley. The Tipperary Foxhounds, still very much in existence, was founded by William Barton, an excellent horseman. He had three sons and five daughters.

Four of the five daughters married. They were Deborah, Mary Frances, Catherine Grace and Anne Margaret, who married respectively, John Wade of Clonebraney, Co. Meath, Charles Shaw of Bushy Park, Dublin, Lt. Col. Sir Robert Shaw of Bushy Park and George Gough of Rathronan, Co. Tipperary. The unmarried daughter was Emily Martha who seems to have died in infancy.

His second son Samuel Henry succeeded to Grove on the death of his eldest brother Thomas Barker J.P., of Grove, a bachelor, who died in 1871.

Samuel Henry who was educated at Harrow and Trinity College, Dublin, married an heiress, Mary Frobisher of Cheltenham, and they had two sons, the younger of whom succeeded to Grove on the death of his father in 1891. The eldest son, William Henry Hugh Barton died unmarried in New Zealand. It fell to the lot of Samuel Henry to supervise the sale of the Grove lands to the tenants following the various Land Acts at the turn of the century.

Samuel Henry's second son was Charles Robert, a career Army Officer. While Charles Robert remained in the Army he rented Grove to the famous Master of the Tipperary Foxhounds, Mr. Richard Burke M.F.H. who stayed there in residence for twenty years.

Captain Charles Robert, who had served in the Boer War and in World War I, retired from the Army after the War and took up residence at

---

[51] The pump featured in the rallying cry of the Fethard football supporters when they shouted 'come on the two streets and a pump'. Tony Newport Fethard & *Killusty Newsletter*

Grove. He was married to Ethel Cobden of Raheen, Clonmel but they had no family and she died in 1935. He held the posts of Deputy Lieutenant and J.P. during the latter period of British Rule in Ireland. He continued living at Grove with his brother-in-law, Colonel Cobden, who predeceased him. When the Captain died in 1955 Grove passed to the Ponsonbys of Kilcooley.

Before he died Captain Barton sold the ground rents of Fethard to the people of Fethard, many of whom were descendants of the tenants of previous centuries. He and his wife were buried in the family vault at Holy Trinity Church.

Unlike many of the estates, Grove was open to the people of Fethard to enjoy by walking in the Deerpark where there were deer to be seen right up to the end of the 19th century.

While the death of Captain Charles Robert signalled the end of the direct line of the Bartons of Grove there are very many collateral descendants alive today.

As already noted William who was settled at Grove by his father in 1751 had six sons.[52] We have sketched the direct line through Thomas of Grove down to the death of Captain Charles Robert in 1955.

The second son was William of Clonelly, Co. Fermanagh who married Anne Isabella Folliott Warren of Lodge, Co. Kilkenny. He died in 1835 leaving two sons, Folliott Warren and Edward George, who both died unmarried.

The third son was Charles, a career Army Officer who attained the rank of Lt. General in the 2nd Life Guards. He was married to Susannah Weld Johnston, a sister of French Hugh's wife. He had five sons and two daughters.[53] One of his sons, Robert, went to Sydney, Australia, married and had a family but there are no details of this family in Burke's *Irish Family Records*. His eldest son, Hugh William, also a career Army Officer attained the same rank as his father. He inherited the Fermanagh lands of

---

[52] William himself died in 1793. He was under house arrest at the time, in his Château, as he was too ill to be imprisoned with the other British residents of Bordeaux who were all rounded up, because of the outbreak of the war with England.

[53] They were Susannah who married Rev. John Stirling and Anna Eleanor who married Rev. Frederick Denison Maurice, a Professor of English Literature at King's College. Both women had families.

his uncle William. He was married to Mary Johnston of Kinlough House, Co. Leitrim and they had seven sons and two daughters.[54]

The eldest of the seven sons was Charles Robert (b. 1832) and he was settled on the family lands of The Waterfoot, in Fermanagh. He was a Deputy Lieutenant, High Sheriff and a J.P. He was also a Captain in the Fermanagh Militia. His wife was Henrietta Richardson from Co. Fermanagh and they had four sons and six daughters.[55] His eldest son was Lt. Col. William Hugh Barton, of the The Waterfoot, Fermanagh, who fought in World War One. His son John was killed in World War II in North Africa.[56] The family of the second son, Henry Charles is represented today by descendants in the female line notably Hugo Pinch, who has two children, Miles Hugo (b.1972) and Sarah Louise (b. 1970), and Jeremy Grahame, now living in Africa. The third son of Charles Robert was Charles Nathaniel and he is represented today by his grandchildren Charles Robert, Richard Hugh, Bridget Marion, Thomas Adams, Hugh Geoffrey and Phillipa Mary, most of whom were born in the latter half of the 20th century and some of whom have children of their own. Charles Robert's youngest son was Bertram, a career Army Officer who fought in World War One, and served in World War II in Malaya. He is survived by his daughter Ruth Anne (b. 1959)

The second son of the seven was James, an Army Officer (d. 1919) who married Mary the daughter of Sir William Barclay. They had four sons and four daughters, one of whom married.[57] Only the fourth son, Sidney, had any children. He was an able man who was granted a knighthood in 1936. Sir Sidney was a barrister and later joined the Services where he became Consul General in Shanghai from 1922-29 and an Envoy Extraordinary to Abyssinia from 1929-37. His wife, whom he married in

---

[54] The daughters, Florence and Mary married General Erskine Dawson and James Sinclair a J.P. from Holyhill, Strabane, Co. Tyrone respectively. Mary and James had a family.

[55] Three of the daughters married – Mary married Henry Rathborne of Fermanagh and Dublin, Henrietta married Frederick Sladen of Kent and Mildred married Simon Loane of Fermanagh. A descendant of Mildred and Simon now owns the Barton property in Fermanagh, known as The Waterfoot.

[56] Lt. Col. William Hugh had one daughter Ruth who married Lt. Col. Butler. They had one son. Mother and child were killed in a railway accident in 1951.

[57] May Barton married Henry Fulton in 1894. They had three sons and one daughter.

1904, was Mary McEwen and they had two sons and two daughters.[58] His eldest son married Margaret Hartigan from Maryland in the U.S. and they had one son, Hugh, who has three sons all born in the 1960s – Hugh, Patrick and James. The younger son, Hugh David, a very talented man, a Lt. Col. in the Irish Guards, fought in World War II. He lived in Kerry[59] for a time and also in London. He held numerous directorships including Director of the Hong Kong and Shanghai Banking Corporation. He was married to Rose Marie Meyer of Shanghai and Copenhagen. He had one daughter, Susannah, who married Michael Adlington and they have two children who were born in the 1960s – Mark Eric Barton and Hugh Michael Barton.

The other five sons of the seven either died unmarried or if they had married their descendants in modern times are not noted in Burke.

The fourth son of William who was settled at Grove in 1751 was Hugh – French Hugh of whom some notice has been given. Hugh as we have seen was extremely wealthy and acquired the Straffan estate in Kildare, in addition to Cootehall in Roscommon and the Château Langoa in the parish of St. Julien Médoc near Bordeaux.[60] His wife was Anne Johnston of Bordeaux and they had four sons and six daughters. Only one of the daughters married. She was Susan who married the 3rd Baron Clarina and they had descendants. His eldest son died in infancy and Nathaniel, the second son, was settled at Straffan.[61]

The Straffan Bartons: Nathaniel was a Deputy Lieutenant, a J.P. and High Sheriff for the county. He was born in 1799. He married Mary Scott the daughter of a consul at Bordeaux. They had five sons and four

---

[58] Marion the eldest daughter married Baron Filippo Muzi Falconi an Ambassador to Indonesia in 1933. Their three sons, Alessandro, Livio and Marcantonio all married and both Livio and Marcantonio have children who were born in the 1960s. Sir Sidney's youngest daughter, Esme, was married twice. Her first husband was Lt. Col. George Lowther Steer of South Africa and they had one son George Augustine Barton and one daughter Caroline. George, an Oxford graduate, married Sarah Clifford-Wing and has two daughters Sophia (b. 1969) and Isabella (b.1972). Esme's second husband was William Kenyon Jones of Worcestershire, and they had one daughter Marion, who married David Boorstin in 1974.

[59] Westcove House, Castlecove, Co. Kerry.

[60] He bought this estate in 1821 and he later purchased the Léoville Barton estate in 1826.

[61] Hugh Barton spent most of his time in France. He died in 1854.

daughters. The daughters either died in infancy or unmarried. Only two of the sons had descendants. They were the third son Bertram Francis of Straffan and Charles Thomas Hugh who seems to have gone to live in Devon where his wife's family lived. She was a sister of Bertram's wife.

Bertram Francis was High Sheriff for the county in 1903. He was married to Fannie Cutler of Devon. He died in 1904, aged about 74. He was survived by two sons and two daughters. It was during his tenure of Straffan that the estate was carved up as a result of the Land Acts, which gave the tenants the right to buy their holdings. His two daughters were Mary and Isabel who died unmarried. Mary became Mrs. Studdy of Devon and she had descendants living there. Only his eldest son, Bertram Hugh, had descendants. Bertram Hugh of Straffan was a Deputy Lieutenant, J.P. and High Sheriff in 1908. He was the Wine Shipper for Barton & Guestier. A very talented man, he was educated at Eton and Oxford. He married Lilian, the daughter of Sir Frederick Carden, and they had two sons Frederick and Hugh Ronald and one daughter[62]. Frederick, who was always known as Derick, was educated at Eton and Sandhurst and became an Army Officer. He served in World War II. He retired as an Hon. Captain. He married Joan St. Clair Lecky of Ballykealy, Tullow, Co. Carlow, in 1927. They had two sons Christopher and Anthony.[63]

Hugh Ronald, the second of Bertram Hugh's sons, born in 1902 and educated at Eton and Oxford, was awarded a CBE in 1971 and an MBE in 1942. He served in World War II and was awarded the Legion d'Honneur in 1951 and the Croix de Guerre in 1944. After the war he returned to France to the neglected vineyards and began to restore them again. He was quite successful in this and had many memorable vintages. An Oxford graduate he married Phyllis Roadknight of Kent in 1963. He was Chairman

---

[62] Storeen Lily who married Wilfred Sharp of Newcastle-upon-Tyne in 1939. She lived in Killiney, Dublin.
[63] Christopher, a Cambridge graduate, was married twice and has two daughters, Fiona (b.1959) and Angela (b.1972). Anthony, also a Cambridge man, married Eva Sarauw of Copenhagen and they have one daughter Lilian (b. 1956). Their only son Thomas (b.1958) was tragically killed in a car accident in 1990. Lilian, who takes an active part in the business affairs, including the shipping arm, is married to Michel Sartorius. They have two children Mélanie and Damien.

Anthony Barton & Family in the 1970s
(Courtesy Anthony Barton)

of Barton & Guestier.[64] Ronald and Phyllis had no children and in 1983 the properties were made over to Anthony, Derick's son. When Anthony wrote to thank him Ronald replied as follows: ' Do not thank me, thank Hugh. I have never considered it anything but my duty as custodian of the vineyards to hand them on to my heir in the best possible condition.'[65]

The Glendalough Bartons: Thomas Johnston Barton, the third son of French Hugh was settled at Glendalough, Co. Wicklow. He was a Deputy Lieutenant and J.P. for Wicklow. He married Frances Morris the daughter of the Hon. Mary (daughter of the 1st Baron Erskine, Lord High Chancellor of England). They had four sons and four daughters.[66] Three of the sons died unmarried and one of them, Robert, a Captain in the Coldstream Guards, was killed in action in the Zulu wars in 1879. The surviving son, Charles William Barton of Glendalough House was a Deputy Lieutenant, J.P. and High Sheriff. He was married to Agnes Childers and they had three sons Robert Childers, Charles Erskine and Thomas Eyre. They had two daughters who died unmarried. The two younger sons were career Army Officers and both were killed in action. Charles Erskine, a Captain, was killed in France in 1918. He left a widow, Nora Deane-Drake of Stokestown, Co. Wexford. Thomas Eyre, a Lieutenant, was killed at the Battle of the Somme in 1916.

The eldest son Robert Childers, who was born in 1881 and educated at Rugby and Oxford, served in World War I. He joined Sinn Fein and was

---

[64] His father, Bertram Hugh, bought out the interests of his brother and two cousins and left the vineyards and half his Barton & Guestier shares to Ronald and his Straffan estate and the remaining shares went to Derick.

[65] Quoted from the admirable and fascinating brochure of the Château Langoa & Léoville Barton, kindly sent to the authors by Anthony Barton, the present owner.

[66] The daughters were Frances Isabella, Georgina, Anna Mary and Beatrice. They were all married. Frances was married twice. Her first husband Captain James Hart died in 1876 and her second husband was Fletcher Menzies of Kinross. Georgina married George Booth of Larah House, Co. Wicklow and they had children. The last of the Booths was Brigadier Booth who lived at Rainsfort Lodge, Bunclody, Co. Wexford and his sister Miss Booth who lived near Mount Leinster. The Booths were related to the Hall-Dares of Bunclody (Newtownbarry). See *The Wexford Gentry Book 1* by Art Kavanagh and Rory Murphy. Anna Mary was married to Professor Robert Childers and it was her great grandson, Erskine Hamilton Childers who became 4th President of Ireland. Anna Mary has numerous Childers descendants living today. The fourth daughter Beatrice Louise was married to Captain Hugh Massy of Bray, Co. Wicklow and she has descendants living today.

a member of Dail Eireann for counties Kildare and Wicklow. He was on the Irish Peace Delegation that went to London in 1921. He was Chairman of the Agricultural Credit Corporation from 1934- 59 and Chairman of Bord Na Mona from 1935-60. He married Rachel Warren from Boston, but they had no family.

Chateau Langoa (courtesy Anthony Barton)

The 4th son of French Hugh Barton was Thomas Henry of the Dublin Metropolitan Police. He married the Hon. Charlotte Plunket, the 3rd daughter of Baron Plunket, and they had four sons and three daughters.[67] The youngest son Ion Plunket, a commander in the Royal Navy, died young. The second son, Augustine, died relatively young also. He was a Government Auditor for the Oxon district. Aubrey, the third son, went to the U.S. where he married Kathryn Floding of Virginia and they had a family.

The eldest son, Dunbar Plunket, was the most able man of the family. He was educated at Harrow and Oxford. He was created the Right

---

[67] Only one of the daughters married. Sylvia married Arthur Woodgate of Halifax, Nova Scotia and they had a family.

Hon. Sir Dunbar Plunket Barton. He was Solicitor General for Ireland 1897-1900, Judge of the High Court 1900-04, Judge in Chancery 1904-18, Senator of National University of Ireland 1909-37, Trustee of the National Library of Ireland 1920. He was married to Mary Manly of Dublin and they had one son who died young and unmarried.

Bianconi

The Chief Secretary of Ireland once asked Bianconi how, he, a foreigner, had acquired such a distinguished position in Ireland. Bianconi had replied: "Well, it was because, while the big and the little were fighting, I crept up between them, carried out my enterprise and obliged everybody."

There is a good story told about Bianconi and his trusted agent Dan Hearn. In the mid 1830s, Bianconi, accompanied by Dan Hearn was out driving around the country inspecting cars and visiting agents. Occasionally they would have to spend the night away from home. One night coming from Thurles they had to take lodgings at a carman's stage, which was managed by a woman called Biddy Minehan. Biddy had only one room vacant and the two men had to share the bed. Neither could sleep. Dan, who was feeling cold, put his hand under the bed saying, "There must be an iceberg under here". With that he jumped out of the bed and raced down the stairs to the kitchen where the carmen were smoking and drinking. He then shouted up the stairs "come down, Mr.B., come down out of that". Bianconi immediately jumped out of the bed and went down to see what the commotion was. "Did you see it?" asked Dan. "See what?" "The Devil" whispered Dan, shaking with fright. "Where?" queried Bianconi. "Under the bed," was the frightened reply. Biddy Minehan came forward. "I had no place else to put it your Honour." "Put what?" enquired Bianconi. "The corpse, your Honour," she replied, "we were going to have a wake when you came asking for lodgings, and I thought it would be hard to lose the chance of a few shillings, so having no bed to spare I just slipped the corpse under the bed"

One day, while being driven in a carriage in London, Bianconi noticed a rather stout man trying in vain to hire a carriage. He ordered his driver to pull over and invited the man to travel with him. The grateful stranger got in and enquired the name of his generous host. Bianconi told him his name. "The great Bianconi!" he exclaimed. Bianconi then, politely, asked his passenger what his name was. "Rothschild", was the reply. Bianconi regretted all his life that he hadn't the presence of mind to say "The great Rothschild!"

This extraordinary man, a penniless immigrant Italian, became a very wealthy man who made the transition to become one of the gentry of Tipperary in a seamless and effortless manner.

While this had been done before by numerous families including the Bagwells and Grubbs of Clonmel, it had taken at least a couple of generations to achieve what Bianconi did in his own lifetime.

He arrived in Ireland in 1802 at the age of sixteen. He was brought over from Italy by Andrea Faroni, a man who made prints of famous pictures. Faroni brought three other young apprentices with him. Originally he had intended to go to London, but for some strange reason he chose to go to Dublin instead. Upon arrival he collected any money the apprentices had and used it to set up his business. Bianconi had a hundred gold coins, which had been given to him by his family and friends and this was reluctantly handed over.

Faroni set up shop in Dublin and began to manufacture prints. He sent young Charles out into the streets of Dublin to sell the prints. The young lad knew no English except what he had been told to say "buy, buy, buy".

Within a short time, when his command of the language improved, his master sent him out to the countryside towns to sell his wares. He travelled to most of the counties and towns in Leinster and to Waterford and Tipperary in Munster. His master supplied him with two pounds worth of pictures and four pence subsistence money.

Later one of the other apprentices was sent with Bianconi but he became restless and ran away. Another boy, Ribaldi,[68] was sent in his place and they continued selling their wares in the country towns.

---

[68] Ribaldi eventually became a retailer of mirrors and set up shop in Limerick and later moved to London. The fourth lad, Castelli, opened a picture shop in Waterford and became quite prosperous.

One day, in Passage, in Waterford, Bianconi was arrested for selling a picture of Napoleon, although the Peace of Amiens had been declared the previous year. He was suspected of being a French agent. Fortunately for him the magistrate decided to release him without charge.

When his apprenticeship was over in 1804 Faroni gave his apprentices their money, which he had held in trust. Bianconi immediately began to invest his money in buying prints and in making a box with shoulder straps to carry them. After some months of trudging the roads with the very weighty pack he decided to settle down for a few months and did so in Thurles. There he met a young man who was to become his life-long friend. He was Toby Mathew, later to become Fr. Theobald Mathew, the apostle of Temperance.

He didn't stay very long in Thurles and soon moved on to Cahir, where he stayed a while with a family named Baldwin. From there he went to Carrick-on-Suir where he opened his first shop. Because he needed to go to Waterford for his supplies he found the journey by boat intolerable. It only went once a week and on one occasion he was soaked with the rain, as a result of which he developed pleurisy. When he had recovered he decided to move to Waterford. He got an introduction to Edmund Rice, the founder of the Christian Brothers, who took it upon himself to continue Bianconi's education.

After two years in Waterford he made up his mind to move to Clonmel. At that time, in 1809, Clonmel was a prosperous trading town of some 18,000 inhabitants. There were breweries, distilleries and factories producing cotton and linen goods.

He opened a shop in a good location and began trading. His landlord was Bagwell of Marlfield. He was a good listener and became interested in the local politics. He became friendly with the Grubbs and other Quakers.

His business thrived and he was very fortunate in getting a contract to buy up all the golden guineas hoarded by the peasantry. He made substantial profits from this venture and he continued to expand and reinvest in his business.

Charles Bianconi now found that he had to travel to Dublin occasionally on business. There he met and became friendly with the Patron of the Italians residing in Ireland. The Patron, Signor Del Vecchio, lived near the sea in a house rented from a Mr. Philpot Hayes, a wealthy stockbroker, who also lived close by. Bianconi became quite friendly with the Hayes family and there he met the five-year-old Eliza Hayes who was to become his wife.

It was at the Hayes household that Bianconi met Daniel O'Connell for the first time. O'Connell said of this meeting later that he found a young man 'looking up at me with a face seen only on a Roman coin'.

Down in Clonmel Bianconi was making his presence felt too. The public library was a place where Catholics were expected to talk in whispers while the Protestant had the right to express their views in louder tones. One day Bianconi began an animated discussion in a loud voice and was joined by others. From then on Catholic and Protestant stated their views on equal terms.

The next big milestone in Bianconi's career was his idea of starting a public transport business. It was 1814 and the war in Europe was over. Grain prices had fallen from an astronomical 3s.8d. per stone to 1s.per stone. Army horses were plentiful and cheap. As there was a tax on private vehicles many of them were laying idle.

In June of the following year his first coach set out from Clonmel to Cahir carrying the mail for Cahir post office at half the fee normally paid by the Government. Passengers were slow to avail of the service and Bianconi had to resort to a ruse to promote interest in the venture. He bought and outfitted another car without letting anyone know he was the owner. The two cars began racing each other. Bets were made as to which car would arrive first. Soon people began travelling in both cars to enjoy the race at first hand.

He now extended the range and routes of the cars and went west as far as Limerick and north to Thurles and Cashel. Soon after he initiated a service to Waterford.

Staff had to be employed and complex organizational ability was needed. Bianconi was up to the task and soon his cars became known the length and breath of the land. They were called Bians for short and on occasion the man himself was called Bian, which he took as a compliment.

In a remarkable incident in his life in 1826 Bianconi became embroiled in the bitterness of Irish politics. Lord George Beresford, the

Arriving at the end of a stage

brother of the Marquess of Waterford, stood for election in that year. He hired Bianconi coaches to bring his voters to the polls. As there was no liberal candidate Bianconi agreed to have his coaches used for this purpose. At the last minute Mr. Villiers Stuart came forward to oppose Lord George and support Catholic Emancipation. O'Connell supported Mr. Stuart. In those days it took three days to complete the polls. On the first day the Bians carrying the Beresford voters were attacked and heaved over the bridge. Bianconi himself, though a firm supporter of the liberals and a member of the Catholic Association, was pelted with mud.[69] He immediately contacted the Beresford agent and terminated the agreement as he could not, he said 'risk property and the lives of his drivers'. The agent concurred. Bianconi then put his coaches at the disposal of Villiers Stuart who won the election comfortably.

The following year, when Bianconi was forty years old, he married Eliza Hayes. In the marriage settlement made with her father Bianconi

---

[69] He was also a member of the Order of Liberators, a society formed by O'Connell with a view to conciliate Irishmen of all classes and creeds, prevent feuds and faction fights and to discourage secret societies. As the head of the Order, O'Connell was accorded the title of 'The Liberator'.

settled £2000 on his wife and children, while Mr. Hayes settled £1200 on his daughter. They were married in Dublin, in the Hayes house, by Archbishop Murray, a family friend.

After the wedding they went to Clonmel where they were met by a huge crowd of well-wishers. In time-honoured fashion the horses were unharnessed and the coach was drawn through the streets of Clonmel by the cheering workmen. From the balcony in their apartment the bride and groom looked out and were cheered even more loudly. Then the fiddles started up and the Bians (coachmen and workers) sang a song specially composed for the occasion called "The Coachman's Song".

'Now welcome lovely lady,
To this country by the Suir,
Where yer fine man started going
The Bians that will endure.
'Tis we are proud to greet ye
And we hope ye are the same,
For before the God Almighty
Ye're a great and lovely Dame.

And to ye, yer honour, Sir,
We sing our song as well,
To wish ye years of plenty
In this grand and lovely dell;
To tell ye that we'll always
Take our horses to the end,
And may ye meet but happy days
Round every single bend.'

In the next year, 1828, Bianconi's daughter, Catherine, was born and Daniel O'Connell was elected an M.P. for Clare. As in the election of Villiers Stuart the Bianconi cars brought the Clare voters to the polls. Within a year the Catholic Emancipation Bill was passed.

Bianconi, a Catholic, was still considered an alien, as Daniel O'Connell pointed out to him at a dinner in Merrion Square. As such he could not purchase land in Ireland. O'Connell offered to approach Sir Robert Peel the Prime Minister with a view to introducing a Private Bill to have Bianconi naturalized. As this procedure would be very costly he suggested an alternative. Bianconi drew up a memorial for the Viceroy showing how he had come to Ireland and the path his career took since then. He was directed to obtain testimonials from the principal magistrates in the district and a certificate from at least one member of the Privy Council. He was naturalized in 1831 by Royal decree.

In 1833 he went to London to seek contracts from the Government for the conveyance of cross mails. He had contacts in the Whig government and was able to get an interview with the Postmaster General, the Duke of Richmond. He took an instant liking to Bianconi and when Bianconi returned to Ireland he had the contract for the mails.

Dropping a Passenger

Shortly after this he was notified of his father's death and discovered that he had been left a quarter of his land holdings in Italy. Bianconi travelled back to Italy taking only one servant. He stayed with his family there for a couple of weeks and made over the property to his nephew. He paid substantial sums to save his nephews having to join the army and set up a fund for their education.

Back in Ireland he moved house to get his complaining household away from the stables and coach yards. He bought a property, which became known as Spring House. Many famous people came to dine there including the Liberator, Lord Monteagle, and most of the Tipperary M.P.s such as Thomas Wyse, Richard Lalor Shiel, Mr. Justice Ball and Lewis Perrin who became Chief Baron Wolfe. Other members of the O'Connell clan came to visit too, brothers[70] and nephews of the Liberator, who himself often stayed there days at a time.

In 1835 Daniel O'Connell formed the National Bank of Ireland and became its first Governor. It was intended to help the poorer people to avail of banking facilities. The Clonmel National Bank was opened in the same year and Bianconi became one of its directors and principal shareholders.

Sometime shortly after this O'Connell was found to be in financial difficulty himself and it was Bianconi with two other friends who sorted out his affairs.

Bianconi at the time of his marriage

_____

[70] One of these was John of Grena, a huge man who bore on his face the scar of a bullet wound received in one of his eighteen duels.

Despite his generosity in some ways he could be mean. There is a story that he brought back a tea urn from London and brought it to Hearn's[71] hotel where he gave it to Judy, the barmaid. A day or two later he called and told Judy she owed him 5s 9d. She enquired what that was for. "For the tea urn", he replied. Judy was flabbergasted and said she thought it was a present. "Not at all," said Bianconi, "come pay me what you owe me". She gave him 5s 8d. which was all the money in the till. The next day he came back looking for the balance of 1d.

Bianconi did not see eye to eye with O'Connell on the Repeal of the Union. He felt that rule from Westminster was fair and impartial especially under a liberal government. Nevertheless his personal loyalty to the Liberator was such that he never openly criticized his policies.

He was elected Mayor of Clonmel in 1844 and had to buy his own robes of office and chain as the other robes and chain had been removed by the Tory corporation, along with all the legal books of reference. He also provided a stand for the Corporation regalia, which consisted of a sword with a Toledo blade and two silver maces dating from the reign of Charles II. He wrote to O'Connell to ask him how to discharge his civic duties and what legal books he should consult. O'Connell replied as follows – ' if you wish to discharge the duties of mayoralty with perfect satisfaction, act upon your own sound common sense and do not look into any law books'.

He was the first Catholic Mayor of Clonmel to wear his mayoral robes to Mass. It was pointed out to him that this was in contravention of the law but Bianconi persisted and the matter was overlooked by the authorities.

As Mayor he was also a Justice of the Peace and as such presided over the Borough Petty Sessions, assisted by two Resident Magistrates. He was reputed to be just but firm in his dealings with the petty offenders who came before him. He was very generous to the poor and needy and gave considerable sums to have National Schools built in the town.

In 1846 the Longfield estate, which Bianconi had admired from his youth, came on the market. The owner, Captain Edward Long had become

---

[71] This was Dan Hearn's hotel. Dan was one of Bianconi's most trusted men and when Bianconi had moved out of his home in Clonmel Dan Hearn and his wife moved in and started up a hotel there.

depressed after the murder of his father. This combined with the reduced rents due to the famine made him decide to leave Ireland. Bianconi paid £22,000 for the beautiful house and estate.

Longfield (courtesy Irish Architectural Archive)

When he moved to Longfield with his family he was met by the Cashel Temperance Band and cheering crowds of employees, tenants and servants. This was extraordinary in the time of the famine. A great party was held on the lawn with singing and dancing and refreshments. An address of welcome was read and in reply Bianconi emphasized the need for everyone to do their duty properly, landlord and tenant, mechanic and labourer. He exhorted everyone to obey the law and to be temperate as recommended by his good friend Fr. Mathew and by the Liberator.

One of the first things Bianconi did was to send to Italy for experts to lay out an Italian garden. He also planted a rose garden with white and yellow roses to represent the Joyful Mysteries of the Rosary and red roses for the Sorrowful Mysteries.

Here he entertained the Grubbs, the Maudes of Dundrum and the Coopers of Killenure, while he in turn was entertained in other Big Houses. He was particularly pleased to have been invited to the Viceregal Lodge where he was entertained by the Viceroy, the Earl of Bessborough.

During the worst years of the famine he was in a position to alleviate the rents of the tenants and provide works, such as building a demesne wall, to enable the poor to earn money. He also set up a soup kitchen and provided meals of macaroni and got a Frenchman, who lived in Cashel to give lessons to the people on how to cook the Italian food.

Because his eldest daughter Catherine developed tuberculosis in 1850, Bianconi was advised that she should spend time in a warm climate so he decided to bring his family to the Italy. This time he travelled in style bringing three coaches, his own horses and a large number of servants. He was to spend three years in Italy while his daughter languished in her illness. The family was given an audience with the Pope and Bianconi's son, Charles, was made a papal Chamberlain. This was a signal honour and it entailed young Charles having to attend the Papal Court at certain times of the year dressed in an exotic medieval type of dress.

Daniel O'Connell had died in 1847 and in accordance with his wishes his heart was buried in Rome. Bianconi commissioned a monument, which was erected in the Church of St. Agatha, which is in the Irish College in Rome, to remember his great friend. This is the inscription which he had written on the monument:

This Monument contains the Heart of
O'CONNELL
Who, dying on the way to the Eternal City, bequeathed
His Soul to God, his Body to Ireland,
And his Heart to Rome.
He is represented at the Bar of the British House of Commons
1829
when he refused to take the anti-Catholic declaration
in these remarkable words;
"I at once reject this declaration: part of it I believe to be untrue,

and the rest I know to be false."
He was born on 6th August 1776; died 15th May 1847.
Erected by Charles Bianconi, Esq., the faithful
Friend of the Immortal Liberator
And of Ireland, the land of his adoption.

After Catherine's inevitable death in 1854 the Bianconi's returned to Ireland. Within a short time Bianconi had a special Mortuary Chapel built at Boherlahan and the body of Catherine Bianconi was brought home from Italy and interred there.

With all his energy and enthusiasm Bianconi threw himself into the work of improving his estate. All the tenants' houses were slated and wells were sunk in their yards. He bought more land and tried to improve the tillage system. His business still thrived and he spent money generously on worthwhile projects. He became involved in the founding of the Catholic University and bought a house at 86 St. Stephen's Green for that purpose.

The crowning glory of his social aspirations was when he was appointed Deputy Lieutenant of the county in 1863. Already a Justice of the Peace this new position brought him into contact with the highest aristocracy in the land. His landholdings of 9,000 acres put him on a par with the biggest landowners in Tipperary.

The following year, 1864, brought nothing only pain as his only son Charles died in that year. Charles, a spendthrift, had married Eileen FitzSimon, a granddaughter of Daniel O'Connell, by whom he had three daughters. His lavish spending soon led to bankruptcy and Bianconi was reluctant to pay his son's debts. They became estranged and young Charles had to flee to Belgium to escape his creditors. Bianconi was eventually prevailed upon to pay off most of the debts, but the rigours and trauma of his position told on the health of young Charles. He was buried in the family vault at Boherlahan.

His surviving daughter, Mary Ann, fell in love with another O'Connell, Morgan, the nephew of the Liberator. Though much older than Mary Ann, known as Minnie, he was a charming man, and while Bianconi was at first opposed to the marriage, he at last consented and the two were married in the Catholic University Church in Dublin, in 1865. They had one daughter who died young and a son John, who later inherited the Bianconi fortunes.

Bianconi, himself, though in excellent health, fell from a car, when a strap of the harness suddenly snapped, and broke his thigh. He adjusted to life in a wheelchair and lived another ten years, dying in 1875. He was almost ninety years old.

Young John O'Connell was only a boy of four at the time of his grandfather's death. His own father, Morgan, had died suddenly a few months before Bianconi. When he became of age he took the name Bianconi in accordance with the wishes of his grandfather.

He married his cousin, Arabella Burke Hayes and they had only one daughter, Mary Anne, (Molly) who was the co-author of the very fine book *Bianconi King of the Irish Roads*.

Butler of Cahir

This strange tale is recorded in Dorothea Herbert's book *Reminiscences*. 'Lord Cahir's mother was a poor mendicant woman in the town of Cahir for many years and winnowed corn for her subsistence. When the late Lord Cahir died his expectants found out that this old woman's children were next heirs to his Lordship. They had them kidnapped and secretly conveyed to France where they were reared in miserable poverty. Mrs. Jefferies[72], a sister of the Chancellor, Lord Fitzgibbon, passing through Cahir, heard at an Inn, the history of the old beggar woman and her two children.

She sent for the woman and took notes of her tale, which she laid before the Chancellor. On further investigation the whole was proved to be fact and the Chancellor procured warrants for bringing the children over (to England).

Mrs. Jefferies' daughter was in a convent in France and when Mrs. Jefferies went over to bring her daughter home she undertook the guardianship of the children. They were found in a miserable garret, all overgrown with hair. Mrs. Jefferies had them educated and then made a match for her daughter with the young Lord Cahir[73].

The Chancellor was much enraged with this proceeding and threatened to imprison his sister and niece for inveigling the young heir but Mrs. Jefferies' cleverness got her over it.

---

[72] Wife of John Jeffreys, Blarney, Co. Cork.

[73] His name was Richard Butler and he was reared as a Protestant.

They all came to Ireland and took Dowager Lady Cahir from her winnowing sheet to enjoy her new title and live with her son. They now settled at Cahir.

Lady Cahir was a beautiful little creature, wild with spirits and very affable, but she cursed and swore tremendously. In the metropolis she was chief leader of Fashion and Ton, an uncommonly elegant woman.'

Lord Cahir was restored to his estates by a special Act of Parliament in the reign of Queen Anne. He was confirmed in his estate of 10,000 acres. The restriction on Catholic inheritance was not apparently enforced in his case.

The Butler association with Cahir began with James Gallda Butler, the illegitimate son of the 3rd. Earl of Ormonde who was born around the year 1400. His mother was Catherine, the daughter of the Earl of Desmond.

James Gallda, of Cahir, was appointed by his brother, the 4th Earl of Ormonde, to be the keeper of the county with the right to maintenance of the necessary troops.[74] This appointment was disastrous as James Gallda had his own agenda and was closely involved with the Desmonds who were rivals of the Ormondes in Munster.

This rivalry ripened into enmity when the War of the Roses broke out in England between the Houses of York and Lancaster. The Ormondes supported the House of Lancaster and the Desmonds that of York. That bitter English war found expression in Ireland when the forces of the Butlers of Ormonde and the Fitzgeralds of Desmond fought a battle at Pilltown in 1462. On that occasion the Ormondes were defeated.[75]

When Piers Rua, whose mother was Sadbh Kavanagh, daughter of the King of Leinster, became the 8th Earl he set about bringing peace between the warring factions. His efforts culminated in what became known as the Composition of Clonmel, a fairly straightforward treaty between the various interests.

As to the Cahir Butlers there were two main items of the agreement that concerned them particularly. The arbiters directed that the Earl should deliver the manor of Cahir with its appurtenances to Edmund Butler, the

---

[74] Eoghan O'Neill *The Golden Vale of Ivowen*

[75] This long running dispute continued intermittently until 1565 when the last private battle fought in Ireland took place at Affane, Co. Waterford. The Desmonds were defeated on the day.

Baron of Cahir, on condition that Edmund and all his heirs 'shall be in all things faithful to the Earl and his heirs'. The other agreement stated that whenever any stranger should attack Edmund or his country, then all horsemen, Scots, footmen, gentlemen and husbandmen were to rise in defence of Edmund and Mac Ui Phiarais (the ancestor of the Butler Barons of Dunboyne), provided that no regular war would begin or continue without the consent of the Earl.

Another important section deprived the Cahir Butlers of some of their illegal revenues such as coyne and livery and cudihy[76] for his followers. Henceforth they were not allowed to keep their own private army or exact forced labour for the building or repair of their castle or houses.

Edmund was the son of James the first 'Baron'[77] of Cahir. His second son James was soon in breach of the Composition and in 1519 he was arrested and detained by Piers Rua. He seems to have appropriated the goods, profits, rents and tithes of the rectory of Tibroughney. He was released on condition that he restored the goods to the rectory. Eight of the foremost men of the area had to pledge £100 each for his good behaviour.[78] James was later made Sheriff of the county.

A few years later, Thomas Butler, the heir to the manor of Cahir was in dispute himself with Piers Rua and on this occasion had to reaffirm the articles of the Composition of Clonmel. It would seem that he had resorted to the coyne and livery and taking of cudihys as well as forced labour and unfair exactions. Thomas's friends, too, had to sign pledges of good behaviour, but this time it was much more severe. They had to sign pledges of £500 each.[79] Thomas Butler was created (officially) 1st Baron of Cahir by the king in 1524.

---

[76] From the Gaelic *cuid oiche* or night suppers.

[77] They were given the title of Baron by the Earl of Ormonde to signify their lordship of the manor of Cahir but later in 1524 they received the official title of Baron from the King.

[78] These were Thomas, Geoffrey and John Prendergast, the Treasurer of Lismore, William, Thomas and David O'Lonergan and John O'Donnell.

[79] In addition to many of those mentioned above others who signed and pledged the £500 were St. John of St. Johnstown, John Comyn of Kilconnell, James Og Wall, James Keating of Moorestown, James Walsh of Rathronan, James Laffin of Greystown and numerous Butlers.

Cahir Castle (courtesy Irish Architectural Archive)

The Barons of Cahir seemed to continue living in peace until the death of James the 9th Earl of Ormonde in 1546.[80] The new Earl, Thomas (Black Tom), was only a boy of fourteen and the Butlers of Cahir and Dunboyne became restless and ambitious. Their followers committed many robberies and thefts from the Earl's lands during the period.

The Lord Deputy of the time was prevailed upon to try to settle the affairs of the disputing Butlers and in 1549 he appointed commissioners to enquire into the affair and recommend any solutions. They found that the Dowager Countess of Ormonde (the mother of Black Tom) had suffered unjustly at the hands of the Cahir Butlers. They ordered that the Baron of Cahir should pay compensation to all those injured and restore any goods that had been stolen or repay their value. Failing that he was ordered to deliver up a number of his followers who included many O'Donnells, Prendergasts, Hogans and Lonergans.

---

[80] He was poisoned along with his stewart and sixteen of his servants at a supper at Ely House, Holborn.

Not much is known about the Barons of Cahir until the middle of the 17th century when George Mathew of Thurles married Eleanor Butler, the daughter of Lord Dunboyne and widow of Lord Cahir (another Butler). George raised her young son, the 4th Lord Cahir, and when he was of age married him off to his niece, Elizabeth.

In common with the all the Butlers, including the Earl of Ormonde the Cahir lands were declared forfeit after the Cromwellian wars but were restored in 1662 when Charles II was restored to the monarchy in England.

The Butlers were held in high esteem by the people of Tipperary and during the years following that terrible upheaval poems were still written in praise of the Butlers of Cahir.[81]

Since the Cahirs were Catholic they were lucky to have held on to their lands during the penal times. The 5th Lord Cahir, Theobald Butler, had only one son, Thomas, so the provisions of the penal laws on inheritance did not affect him, as he inherited before 1703. However Thomas, the 6th Lord Cahir, had five sons and in theory the estate should have been divided amongst them. To avoid this happening sophisticated legal devices were used. The estate was vested in trustees and subsequently mortgaged at various times in the 1750s with the proviso that it would not revert to the owner until the borrowed money was repaid.[82] In effect this meant that the person or institution that advanced the money was the legal owner for the time being. Lord Cahir was conveniently absent from the area at this time and his agent was a very competent man, named Martin Murphy from Waterford.

When the 6th Lord died in 1744 he was succeeded by James his eldest son. James now became the 7th Lord. As well as having four brothers, James had two sisters, both of whom died unmarried. One of his brothers died young and another seems to have remained at home and died unmarried also. The Lord Cahir was an absentee landlord[83] who had an income of £10,000 in 1775.

---

[81] The fact that the Butlers gave long leases to other pre Cromwellian Anglo Irish and Irish families was a major factor in their popularity.

[82] ibid.

[83] He came to live for a period at Cahir Castle in the mid 1770s. - T. Power in *Land, Politics and Society in 18th century Tipperary*.

By virtue of the fact that he spent most of his time abroad he escaped the turmoil of the 1760s when the polarized attitude of the Protestant Gentry culminated in the judicial murder of Fr. Sheehy.[84] It is significant though, that one of the co-accused of Fr. Sheehy, James Farrell, who with Edmund Sheehy and James Buxton was hanged in Clogheen in 1766, was a close relative of Lord Cahir.[85] The fact that the head tenants on the Cahir estate were the Catholic Keating, Baldwin and Nagle families made the Protestant gentry nervous. A report on the trials of 1766 remarked of them that 'they were very respectable as they lived in affluence and with reputation, associated with the gentlemen of the neighbourhood with whom they lived in the highest hospitality, frequently receiving and returning visits'.[86] Robert Keating, James Nagle and John Baldwin had been arrested on suspicion of involvement with the Whiteboys and of plotting a French invasion. All three were charged with treason but were acquitted.[87]

There was general distress in 1784 as a result of bad weather conditions leading to the death of cattle. This in turn resulted in ruin, emigration and farms being abandoned or surrendered, as the tenants could not pay the rents. Lord Cahir, to his credit, cancelled arrears, accepted surrenders and abated former rents. The bad weather of 1784 was only a hiccup as the level of income on the Cahir estate grew from £10,000 in 1775 to £36,000 in 1809. The Butler owners also benefited from the rents of Cahir town.[88]

As with many Catholic gentry families younger sons often went abroad and entered the French (military) service. So it was with Pierce Butler and Thomas[89], brothers of the 7th Lord Cahir.

James was unmarried and when he died in 1786 the estate passed to his brother Pierce. Since the penal laws on inheritance had been repealed in 1778 there was now no difficulty in the succession.

---

[84] For a full account of the Fr. Sheehy case see Bagwell in this volume.

[85] Eoghan O'Neill in *The Golden Vale of Ivowen*

[86] *Gentlemen's and London Magazine*

[87] T. Power in *Land, Politics and Society in 18th century Tipperary.*

[88] ibid

[89] Thomas was sent to France to enter military service at the age of 16, in 1737. The following year he was made second Lieutenant in Dillon's regiment and was later promoted to Captain in Lally's regiment. He fought at the Battle of Fontenoy. – Ibid.

The Act of 1778, which gave an enormous measure of relief to the Catholics, was widely welcomed by the Catholics in Tipperary. The main features of the Act were (1) the removal of the requirement that Catholic property had to be divided among the surviving sons. (2) Leases could now be given for more than 31 years. (3) The removal of the decree that a son who converted would get immediate possession making his parent a tenant for life only. The Act would only apply to people who took the oath of allegiance. In Tipperary county over 900 people took the oath. This number probably represented the vast majority of Catholic landowners in the county and included Archbishop Butler and many of his clergy.

As a result of the passage of the Act two tenants of Lord Cahir, James Nagle of Garnvella and Robert Keating of Knockagh had their interest in leases confirmed.[90]

With the re-emergence of considerable agrarian unrest, the American war of Independence and threatened French invasions Volunteer Corps were founded all over Ireland. The corps on the Cahir estate was composed of Catholics and was commanded by Pierce Butler, Lord Cahir's brother. Each corps was comprised of about forty rank and file members drawn from the head tenantry or from friends or associates of the colonel.

When James Butler died he was succeeded by Pierce Butler, who only survived his brother two years and died in 1788. The estate then passed to James Butler of Glengall, the 9th Lord, a cousin of Pierce. James died in the same year as Pierce (1788)[91]. His son Richard became the 10th Lord Cahir and 1st Earl of Glengall and we have recounted his story at the beginning.[92] He was twenty-five years old at the time of his succession.

The Cahir estate did not go unnoticed in the period of unrest when the Whiteboys were active. In 1800, Alexander Mollison, Lord Cahir's steward, was murdered. It would appear from some local evidence that the instigators of the rural unrest in the area were the tenants on the Cahir estate. This situation may have arisen because prior to 1800 the estate

---

[90] T. Power in *Land Politics and Society in 18th century Tipperary*
[91] He had two brothers in the church who may have been responsible for the abduction of the young Richard Butler.
[92] His mother Dame Sarah Baroness Cahir converted to Protestantism in 1789 – *Inch Papers*

agent,[93] who had granted long leases, was replaced by Scott, an attorney and later by Mollison.

Richard the restored heir made an unsuccessful attempt, in the early 1800s to reduce the period of the leases on his lands, where the middlemen held leases of 61 years. The middlemen in turn sublet extensively so that the estate was divided into an array of small sub tenancies from which the middlemen reaped large profit rents. One of the later Lord Cahirs, possibly Richard, said that 'the estate was loaded with paupers' and the leases were 'shamefully abused with the lands being sub-let and ruined and the farmers pauperized by the leasees'.[94] The Cahir estate leases did not change until the 1840s when the long leases expired.

Lord Cahir carried out extensive improvements to his estate where he embellished two miles of a demesne on either side of the Suir. A visitor later remarked that 'finely planted and well stocked with deer the scenery was bold and romantic and the river a fine deep stream gliding through a rich and fertile land'. He had his own band, which played in the town square of Cahir and was known as Lord Cahir's band.[95]

Just as the appointment of more professional agents in the 1780s can be viewed as a reassertion of the landlord's power, so also can the revival of manor courts in that decade. These institutions were largely medieval in origin though some came into existence in the seventeenth century. About 1650 there were thirty-seven locations, which had manorial jurisdiction, but by the 1830s this number had fallen to six.

Functionally the manor court was divided into a court leet and a court baron. In the former, which was convened twice yearly by the manor's seneschal, who was appointed by the landowner, matters like land boundaries, roads, regulation of markets, weights and measures were dealt with. The court baron, also summoned by the seneschal, adjudicated in cases concerning the recovery of cash debts (£5 or under), promissory notes (£10 or under), and trespass. The court proceedings for the manor of Coolkill near Thurles in 1790 show it to have been mainly taken up with disputes between tenants, adjudicating small debts, and awarding costs.

---

[93] This may have been Martin Murphy, the merchant from Waterford.
[94] T. Power Land, *Politics & Society in 18th century Tipperary*.
[95] M.O'Connell Bianconi and S.J. Watson in *Bianconi King of the Irish Roads*

Lord Cahir appointed a seneschal for his three manors in 1802, as did Lord Llandaff for his manor of Thurles in 1817. The revival of these courts reflected the desire of certain landlords to reassert control over their estates, which in Lord Cahir's case had been sharply diminished in the 1780s.[96]

Richard Butler stood for election in 1818 and topped the poll ahead of the Mathew candidate with Prittie coming a close third. He resigned the seat however, in the following year, as he had been elevated to the peerage as the 1st Earl Glengall. He was opposed to the plan to divide Tipperary on the grounds that the cost would be exorbitant. He had survived a duel in 1826 arising from his being allegedly libeled in *Age* magazine.[97] He supported Catholic Emancipation and in 1828 he had given a free site and a substantial sum of money towards the erection of a Catholic chapel at Dunhill. This was at odds with his attending a 'Protestant' dinner in Morrison's Hotel in honour of the Earl of Winchelsea in the course of which 'he confessed his error' in voting for Emancipation.

Richard and his wife were very prominent at all the social functions in the county and as we have seen his wife, apart from being elegant was lively and extrovert. They were the leading figures at the Cahir Ball in the Assembly Rooms. Richard was the President of the Tipperary Agriculture Society and was chairman of many of the local bodies.

Richard had one son Richard and on the death of the 10th Lord Cahir and 1st Earl of Glengall, he became the 11th Lord and 2nd Earl. He married Margaret Mellish of Essex in 1834, in London. After a prolonged honeymoon abroad they arrived back in Cahir where they were met by the usual cheering crowd of tenants, who unharnessed the horses and pulled the carriage themselves. These scenes of jubilation were accompanied by the firing of cannon.

The new Earl spent much of his time abroad. He had a yacht built, a craft of some 500 tons, which was launched at Cowes the following year. He named it *The Margaret* in deference to his wife.

---

[96] This loss of control was evidenced by a rise in lawlessness. Lord Cahir's stewart was murdered in 1799. – *Finn's Leinster Journal*
[97] D. Murphy *The Two Tipperarys*

The Swiss Cottage, early 1800s (Courtesy Dept of the Environment)

A combination of bad luck, the Famine, foreign holidays, the town house (now Cahir House Hotel), a marine residence in the Isle of Wight, a London house at 34 Grosvenor Square, the building of St. Paul's Church of Ireland and an Erasmus Smith school in Cahir debilitated his finances. He went bankrupt in 1855 and the estate had to be sold. John Sadleir, the unfortunate banker from Tipperary, bought the estate for £68,000.[98]The Earl's daughter Margaret and her husband Richard Charteris re-purchased the estates later.[99]

The last Earl who died in 1858 and his countess who died in 1864, were buried in the grounds of St. Paul's Church, together with a daughter and his mother.

---

[98] When the Joint Stock Bank of Tipperary crashed in 1856 he committed suicide. At the time of his death he had an overdraft of £250,000.
[99] D. Murphy *The Two Tipperarys*

Lady Margaret erected a fountain in Cahir in 1876. The purpose of the fountain was to supply water to the town centre. It was piped from the Galtee Mountains. The fountain was erected as a memorial to her husband the Hon. Richard Charteris.

Between 1876 and the end of the century the Charteris Estate was responsible for the building of the town reservoir. Water was then supplied on tap to the houses of the town for an annual charge. The local council paid the Charteris estate for the water up to the early 1960s when the estate was finally sold.

Carden of Barnane

On Sunday, 2nd July 1854 a covered carriage containing four ladies was being driven by James Dwyer towards the entrance gates of Rathronan House, near Clonmel. The ladies, who were returning from Sunday Service in nearby Rathronan Church, were Jane, Eleanor and Laura Arbuthnot, three sisters, and Miss Lydon. Jane was married to Captain Hon. George Gough, son of Field Marshal Viscount Gough. Eleanor and Laura were both unmarried, and lived at Rathronan House as well as at St Helens, the Gough residence near Dublin. Miss Lydon was governess to the Gough children. The ladies, sitting two opposite two, were chatting gaily until they noticed John Carden riding his horse close to the carriage. That did not unduly alarm them, as John, the bachelor landlord of Barnane, on the slopes of the Devil's Bit, had been in the habit of turning up at functions which Eleanor was attending for the past two years. He was infatuated with her. It was only when they sighted a two-horse brougham at the entrance gates and a number of strange men near it that they became alarmed.

Suddenly the carriage was surrounded, the horses' traces cut to immobilize it, and Carden, now dismounted, was reaching in and forcibly trying to take Eleanor out. Jane, who was pregnant, succeeded in getting out while Miss Lydon and Laura did their best to ward Carden off. But he succeeded in dragging them out, and then as he reached in to a terrified Eleanor he said, "Eleanor, it is you I want." He had the struggling, screaming girl almost out when he was half stunned by a blow to the head by an employee of Rathronan House who had arrived on the scene. One of Carden's men then made another attempt to pull Eleanor out, but James Dwyer pulled him off, and by then other Rathronan employees were at hand.

Seeing that his planned abduction had failed, Carden and his men made off madly in the two-horse brougham, in which he had hoped to be conveying Eleanor away. His outside driver, Pat Kenneally, kept urging on the two horses as they sped along the Clonmel-Cashel Road, then on to Holycross via Boherlahan. Then, as they were heading towards Ballycahill and Bouladuff, they were halted at Farney Bridge by Sub-inspector George McCullagh, who had overtaken them at that point. One of Carden's horses collapsed there and died of exhaustion. The wounded Carden was arrested and conveyed to the County Gaol in Clonmel.[100]

The bungled attempt at abduction was the main talking topic all over Tipperary and beyond it. Abductions among 'the lower orders of the society' of the time were not uncommon, but for one of the gentry to be involved in abduction was sensational. Judge Nicholas Ball, who addressed the grand jury at the Tipperary South Riding's assizes a few weeks later, referred to the crime as exceptional, because the principal perpetrator was "a person of considerable station and property".[101] The grand jury decided at that summer assizes that John Carden, their magistrate colleague, should be indicted to stand trial for felony, the felony in question being the unlawful and forceful abduction of Eleanor Louisa Arbuthnot with intent to marry her against her will and with intent to violate her. Carden pleaded 'not guilty' in response. If convicted of such a felony he could receive the death sentence or transportation for life.

The trial commenced in Clonmel on Friday 28th July and ended on the following Monday. The *Times* reported that for the days previous to the trial the gentry were "pouring into the town", and that on the day of the trial there was "continued rolling of carriages towards the Courthouse". The courthouse galleries were packed. The *Times* commented, "For years past no event of a non-political cast has created greater excitement than the adventurous attempt of the lord of Barnane to possess himself, by means beyond the pale of the law, of a bride endowed with all the requisites,

---

[100] Nancy Murphy, The Apologia of an Abductor, in Tipperary: A Treasure Chest, 1995, p. 60

[101] Ibid. p. 59

personal and pecuniary."[102] John Carden was 43 years old, and Eleanor was only 21. She was a native of Surrey and said to possess a fortune in excess of £30,000.

Eleanor stated in the course of the trail that she had 'never encouraged Mr. Carden'. Carden was found not guilty of the felony for which he was charged, but guilty of the attempt to commit it. There was a second charge of felonious assault against him, that he had hit and seriously injured John Smithwick with a scull-cracker, during the affray at Rahronan. He was found not guilty of that assault. Sentence was not pronounced until the second case was dealt with, and then Judge Ball handed down his sentence of two years imprisonment with hard labour, adding that Carden 'was found guilty of an attempt to commit a felony hardly in a single instance known to have been perpetrated by any person of the class of society to which you belong.' [103]

According to the *Times* report, when the verdict was announced there were loud cheers in court, and 'many ladies in the gallery enthusiastically waved their handkerchiefs'. When the verdict was known outside the courthouse, where a great crowd had gathered, 'three vociferous cheers were given for Carden of Barnane'. His supporters became known as 'the Cardenites'.

Carden served the full two-year sentence. His fellow magistrates in Tipperary, and Lord Donoughmore in particular, made representations for shortening the period of detention, but to no avail. John Rutter Carden was then becoming a nationally known figure. He was already a controversial one, at least in the context of North Tipperary, and was dubbed Woodcock Carden because he was allegedly fired at so many times and was as hard to hit as that elusive game bird. He was described as "a compactly built, muscular man, no more than five foot six inches tall". He was considered good-looking. His father, also called John, was known in his younger days as Killing Jack, a nickname thought to refer to his good looks and their effect upon young ladies. John Rutter was only eleven when his father

---

[102] Hugh A.S. Disney, The Disneys of Strabannon, privately printed, and quoted by Arthur Carden, in his article *"Woodcock" Carden—a balanced account*, in Tipperary Historical Journal, 2000, p. 127

[103] Murphy, op. cit., p. 62

died, and his English mother, Ann, nee Rutter, (hence John's full name), "a formidable woman", ran the estate until he took over around 1838.[104]

The old Barnane towerhouse, recorded as inhabited in 1654,[105] was used as a dwelling up to about 1750 by the early generations of Cardens of Barnane. The first Carden to settle in Barnane was Jonathan, grandson of 'the Patriarch', John Carden, who moved to Tipperary from Cheshire about 1665, and settled in Templemore.[106]

Templemore (courtesy Irish Architectural Archive)

---

[104] Arthur Carden, "Woodcock" Carden—a balanced account, p.121; Arthur Carden, Cardens of Barnane, Part 11, Typescript, 1995, County Library, Thurles, p. 43. Ann was the only child of Henry Rutter of Lincoln and as such inherited a considerable fortune, "with which she paid all the debts and charges on Barnane". Arthur Carden, Carden of Barnane, Working Draft, 2003, p. 8

[105] Civil Survey, 1654, Co Tipperary, Vol. 1, p. 24

[106] Carden, The Cardens of Barnane, Part 11, p. 43. It has been suggested that the Cardens came from Lincolshire rather than Cheshire. Arthur Carden, Carden of Barnane, Working Draft, p. 8

Jonathan, as the eldest son, should have inherited Templemore, and it is thought he was disinherited because of his marriage to a Catholic named Bridget Bagot. It was his younger brother, John, who inherited Templemore and founded the main branch of the Tipperary Cardens. Soon after coming of age Jonathan leased the "castle, town and lands of Barnane". Jonathan died in 1703 aged only 28, and he bequeathed his estate to his wife and son, John III, who was then only three years of age.

Barnane (courtesy I.A.A.)

Jonathan's acquisition, the "castle, town and lands of Barnane", on the southern slopes of the Devil's Bit, was named after the fabled gap, the *bearnán,* in the summit of the mountain range behind the towerhouse. It is thought that a two-storey house was built around 1750 near to or adjoining the towerhouse. When John III came of age around 1720 it seems he commissioned a survey of the estate, which then consisted of 1510 acres, plantation measure. The estate map shows a three bay, three storey house in the vicinity of the old graveyard, and this may have been built by John III.[107] His son, John (Killing Jack), the holder of Barnane from 1789 to 1822, became prominent in Tipperary affairs through being appointed as High Sheriff of the county in 1796 at the age of 28. He was also a J.P. Around that period he may have built the first two storey house incorporating at least in part the old tower house, and added a lake below it.[108] He did not marry until 1809, when he was 37, and his marriage to the heiress, Ann Rutter, enabled him to lease more parcels of land.

After his death at the young age of 48 his wife Ann bought out the lease of Barnane, and also may have embarked on the building of the new mansion at Barnane, possibly even before her son, John Rutter ("Woodcock") came of age in 1832. This was the Tudor-style mansion with parapet walls, which survived up to the 1930s. It had thirty bedrooms and is generally thought to also have incorporated portion at least of the old towerhouse. John Rutter did much landscaping, and added to the mansion, one notable addition being the conservatory to east side.

There had been a clearing of some parts of the Barnane estate during Woodcock's minority, and when he took over he embarked on the policy of recovering and embellishing as demesne land the lands around his residence, which had been let to tenants and fenced into small fields. This led to a deepening of resentment among the tenants, even though they were made offers of outfarms or financial compensation. The *Tipperary Vindicator* of October 1844 claimed he had evicted twenty families over

---

[107] A tracing of this estate map is reproduced by Arthur Carden in his article Templemore houses and gardens—drawings by Robert Smith, in Tipperary Historical Journal 2002

[108] A drawing of this early house and its setting by Robert Smith, done in 1819, is reproduced by Arthur Carden in his article referred to in footnote 3, and in his Carden of Barnane Working Draft, June 2003, p.9

twelve years.[109] Woodcock asserted before the Devon Commission that no
tenant ever left his property without compensation. He was an 'improving'
resident landlord who was also determined to take over farms which had
been broken into increasingly smaller, run-down units, hardly capable of
supporting families at all, not to mention capable of bringing in rents. It
seems his policy was to combine the holdings into more economic units
and let them to efficient tenants, and farm more of the land himself,
converting it from tillage land to pasture and plantations. There is mention
also of Woodcock's extensive model farmyard, where he had ambitions of
establishing an agricultural school.

The Irish correspondent of the London *Times* who visited Barnane
in October 1845 recorded[110] the deepening resentment among the poor
tenants who were reluctant to give up their poor-quality mountainy
holdings on the estate, even though those holdings were offering only "the
most wretched means of subsistence", and they were being offered
financial compensation, and, in some cases at least, alternative houses and
employment in another part of the estate. It was a striking example of the
resentment of the tenant farmer, no matter how small a stake he had in the
land, even marginal land, to give up, at the wish of his landlord, his status
as such for that of a mere labourer. The *Times* reporter also stated that
intimidation of the Barnane tenantry was rife, so much so that when
Woodcock offered 5 shillings a day to get his potatoes dug, his own tenants
were too cowered to take up the offer, and he resorted to bringing in some
Protestant labourers from Shinrone, Co Offaly, to do that and other
harvesting. Those workers had to get police protection.

The potato blight had hit the Barnane crop in that first year of the
blight, destroying at least a quarter of the crop in the area. This no doubt
added to the sense of grievance among the Barnane tenantry. Woodcock
walked his lands accompanied by two men with guns. The serving of three
ejection notices on the expiry of leases the previous November led to the
murder of his wood-ranger, and he himself was targeted again several
times, his horse being shot in one incident.

[109] Murphy, op. cit., p. 62
[110] Quoted by Carden, in "Woodcock" Carden—a balanced account, p. 123

It is said that Woodcock first met Eleanor Arbuthnot in 1852, and that this marked the beginning of his infatuation with her. She was only eighteen at the time.[111] She subsequently visited Barnane with the Goughs, and Arthur Carden, Woodcock's great great grandnephew, maintains that "despite all the denials, there can be little doubt that Eleanor encouraged Woodcock when she and her family first visited him at Barnane".[112] Whether she retained any amorous feelings for him, either before or after the abduction and his imprisonment, remains an open question. No documentary evidence has come to light within the family as to her opinion of, or attitude towards him.[113]He asserted that, despite the crude manhandling he subjected her to at Rathronan gateway, she was a person "for whom in my inmost heart I entertain the tenderest affection and the most entire respect". It is thought that he made some of his additions to Barnane House in the expectation that his planned abduction would be a success.

The extent to which she was manipulated by members of her immediate family also remains controversial. It would seem that it was that perceived manipulation which provoked Woodcock into forming his elaborate and detailed scheme to abduct her. In his 40-page Apologia, published as *A Letter to the Public* in 1858, after another court case in which a later conspiracy to abduct charge against him was withdrawn, he claimed he believed she was forced by her relatives to suppress her true feelings toward him. His unrequited love for her apparently remained undimmed, and his pursuit of her for the remainder of his life has been compared to Dante's pursuit of Beatrice. He found that some of his movements and those of his emissaries were under police surveillance.

In 1859 he stood unsuccessfully for election to Westminster for the borough of Cashel. By then he had added "extensive and costly Turkish baths" at the west end of Barnane House.[114] Then in 1860 he let most of his land, except the house and demesne. He also disposed of around 900 acres of his lands in the Loughmore area in the Encumbered Estates Court, and purchased Killoskehane estate (containing 1,305 acres including its castle

---

[111] Carden, "Woodcock Carden—a balanced account, p. 125
[112] ibid. pp. 127-8
[113] Murphy, op. cit., p. 69
[114] Carden, op. cit., p. 129

residence), which adjoined Barnane. By the terms imposed by Trustees from whom he borrowed some of the purchase money, he was obliged to continue the policy of getting sitting tenants to surrender their holdings for compensation.[115] This ensured his unpopularity up to the end of his life. He was called the 'Tipperary Exterminator' in the nationalist press

He died of 'congestion of the liver' on 21 February 1866, aged 55, and unmarried. Eleanor was to outlive him by thirty-five years, and she too died unmarried. The *Irish Times* reported that at Woodcock's funeral, "Upwards of 200 tradesmen and labourers walking in procession with scarves and hatbands across the large and beautiful demesne, he so much loved, formed a very impressive and melancholy sight..."[116] The procession headed to the little graveyard on the estate surrounding the remnant of the medieval parish church. One of the psalm quotations carved on his headstone surmounted by a spire reads *I acknowledge my transgressions and my sin is ever before me. Ps. LI.*

This verse from the 'Miserere' psalm may have been the choice of his younger brother and successor, Andrew, an army man, described as "a Low Churchman and strict disciplinarian". Andrew joined with obvious gusto in the efforts to round up some Fenians who were reported to be rallying in the upper regions of the Devil's Bit in early March 1867. The first change he brought to Barnane House was to convert Woodcock's Turkish bath building into a chapel. He obtained a licence to hold religious services there, which were held on alternate Sundays with Kilfithmone Church. In the 1876 Land Owners survey, Andrew was recorded as having 2,709 acres valued at just over £2,000.

It fell to him and his successor, his son and namesake, Captain Andrew Murray Carden, to deal with the campaigns for rent reductions and the political campaigns against landlordism itself, organized by the Land League and the United Irish League. Apparently the land agitation was most intense in the Killea area of the Devil's Bit, which is to the north of Barnane, and this is immortalized in the well-known poem, Carden's Wild Domain, composed probably in the late 1870s by Timothy Corcoran (1857-1928), of Curraduff, near Templemore. The early verses eulogize the

---

[115] Murphy, op. cit., p. 67
[116] Carden, op. cit., p 129

Carden estates as idyllic hunting ground, and the final verses, given here, bemoan the emigration then rampant, and call for an end of landlord control of land:

> *It grieves me sore to see such land oppressed by tyrant laws,*
> *To strike a blow for this fair land would be a righteous cause,*
> *To see our sons and daughters fair compelled to cross the main*
> *And leaving Paradise behind, in Carden's Wild Domain.*
>
> *Behold my friends your native glens; behold their grandeur too,*
> *Remember well tradition tells, that there's the place for you,*
> *From the landlords and their agents, our rights we can regain,*
> *And plant our homesteads once again, round Carden's Wild Domain*
>
> *So rise up, me bold Tipperary boys, and hasten to the fray,*
> *And join your gallant comrades from Drom and brave Killea,*
> *We'll free the land St. Patrick blessed, and break the tyrant's chain,*
> *We'll hunt and fish and reap the fruit, on Carden's Wild Domain.*[117]

Captain Andrew, who was unmarried, lived a lonely life in Woodcock's mansion, where many of the rooms were shut up. In his latter years he spent much of his time in the Kildare Street Club in Dublin. Killoskehane estate was acquired by the Land Commission early in the 20th century, and divided among small local landholders. Andrew availed of the 1903 Wyndham Act, which enabled landlords to sell their tenanted farms to the tenants, to make 2,327 acres of the Barnane estate available for sale in 1908. Agitation was being mounted at the time by the Drom branch of the United Irish League, and most of the estate was then divided into 35-acre farms.

Andrew died in June 1932, at the Kildare Street Club. He was the last of the Cardens to live in Barnane House. After his death further land divisions occurred. The last to use the house as a residence was Walter P. Thompson, to whom Andrew had leased part of the mansion. Thompson

---

[117] Timothy Corcoran was a seminarian in St Patrick's College when he composed Carden's Wild Domain, and is said to have become involved with his brother James, also a seminarian, in the land agitation. Both were ordained in the United States and served in the dioceses of Dubuque, Lincoln, and Chicago

later bought the house and demesne, and one of his enterprises was importing second-hand cars from England. In the late 1920s Barnane became an old car scrap yard. When Thompson's enterprises finally failed, he sold the lead from the roof and pulled down much of the house. He invited the Irish military then occupying Templemore barracks to experiment with blowing up parts of the house and the old towerhouse. He also sold the timber of the demesne. By 1944 Barnane House was dismantled to its foundations.[118] The property was purchased by J.C. Lupton of Templemore, and his son and family live there now in a bungalow built on the site. Some of the extensive farmyard walls and buildings survive, including the castle-like gardener's house, meshed into the south-west corner of the still intact walled garden.

---

[118] Murphy, op. cit., p. 68; Carden, Carden's of Barnane, Part 11, pp70-71

Damer

What good is Damer with all his riches[119]
When he has nothing in his breeches!

Of all the Gentry families that ever settled in Tipperary the Damers were the only ones to become part of the folklore, not alone of Tipperary but of many parts of Ireland. The old saying 'as rich as Damer' is based on a long tradition concerning the great wealth which was amassed by Joseph Damer.

Joseph Damer was born in Dorset in England in 1630. He became a captain in the Parliamentary Army and came to know Oliver Cromwell. According to some writers he was made a special envoy whose duty it was to liaise with Cardinal Mazarin of France. The story goes that it was at this point in his career that he developed an overriding passion for accumulating wealth, following the example of Mazarin. The good Cardinal was so acquisitive that he was said to be worth over twelve million pounds (sterling we presume) when he died.

Unlike many of Cromwell's officers Damer does not appear to have benefited from the distribution of lands after the Cromwellian Confiscations. He seems to have stayed in England and after the Restoration of Charles II he sold his property in England[120] and came to Ireland where huge tracts of land were being sold for relatively small sums

---

[119] This verse was written about John Damer – the 'Great Damer' who although married had no children.
[120] He disposed of lands that he possessed in Somerset and Dorset.

by the former Cromwellian grantees. He was also an agent for Erasmus Smith who had acquired a huge estate in Tipperary after the Restoration.[121]

Joseph Damer bought a large amount of land at Shronell, in Tipperary in 1662. His first business venture was to go into the woollen business, as a sheep farmer. He covered the estate with over ten thousand head of sheep and exported the wool through Waterford harbour. His business with shipping led him to become engaged in the chandlery business. In the course of time he became interested in banking and set up business in Dublin,[122] while retaining and working his Tipperary estate, where his nephew John was his agent. He became one of the most successful of the Dublin bankers and loaned money to the Government on many occasions.[123]

It was well known that he was extremely miserly and spent very little on his own person. When he died the vitriolic Dean of St. Patrick's, Dean Swift, penned a number of verses to mark his passing. One of them said of Damer:

> He walked the streets and wore a threadbare cloak
> He dined and supped at charge of other folk,
> And – by his look- had he held out his palms
> He might be thought an object fit for alms…[124]

Joseph never married and when he died in 1720 he left his entire estate to one or both of his nephews John and Joseph Damer, the sons of George Damer, his brother. According to the records his estate was valued at over £300,000.[125] This included lands in Tipperary, Kilkenny, Galway, Offaly and Kerry. According to one source he left all his lands in Tipperary

---

[121] Erasmus Smith vested more than 12,000 acres of his 46,000-acre Irish holdings, in trustees. They were to found and maintain schools so that 'the poor children inhabiting any part of his lands in Ireland should be brought up in the fear of God, and good literature and to speak the English tongue'. *Oxford Companion of Irish History*

[122] According to Marnane in *Land and Violence in West Tipperary* money lending was the first business Damer set up in Ireland – in Fishamble Street.

[123] There was a dark side to Damer, too, as, according to Marnane he was involved in a number of lawsuits. It was alleged also that 'he was able to combine the supposed destruction of legal documents with his actual possession of various lands to his own advantage.'

[124] The Poems of Jonathan Swift.

[125] To put this in perspective the modern equivalent would be about 350 million Euros.

and in the other counties between his two nephews and a number of smaller legacies to several other relatives including another nephew by a different brother. This nephew was not the flavour of the month when Damer made his will, as he referred to the fact that he had settled his debts of £150 and then left him only a small amount of money. He did leave £5 for the poor of Tipperary town and surrounding district. He also left money to some charities in Dublin.

Despite Swift's summation of his character the following notice of his death appeared in a newspaper of the time:

"On Wednesday last, Mr. Joseph Damer died at his house in Smithfield (Dublin) upwards of 90 years of age, with not above £340,000 and last night was interred in St. Paul's Church in Oxmantown Green, attended by a numerous train of gentlemen as well as by hackney coaches. He never was married but had two nephews, sons of a brother. I am told that the oldest, Mr. Joseph Damer who lives in Tipperary (county) was made his heir. I knew him upwards of fifty years, and though his fortune was all his own acquiring, I believe that it was every penny got honestly. His Purse was open to all he believed to be honest or where he thought his money secure. He never took more than common interest and very rarely that. I look upon his death to be one of the greater losses Ireland could labour under in the loss of any one subject in it."

Because of his astonishing wealth his name spread to the four corners of Ireland and he became part of the folklore, being equated with King Midas, who turned everything he touched into gold. According to Daithi O'hOgain, who researched the folklore manuscripts in Dublin, many stories sprung up in the peasant folktales concerning the origins of Damer's wealth.

One of the stories confuses the timescale and places Damer in the 16th century. According to this story, Damer was a poor English candlemaker who settled in Shronell district. When the monasteries were being repressed in the time of Henry VIII and their wealth was being pillaged, barrels of wax were sold in Tipperary. Damer bought a couple of barrels and found a hoard of gold contained in the middle of each barrel. He then went and bought the entire consignment of barrels. He built a castle and he had one room full of gold.[126]

Another folktale states that the gold that Damer found belonged to an Irish Chieftain who had been forced out of the district.[127]

Yet another averred that the Devil came to Damer and promised him gold in return for his soul. Damer agreed and the Devil was sent into a room where there was a large boot. The Devil was asked to fill the boot with gold. He went away and came back with the gold, which he filled, into the boot. However the boot was still empty and he had to go for more. No matter how often he tried to fill the boot the gold kept disappearing. After sometime the nonplussed demon gave up in disgust and left. Damer had removed the sole of the boot and made a hole in the floor so that the gold went down a sluice into sacks below, which were carefully stored away by Damer's servants. So Damer got his gold and held onto his soul.

The heir John Damer now became an object of envy and to some extent ridicule when Dean Swift christened him 'The great Damer'

John married Margaret Roe a daughter of Andrew Roe of Roesborough in 1724. It would appear that the Roes were cash strapped and more or less 'sold' the daughter to Damer, who must have been much older than his bride.[128] Again according to legend, the marriage was short lived. A variety of reasons have been advanced. One was that Damer became annoyed with his wife, who gave a golden guinea to every beggar man who called to the house, so Damer prevailed on her brother, whom he paid handsomely, to take her away out of the place. Another was that he became very jealous and built a tower in which he imprisoned her, but from which

---

[126] Daithi O'hOgain, in *Tipperary History & Society*

[127] From Kerry a Damer tale concerned a tailor, who made a suit of clothes for Damer. Damer enquired how much he would take off the price. The tailor told him he would give him a reduction if he was allowed to see Damer's gold. After much bargaining the tailor agreed to give Damer the suit for nothing if he were allowed to see the gold. Damer agreed and the tailor was shown the hoard. Damer enquired was he any the better for seeing the gold. "I am the better of it," said the tailor, "because now I see that you get no more satisfaction or pleasure from looking at your gold than I do!" Damer was so amused with the tailor's response that he allowed him to take two fistfuls of the gold.

[128] Damer must have been in his mid fifties when he got married.

she finally escaped and eloped with an officer from the garrison in Tipperary.

Joseph[129] succeeded his brother as the owner of the estates when John died sometime before 1730.[130] He had political leanings and was elected as an M.P. for the county in the by-election of 1735. He had been advanced in the Mathew interest (Tory). The election was not without controversy. The defeated candidate, John Dawson, attributed his failure to certain irregularities, chief of which was the delayed opening of the poll by Theobald Mathew of Annfield, the Sheriff. This delay facilitated the creation of freeholders who voted for Damer. Joseph didn't enjoy his office for long, as he died the following year.

He was succeeded by his son Joseph who was an absentee.[131] It would appear that Joseph's brother, John, managed the estate for a period. In 1740, John, known as 'little John', built a mansion, which is remembered in folk memory, but very little trace is to be seen today. He was supposed to have brought in hundreds of Scots labourers and tradesmen and it was said the house contained a window for every day of the year. The house was called Damerville and was reckoned to be one of the finest mansions in the British Isles.[132]

Locals too were employed in the project, which was ongoing in 1746 when there was a famine. Because of this employment many families were saved from death by starvation. Yet there was local discontent as evidenced in the cutting down of an orchard on the Damer estate at Borrisoleigh in 1760, ostensibly the work of Whiteboys.[133]

---

[129] Joseph had three sons and two daughters, the eldest of whom, Mary, married William Dawson, the first Viscount Carlow. Her son, John, became the first Earl of Portarlington. His son John, the 2nd Earl succeeded to the fortunes and estates of the Damers in 1826.

[130] This must have been the John who bought Roscrea town and almost 3,000 acres in 1722. He paid £22,000 to Robert Curtis who had bought the property from the Ormondes for £3,399 in 1703. The Damers also benefited from the urban rents of Roscrea. - T. Power in *Land, Politics and Society in 18th century Tipperary.*

[131] Joseph was an M.P. in England. In 1753 he was created Lord Milton and in 1792 he was made Earl of Dorchester. He survived until 1798. He had three sons, John, George and Lionel and one daughter, Caroline. Only George and Caroline survived their father.

[132] The house was demolished in 1775 on the orders of Viscount Milton.

[133] T. Power in *Land, Politics and Society in 18th century Tipperary.*

There is a story told of a visit to the house by Liam Dall O'hIfearnain. Liam, an Irish poet who spoke Irish and composed in Irish, became very famous posthumously.

'Liam Dall hated Damer, though he used to go to the mansion to get his dinner there. In fact Damer would give him his living altogether if he'd stop cutting him up in his songs. One day he went there, anyway and Barlow and Butler were two men employed in the service of Damer. Barlow was a Scotch speaker and he had the Gaelic tongue. He came to Liam Dall to the door. "Take your time", says he, "there's a big crowd of gentlemen inside. You'll get nothing at present!" Liam didn't fancy being second-class at all. He knew more than a lot of them. "Oh," says he, "who are the gentlemen?" "Oh, Lowe of Kilshane[134] is there, and Roe of Roesborough and Mr. Damer himself is at home." "Ah, my good man," says Liam, "there won't be a Damer there, nor a Lowe in Kilshane, nor a Roe in Roesborough, but there'll be a Heffernan in Shronell always!" Old Barlow was a good-hearted fellow, but Damer was a regular ould pauper always. "What is that bard saying?" says Damer to Barlow. It was in Irish Liam Dall and Barlow had been speaking and Damer didn't know any Irish. Barlow said to him: "He says Damer has a great table and that it may be always there!" says he. "Oh, let him have his dinner!" said Damer.[135]

John Damer was instrumental in bringing in Protestant textile workers to Shronell in the 1740s where he must have had an industry, probably a woollen processing factory. By the year 1766 there were over 400 Protestant people on the estate. This included some Catholics who had converted, notably head-tenants, such as Kissane and Burke.[136] He also founded a Methodist community there. It is noteworthy that during the first five decades of the 18th century thirteen head-leases were granted to Protestants, although in his lands at Kilnamanagh and Ileagh in the north of the county he had two Catholic head-tenants in Fogartys and Burkes.[137]

---

[134] There was no Lowe in Kilshane in that period, so the story was embellished as time progressed. The Lowes only moved into Kilshane in the 1820s and replaced the McCarthys.

[135] Bealoideas

[136] T. Power in *Land, Politics and Society in 18th century Tipperary*

[137] Ibid.

John must have further annoyed the locals for Liam Dall had this to say about him, but he was probably referring to his religious bigotry rather than miserliness.

"Feoirling ni thabharfadh don tsagart
Dá dtagadh a thabairt on mbás"[138]

Whatever about John,[139] his brother, the Viscount was in fact a liberal spender and vast sums were expended on his estates in Dorset in England. His bigotry, however, did not go unnoticed as he remarked to the government that 'the common papists are insolent and provide themselves with arms'.[140] The Viscount's son, John Damer, was, by all accounts, a real spendthrift. It was said that he put on new clothes three times a day and never wore the same outfit twice. He committed suicide, by shooting himself, in a public house in London in 1776. When his clothes were sold in an auction they fetched £15,000, a huge sum at the time. He was married to Anne Seymour a noted sculptress.

Ann Seymour was the only child of Field Marshal Henry Seymour Conway. She was a sculptress who took lessons from a noted Italian sculptor and studied anatomy just as the great masters had done. She married John Damer who was heir to a fortune of £30,000 a year, in 1767. By 1776 her husband and his two brothers had accumulated huge debts which their father refused to pay. Damer shot himself the same year, in an inn 'having had supper with a blind fiddler and worse company'[141]

His widow was left with a substantial annuity. She continued her interest in sculpting and designed some notable works including the heads of the two rivers Thame and Isis for the Bridge at Henley near her father's house at Park Place. Her father designed the bridge. She met Josephine, Napoleon's wife, and was introduced to the great man. She made him a

---

[138] In rough translation this might read –' He wouldn't give a farthing to the priest if it was to save him from death.'

[139] John died in 1783. He had no family.

[140] This remark was made following the rescue of Rev. Daniel O'Neill, who was being conveyed to Limerick for trial, from Clonmel jail. His crime was that he had conducted the marriage ceremony of Henry Grady and the abducted Susanna Grove. Over 3000 people were involved in the rescue in 1753. Fr. O'Neill continued to function openly as a priest in Cullen for many years after, although there was a price on his head. - T. Power in *Land, Politics and Society in 18th century Tipperary*

[141] The Dictionary of National Biography

bust of Fox, the English Prime Minister, and in return he gave her a diamond snuffbox, which is in the British Museum today. She made a bust of Nelson after the battle of the Nile. She had many influential friends including Horace Walpole (Lord Oxford) who left her his house, after his death, for her use during her lifetime with £2,000 a year for its upkeep. She was a very well known socialite of her time. She died in 1828 and is buried at Sundridge in Kent.

Following the death of his brother in 1783 the Viscount appointed a firm called Coopers[142] as the agents of the estates. Apart from the loss of his brother as his agent, the Viscount was faced with the unrest that was sweeping the country in relation to tenants' leases and the inability of some tenants to pay their rents due to the bad weather conditions of the time.

In 1784 there was a famous case of forced occupancy in the Cullen area on the Damer estate. Damer's head-tenant, a man called English, with his supporters, forcibly occupied Ballinulta, near Cullen, and resisted attempts by the authorities to have them removed. This action arose because of attempts that were being made to by-pass the head-tenants. This case caused consternation among the landed gentry and the Archbishop of Cashel remarked that 'all the gentlemen of the county will be dispossessed.'[143]

The Viscount himself died in 1798 at the great age of eighty-three.

He was succeeded by his second son, George, who became the second Lord Dorchester. George died in 1808 and his sister Caroline became the heiress to the family fortunes. She was a single person and when she died in 1826 the estates and properties passed to the 2nd Earl of Portarlington, her second cousin, who assumed the name of Dawson-Damer.[144]

---

[142] The family originally settled at Killenure near Cashel in the 1740s as part of the household of Archbishop Price. They later rose to prominence in the Treasury Office in Dublin. As well as being agents for the Damer estate they were agents for the Maudes, Cashel See, Erasmus Smith and Lloyd estates. - T. Power in *Land, Politics and Society in 18th century Tipperary*

[143] T. Power in *Land, Politics and Society in 18th century Tipperary*

[144] This man was an Army officer and was present at the Battle of Waterloo when it was said, his horse was shot from under him. When he retired he became a serious gambler and died unmarried in 1845

After the death of the 2nd Earl the bulk of the 18,000-acre estate in Clanwilliam was sold in 1855 and the Portarlingtons retained only 2,900 acres in the area.

The association of the Damers with Roscrea is now very well known because of the wonderful restoration work carried out by the Roscrea Heritage group. Damer House was built in the early 18th century and was incorporated into the Castle grounds.

Damer House (Courtesy Dept. of Environment)

Liam Dall[145] had the last word about the Damers in a satire about the death of John Damer. Here is a translation of a verse that is pertinent:

> Alas Death's angels calling
> Fool John could not evade
> Nor sun nor moon went crawling
> When Damer great was laid
> His passing is not galling
> His Court a chapel made.[146]

---

[145] Liam Dall O hIfearnain a 17th century poet died in 1803 and is buried in Lattin cemetery in an unmarked grave.
[146] Liam Prut in *Tipperary History & Society*

Grubb

Tennis in the summer months provided the daughters of the Ascendancy with as good an opportunity of meeting and attracting young men as hunting did in the winter. 'The girls there were all in short, exceedingly tight white dresses' Lady Talbot de Malahide reported of a County Dublin tennis party in the summer of 1913. 'Nothing was left to the imagination.' Bence Jones[147] went on to say 'They were as bad as Joan Grubb, the young daughter of a Tipperary County family, who followed the example of Mrs. Sadleir-Jackson and rode astride'.

Joan, whose first husband was killed in May 1915 in the Great War, eventually became Mrs. De Sales la Terriere. Bence Jones in his remarkable book *Twilight of the Ascendancy* mentions Mrs. De Sales La Terriere as one of the elderly ladies of advanced years living in decrepit country houses in the late 1950s. He went on to say that she was fortunate in that her castle in County Tipperary[148] was solidly built so that although totally neglected it did not actually fall down. She cooked her dogs' food in the hall and had no vehicle except a horse and trap. She wore a man's cap, jacket and tie, rather in the manner of John Vere Foster[149].

The adventurous nature of Joan Grubb, in riding astride, was a far cry from the sober, level headed, industrious, religious Quaker Grubb

---

[147] Bence-Jones *Twilight of the Ascendancy*

[148] This was Kiltinan Castle, near Fethard, in Tipperary. Joan was a descendant of Samuel of Clogheen through Richard Grubb of Castle Grace. She died in 1969. She had one daughter.

[149] John Vere Foster was actually a lady.

ancestors as portrayed in his very fine study of the family by G.W. Grubb in his book *The Grubbs of Tipperary*.

Kiltinan Castle (courtesy I.A.A.)

The Grubb ladies were by and large an extremely religious and sensible group of people whose lives were dedicated to the spread of the Word of God. A few of them even went so far as to leave their children in the care of their husbands and travel, not alone all over Ireland, but much further afield in order to fulfill their perceived evangelical roles.

One such remarkable lady was Sarah Grubb, the wife of John, who was the grandson of John, the founding ancestor of the Tipperary Grubbs.

She married her husband in 1803 but "she did not allow family cares to restrict her ministerial activities". She was a recognized Quaker minister for 48 years and she was a great traveller and speaker and one of the most extraordinary women in the Society of Friends. Her missionary zeal eventually brought them to England where they finally settled at Sudbury. Their son, Jonathan Grubb, also became a missionary. He sold his extensive corn and milling business at Lexden in Essex and spread the gospel in Eastern countries and in Ireland, Wales and the Shetland Islands. This family was known as the Burlingham Grubbs, so called after the second wife of Jonathan Grubb. They had numerous descendants,[150] many of whom followed in the footsteps of Jonathan and became ministers in the Society of Friends.

Ann Grubb, an eighteenth century beauty, fell in love with Lieutenant Frederick Close who was stationed at Clonmel with the 96th regiment. Her uncle, Joseph Grubb, as a sincere Quaker, disapproved of the military profession and wished her to marry someone else. One Sunday night in February 1826 the two lovers met secretly on the tow path beside the river, and were seen no more until their bodies were washed up three weeks later. There were many rumours; some of murder and others of an elopement, but the truth was never discovered. Her beauty was noticed by the novelist W.H.Maxwell, who described her in the following way, under a fictitious name –

> 'A lovelier face I never looked at - scarcely nineteen years old, tall, and with gentle hazel eyes. Her golden brown hair was parted Madonna-like, which her silken cap could not fully hide. Notwithstanding her costume the roundness of her arms and the symmetry of her beautiful waist and bosom could not be concealed. The outline of her face was strictly Grecian – her complexion pale and delicate, whilst her ripe red lips seemed as if some Clonmel bee had stung them newly. Were anything wanting to make her quite irresistible her voice was so musical and so modulated, that the listener held his breath to hear.'

The Grubb story is quite extraordinary in that it is a tale of rags to riches that spans over three centuries.

---

[150] Dr. Isabel Grubb, a distinguished author, who lived in Waterford and who was born in 1881 was one of his descendants.

As the name implies the family were of European origin, but the John Grubb who came to Ireland was a Cromwellian grantee. He was settled at Annis Castle on 1000 acres in South Kilkenny, near New Ross. The castle was a ruin and John and his wife, Mary, had to settle in a nearby house. He set up a linen business in an existing mill on the property and in 1676 the family became Quakers. John and Mary had one son Samuel and five daughters. John got married a second time after his first wife died. He was in his sixties and the children of his first family were already adults. John and his second wife moved from Annis Castle to Meylerspark, in Co. Wexford, but also near New Ross.

Samuel himself got married and had two sons, William and John. William went to America with William Penn, the founder of the state of Pennsylvania. William Grubb went on to become the ancestor of a large number of Grubbs in America. The younger son, John, inherited Annis Castle. He had four daughters and when he died in the mid eighteenth century the castle and lands passed out of Grubb ownership.

Meanwhile John the elder and his second wife found life at Meylerspark difficult and when John died, his son, also called John, a boy of sixteen, continued to work the family linen business with the help of his mother's family. He got married and had ten children. A downturn in the linen trade led to a period of extreme hardship. John was forced to sell whatever he had and move to county Tipperary, where a fellow Quaker rented him a small farm, at Magorban, halfway between Fethard and Cashel.

John's economic affairs continued to disimprove and the family were relying on help from their Quaker friends. John got an offer of work. He was asked to go to America to supervise the building of a ship. His wife and ten children were left at Magorban, living in little better than a hovel. John went to America in 1727 and after three years the ship was almost completed, but the owner said there was now no money to pay for the completion. The owner, upon inspecting the ship, found that it was somewhat bigger than the specifications and refused to pay his three years wages to John. To add insult to injury John was accused of pilfering from the ship's stores and committed to prison in New Jersey in 1730. He spent a year in jail. Upon his release some of his Quaker friends gave him his passage money and he sailed home to Ireland.

He arrived to find his wife and children in dire poverty. The hardships of his life and the disappointments led to his premature death three months later at the age of forty-nine. Four of his children had predeceased him, but four sons and two daughters survived. The eldest of the four sons, Joseph, was the man who built the family fortunes.

Joseph was one of those people who, as well as being intelligent and handsome, was lucky and made his own luck. His first job was in a mill in Clonmel. There he learned everything about the milling industry. His marriage to Anne Greer, a wealthy heiress, the daughter of a successful Quaker merchant, proved to be the turning point in his life.

Within a short time he was able to buy his own mill. At the same time he took care to get his brothers into gainful employment. John worked in a draper shop in Clonmel and later was able to acquire his own business. William married a girl who inherited a farm at Woodhouse and he became a farmer.

By the time he died in 1782 Joseph Grubb owned all the mills along the Clonmel bank of the Suir and Anner mills two miles from the town. In the process he had toppled one of the gentry families of Clonmel, the Moores of Marlfield[151] who were forced to sell Marlfield to the Bagwells.

Grubb's house at Anner Mills was attacked by Whiteboys in July 1775. It was said of the attackers – 'they were far above the lower order of people, were decently dressed and spoke the English language very well'. In another incident the houses of M. Reilly and J. Casey, tenants to Thomas Grubb near Clonmel, were attacked by forty or fifty men. Casey by prearrangement with his attackers was absent, but Reilly was flogged because he was to succeed the following March to the old tenant.[152]

Samuel Grubb, the second son of Joseph, who had founded the family fortunes, and his wife Margaret[153] were severely traumatized in 1798. Thomas Judkin Fitzgerald arrived in Clonmel that summer to put

---

[151] The Moores were heavily involved in the milling business also.

[152] T. Power in *Land, Politics and Society in 18th century Tipperary*.

[153] She was Margaret the sister of Abraham Shackleton, the Quaker schoolmaster of Ballitore, in Co. Kildare. During the period of the Insurrection the school in Ballitore, which was attended by the Grubb children among others, was closed. That was the reason the Grubbs employed the French tutor for their children. Many of the later Grubb children were educated at Ballitore.

down the insurrection. Acting on information, which was totally inaccurate, he arrested an unfortunate Quaker, called Wright, a French tutor to the Grubbs, dragged him out onto the street and had him flogged so badly that it took him many years to recover. Samuel and Margaret, with other Quakers watched and prayed in the street as the punishment went on, but were powerless to help. After that episode they determined to move out of Clonmel. They went to Clogheen, fifteen miles from Clonmel, near the Vee and set up a milling business there. As time progressed they brought their sons into the expanding business in Clogheen while the eldest, Abraham, was left in Clonmel to look after the corn and butter business there.

As they prospered they bought more property and some beautiful houses in the Clogheen area. Samuel and Margaret applied for and received a Coat of Arms with the motto "Bonne et Assez Belles" which roughly translated means "Goodness and enough Beauty", a reference to the many beautiful Grubb ladies. In keeping with the new crest, which was worn later on signet rings by their descendants, Samuel and Margaret ordered two large canteens of cutlery for use by the family at Clogheen, and on their marriages his children were each presented with George III silver, mint marked with the Grubb crest.

The Quakers founded the House of Industry in Clonmel in the early part of the 19th century. This was a building 'that redounds immortal honour on the Society of Friends, and especially on Robert Grubb, whose unremitting labours and charitable exertions toward ameliorating the situation of the poor inhabitants of Clonmel, will never be forgotten'.[154]

Robert was the 5th son of Samuel Grubb, Joseph's second son. Robert was born in 1790. He never married but became famous in Clonmel because of his charitable works. The House of Industry, which was built outside the West Gate of the Town, was a place of refuge and confinement for vagrants and for the poor and helpless.

Thomas Grubb, Robert's brother, became famous too. He was the man who devoted his life to making the Suir navigable for barges and boats from the sea at Waterford up to Clogheen and Cahir. In the early part of his life he worked in his father's mill at Clogheen, where he soon realized the difficulty of exporting goods from the Golden Vale. He got married to

---

[154] *Bianconi King of the Irish Roads*

Elizabeth Haughton, in 1819, and with her he received a considerable dowry. He invested in a large amount of real estate at the Quay in Clonmel, where he built up a prosperous trade in river transport. He had seven sons and he employed them all in his business ventures which included horticulture and boat building. Thomas Grubb's two elder brothers, Richard and Samuel, both married very well and received considerable dowries, which they used to purchase large estates at Cahir Abbey and Castle Grace. They also had large families and it was not unknown for as many as sixty Grubbs to be seen out hunting together near Cahir or Castle Grace.

Another prominent Grubb was Thomas of Dublin, a second cousin of Thomas of Clonmel, just mentioned. He was a Fellow of the Royal Society of Dublin. He was a noted optician and constructed reflecting telescopes and fine instruments. Like his cousin, he had a large family and one of his sons was Sir Howard Grubb of Dublin (1844-1931), a Trinity College graduate of science and a leading astronomical instrument maker who was knighted in 1887.

Richard Grubb of Cahir Abbey settled into the life of a country squire and was soon invited to become a J.P. There is a remarkable resemblance between the characters of Richard Grubb and that of Charles Bianconi who was on the bench in Tipperary at that time. They both came from working backgrounds, they were both genial and friendly, caring of their families and tenants and both came from a deeply religious background. Richard had distanced himself from the Quaker community and this meant inevitably that they no longer regarded him a member of the Society of Friends. Though saddened by this episode in his life, his compassion for his fellow man, especially those unfortunates who were summoned to appear before him, was increased, if anything, by his own misfortune. Richard's family all grew up and married. Their numerous descendants went away to live in England, Australia and Canada. Others joined the British Army and one, Alexander, fought in the Maori Wars in New Zealand.

Frederick, Richard's third son, was the man who was to inherit Cahir Abbey but after Richard's death the Abbey had to be sold to pay the mounting debts. Frederick emigrated to California where he died in 1919.

Grubb photos said to be the oldest photographs in Ireland.

Alexander, his second son, joined the Army and while in Gibraltar wrote home to say he had become engaged to Sara Watkins, the only daughter of a Vicar from Middlesex. The Vicar's wife, Mrs. Watkins was an extremely wealthy woman in her own right and she requested a visit to Cahir Abbey to meet the Grubbs. Alexander married Sara and later as a retired Army officer, served on the bench in Kent. Alexander's son and grandson both named after him, also served as Justices of the Peace.

One of the outstanding events in Lieutenant Colonel Alexander's life was his being invited to King Edward VIIs levee for officers at St. James' Palace, with his four sons- Captain A.H. Watkins Grubb, D.S.O., R.E., Headquarters Staff, Captain Herbert Watkins Grubb, the Border Regiment, Lieutenant W.B. Watkins Grubb, R.N., and Lieutenant R. Watkins Grubb, R.N.

The outstanding event for the Grubb ladies was when Mrs. Sara Grubb presented each of her daughters and daughters-in-law to the King and Queen Alexandra at Buckingham Palace in 1909 and again in 1910.

Captain Herbert Watkins Grubb remained a career Army officer, attaining the rank of Lieutenant Colonel. He had the distinction of being the last uniformed British Army Officer to take the salute in Ireland before Southern Ireland became a Republic. His long army career brought him to South Africa (the Boer War), India, Burma and France (World War 1).

Lieutenant Colonel Herbert had two sons, one of whom became a clergyman and one a Major in the Army. The Major served in World War II in France, North Africa, Italy and Holland and took part in the parachute jump at Arnhem in 1944. He married Elizabeth Canter in 1948 and they had two children Martin John Grubb, an army Lieutenant, who served in Northern Ireland in 1971 and Rosemary (Grubb) who began nursing in London in 1972.

The Grubbs of Castle Grace

Castle Grace was an estate of about 2,000 acres at the time it was bought for Samuel Grubb, the third son of Samuel and Margaret Grubb mentioned above. Castle Grace lies in the foothills of the Knockmealdown Mountains and it is said, received its name from Raymond le Gros, the famous Norman invader. The ruins of the 12th century castle still remain on the banks of the Tar river (shortened from Ouentarr). The estate was bought in 1820 when Samuel junior married his second cousin Deborah Davis. He built a new corn mill near where the river Tar joins the Suir and shortly afterwards he built the house which is currently the home of Mr. Nicholas Grubb and his wife and family.

Castle Grace 2003 (Courtesy Mr.& Mrs. Grubb)

Samuel and Deborah had six sons and three daughters. The three girls, Sarah, Elizabeth and Louisa, married Thomas Andrews, Edwin Taylor and Charles Barrington respectively. One of the sons, Samuel, died young and the three younger sons remained bachelors. They lived at Maryville, Cashel. Maryville became the Deanery of Cashel and later a hotel. Samuel and Deborah were very active during the famine and spent a considerable part of their income relieving the poor. Samuel died in 1859 and Deborah survived to see the introduction of the Land Acts in 1885.

The eldest son, Richard Davis Grubb who was born in 1820 married his first cousin Margaret Grubb, the daughter of Thomas of Clonmel, in 1851. Both Richard and his wife died at a comparatively young age. Richard died in 1865 and his wife died in childbirth ten years before him, leaving two small children, Margaret[155] who was born in 1853, and Samuel

---

[155] She married John Russell Mechem.

Richard who was born in 1855. The two children were reared by their grandmother Deborah and their father.

Samuel Richard got married in the same year that his grandmother Deborah died, 1885. His wife was Hannah Binney who was from the Isle of Man. Samuel, a J.P., was High Sheriff of Co. Tipperary in 1914. He died in 1921. In accordance with his wishes he was buried in the Knockmealdown Mountains and a large stone cairn marks his grave. Samuel and Hannah had one son, Richard Raymond de Cruce and one daughter. The daughter was Joan who has already been mentioned at the start of this article.

Richard Raymond de Cruce, J.P., who was born in 1886, attended Wellington College in Berkshire and entered the Army. He fought in World War I and also in the Second World War. In between the wars he commanded the 3rd Hussars. He retired as a Colonel and lived until 1970. He married Ruth Leney of Saltwood House, Hythe, Kent and they had two sons, Richard (b. 1915) and Patrick de Cruce Grubb, the father of Nicholas mentioned at the start of the section about the Castle Grace Grubbs.

Richard was a test pilot with the R.A.F. and he was killed in an accident over the Irish Sea in 1934.

Patrick, like his father, attended Wellington College and became an officer in the Army. He was captured during the Second World War and remained a prisoner of war for two years 1941-42.[156] He retired from the Army after the War and set up a number of businesses at Castle Grace, including a packaging business and a horse box manufacturing company. He was married in 1947 to Vivien Woodhouse of Dungarvan. Vivien is still living in Tipperary and runs a Stud Farm. Their two sons, Richard (b.1948) and Nicholas (b.1950) were both educated at Wellington College and later attended University in Belfast.

---

[156] He was shot in North Africa and presumed dead but survived and was treated most humanely by the Germans, and eventually was returned to England. His grandson Alexander has written a superb account of his experiences in the Appendix on page 233.

Hely-Hutchinson

Towards the end of April 1916, Lord Donoughmore, the 6th Earl, and his wife, who were now living mostly in England on account of their wartime activities, crossed over to Dublin for his Investiture as a Knight of St. Patrick.[157] The ceremony took place in the Viceregal Lodge in the Phoenix Park. During the ceremony the Viceroy was giving himself kudos for the sterling way in which he was fulfilling his role. Lord Donoughmore winked over his head at Maurice Headlam an English Civil Servant and friend of the Donoughmores. Both men knew that Sinn Fein had become very active and had staged a mock attack on Dublin Castle, which had been swept under the carpet by the authorities. After the ceremony they travelled to the ancestral home of Lord Donoughmore, Knocklofty in Tipperary.

Captain Anthony Maude[158] and Maurice Headlam spent Easter at Knocklofty with the Donoughmores. A career civil servant, Maurice Headlam, became very friendly with Lord and Lady Donoughmore, whom he had met in the Club, in Stephen's Green. Maurice spent many a happy day down in Tipperary fishing and shooting with the Donoughmores. He said that the best salmon fishing in Ireland was at Knocklofty on the lower Suir above the town of Clonmel. Both Lord and Lady Donoughmore were experts at fishing.

It was a bit of a picnic, that weekend, as the house was mostly under dustsheets, but they enjoyed the fishing and the peace and quiet of the Suir valley. All four, left on Easter Monday taking the Dublin train from

---

[157] Lord Powerscourt and Lord Middleton were also invested – *Bence Jones Twilight of the Ascendancy.*

[158] Secretary of the Irish Church Representative Body who lived in Clondalkin.

Clonmel. At Thurles the train stopped for longer than usual. They whiled away the time playing bridge. Then someone came and told them that there was a rebellion in Dublin and that the train would go no further. Nobody seemed to know what had happened. The Donoughmores, who were intent on returning to England, decided to take the next train south hoping to catch the boat from Rosslare. They could only get as far as Clonmel, so they went to Marlfield where the Bagwells[159] gave them lodgings for the night. It would seem that the Bagwells decided to travel back with the Donoughmores, possibly with the intention of going to England also.

Knocklofty 2003 (Now a hotel)

---

[159] John Bagwell, the scion of the family was the General Manager of the Northern Railway and he had a home on Howth Hill in addition to Marlfield.

They were driving by car and as they came down Harcourt Street they were stopped and informed that Stephen's Green was in rebel hands. They turned around and as they went back up Harcourt Street they heard rifle fire. A bullet came through the hood of the car, went through Mrs. Bagwell's shoulder, through the upper part of her husband's arm and through Lord Donoughmore's great coat, giving him a flesh wound and out through the windscreen.[160] They were driven to the home of Sir Frederick Shaw at Bushy Park in Terenure and were treated for their wounds by a Dr. Albert Crolly.

Lord and Lady Donoughmore left the next day and went back to Knocklofty, hoping to be able to get to England via Rosslare.

In 1751 John Hely, an ambitious barrister of modest origins from Co. Cork, married Christian Nickson,[161] grandniece and heiress of Richard Hutchinson of Knocklofty, near Clonmel. Hely agreed to pay off the £11,000 Hutchinson debts, received no dowry and was given only a reversionary interest in the estate of over 3000 acres. However in return for adopting the name Hutchinson the estate was to devolve on him and his heirs and he had power to charge it with £2,000 for younger children. In the process Hely obtained a rural estate and a foothold in the landed class. The family, who achieved an Earldom in 1800, was primarily responsible for carrying the Act of Union in Tipperary and was also distinguished for its support of Catholic relief.[162] Indeed as an important visible manifestation of their stance the Hely-Hutchinsons encouraged the commutation of tithes on their estate in the later years of the 18th and early years of the 19th centuries. Liberal non-Catholic landlords could also be responsible for allowing a Catholic chapel to be centrally located within their estates. The Earl of Donoughmore at Knocklofty House had a large chapel located beside his demesne.[163]

---

[160] Maurice Headlam *Reminiscences*

[161] She was from Munny in South County Wicklow. Richard Nixon, a magistrate from south Wicklow was murdered in the rebellion of 1798.

[162] T. Power *Land, Politics & Society in 18th century Tipperary*

[163] Whelan *Tipperary History & Society*

The dynasty was begun by Colonel James Hutchinson[164] who was settled at Youghalarra in the immediate period after the Cromwellian Confiscations. However, after the Restoration of Charles II he was uprooted and had to move to Knockballymeagher, thus settling on what had been in pre Norman times the homeland of the Gaelic O'Meagher clan.

In later times the Knockballymeagher lands were enclosed and became the Rockforest estate, near Roscrea. The second estate he acquired was Knocklofty. The tenants on the estate were mainly Prendergasts and Lonergans, the descendants of the Gaelic owners in Pre-Cromwellian times.

The house was built, disappointingly, in a hollow according to Wakefield. 'The grounds', he wrote, 'are finely planted but the house stands in a most miserable situation sunk in a hollow, with a large walnut tree in front which is the only object seen from it'

Mr. Hutchinson had excavated a lake, at Knockballymeagher, on which reposed ' a canoe of considerable dimensions, hollowed out of a single tree by the American Indians; it was picked up off the Bank of Newfoundland'.[165]

Hutchinson's family seems to have become interested in commerce as we find in 1658, Richard Hutchinson, a merchant at Nenagh, issued his own coin.[166] This man died about 1700 A.D. when his estate devolved on his sister's family in Co. Wicklow.

Apart from the rent rolls, which probably increased significantly in the latter half of the 18th century, The Right Hon. John Hely-Hutchinson had added income from his various offices. In 1775 these were worth £4,900. Born in Cork in 1724 he had been called to the bar in 1748 and became interested in politics. In 1759 he was elected an M.P. for

---

[164] There seems to be some confusion as to the ownership of Knockballymeagher in the 17th, 18th and early 19th centuries. In the pedigree of Hutchinson of Timoney, Roscrea, it would seem that a William Henry Hutchinson (minus the Healy) was of Knockballymeagher in 1821 and his line of descent is shown from Captain James Hutchinson! Perhaps more informative is the name of a J. Hutchinson who was a mere soldier in Captain Sandy's company in *Prendergast's Cromwellian Settlement of Ireland!* Also quite informative is the entry showing Richard Hutchinson, an Adventurer, getting almost two and a half thousand acres in the Barony of Iffa & Offa in compensation for the sum he advanced of £760.

[165] Lewis *Topographical Dictionary*

[166] D. Gleeson *Last Lords of Ormonde*

Lanesborough and for the city of Cork two years later. In the same year he was appointed Provost of Trinity College. He achieved his highest honours in 1777 when he was made Secretary of State for Ireland and Keeper of the Privy Seal.[167]

Barrington tells an interesting tale about a dinner that was held in Trinity College by the Provost, the Right Hon. John Hely-Hutchinson. 'Dr. Barrett, late vice provost, dining at the table of the new provost, who lived in a style of elegance attempted by none of his predecessors, helped himself to what he thought was a peach, but which happened to be a shape made of ice. On taking it into his mouth, never having tasted ice before, he supposed from the pang given to his teeth and the shock which his tongue and mouth instantly received, that the sensation was produced by heat, starting up, therefore, he cried out (and it was the first oath he had ever uttered) "I'm scalded by God", ran home and sent for the apothecary.'

John Hely-Hutchinson's wife, Christian, was elevated to the Peerage in 1783 as Baroness Donoughmore and she survived until 1788. Her husband seems to have lived until at least 1794. They had three sons, Richard, John and Francis.

The second Baron and 1st Earl of Donoughmore[168] was their eldest son Richard Hely. He was made Viscount of Donoughmore in 1797. Like his father, he was in the service, but in the capacity of a military man. He was a Lieutenant General in the army and he was Governor of Tipperary. He never married so when he died in 1825 his interests and honours passed to his brother John.

The second son John Hely-Hutchinson was also a military man and attained a peerage in his own right. He followed in the footsteps of Abercromby and commanded the army in Egypt. He was created *Baron Hutchinson of Alexandria and Knocklofty, Co.Tipperary*. This famous scion of the family was also Ambassador to Russia from 1805-6. He died in 1832 and was succeeded by his nephew John, who became the 3rd Earl of Donoughmore.

---

[167] Like many of the men of his time Hely-Hutchinson could be hot headed. Barrington states in his *Reminiscences* that the Rt. Hon. Hely-Hutchinson, the Provost of Trinity College fought duels with Mr. Doyle, Master in Chancery and others. His son, the Hon. Francis Hutchinson fought the right Hon. Lord Mountnorris.

[168] Made an Earl in 1800 during the push by Government to seal the Act of Union.

Francis Hely-Hutchinson was the third son and he remained in Ireland and became very involved in politics also. He married another Nixon, a daughter of Henry Nixon of Belmont, Co.Wexford. He was an M.P. for Trinity College University and for Naas. Francis will be remembered for his duel with Lord Mountnorris as recorded in Barrington's *Reminiscences*. The duel was fought at Donnybrook, which seems to have been a favouite meeting place for such encounters. In the course of the duel Mountnorris was shot and fell to the ground. However after some time he rose to his feet, both men bowed to each other and went their separate ways. Mountnorris, helped by his second was brought to his home in Dublin and recovered his wound after a month.[169]

In 1774 sixteen immigrant workers, on the Knocklofty estate, were ducked in a pond and sworn 'never to work here again under the severest penalties'. It will be remembered that this was a period of grave agrarian unrest during which the Whiteboys were actively discouraging the employment of people from outside their immediate areas of control. It is not recorded how the Hely-Hutchinsons dealt with the problem.

In the last decade of the 18th century there was a nation-wide movement, in the form of the Catholic Committee, in which Tipperary played a significant role. There were representatives from Carrick, Clonmel, Cashel, Nenagh and Thurles on the county committee. The county delegates were Laurence Smith, a merchant from Carrick, James Scully of Kilfeacle and John Lalor of Long Orchard.

In direct response to this and only a day after the delegates were selected the Protestant diaspora of the county held a meeting of gentry, freeholders and clergy that was very well attended. The meeting formulated an address to the two county M.P.s, John Bagwell and Daniel Toler instructing them to 'vigorously oppose all attempts at innovation or alteration in Church and State' and to support the constitution. Provision was made to collect signatures from the freeholders of the county. When that was done there was found to be only 600 signatures in all, less than forty per cent of the total. What was significant about this meeting was that

---

[169] Duelling seems to have been part and parcel of the life of a squire at that time. The first two questions asked of a young man, seeking a wife, so as to ascertain his respectability were 'What family is he of?' and 'Did he ever blaze?'

it showed clearly that less than half the Protestant interest in the county was opposed to Catholic Relief.

One of the most influential proponents of Catholic relief was Lord Donoughmore. When the petition of 1792 was in preparation he played an important role in seeing that the contents were acceptable not alone to the convention but also to the English side. He was also the chief spokesman in favour of relief in the House of Lords. He had able support from people like Francis Mathew (Lord Llandaff) and Lord Lismore (Cornelius O'Callaghan)

Lord Donoughmore was highly instrumental in keeping the south and south west of the county under control in 1797. He held a meeting of the gentlemen of the area in Clonmel where they resolved to keep the disturbances from spreading from nearby Waterford with the creation of a fund of £1000 to reward informers. By the end of the year he could report to the government that everything was perfectly quiet in the district and would continue so.

John Hely-Hutchinson a nephew of the 2nd Earl of Donoughmore was defeated in the elections of 1830. He and Henry Prittie had been the sitting M.P.s for the county since 1826. In this election Henry Prittie (brother of Lord Dunalley) was returned as an M.P., with Thomas Wyse of Waterford, who defeated John. Although the Hely-Hutchinsons were pro Catholic relief and had been for many decades, Wyse was returned by the voters because he was a Catholic. Prior to entering politics, John was a career Army Officer and fought in the Peninsular War and at the battle of Waterloo.

In the election of 1831 Wyse and Hely-Hutchinson were returned unopposed. John, who was a Lieutenant for the county and a member of the Privy Council held the seat until the following year when he succeeded to the title of Lord Donoughmore on the death of his uncle. It is unclear as to why Henry Prittie did not stand as he only succeeded his uncle as 3rd Lord Dunalley in 1854.

Both Wyse and Hely-Hutchinson lost their seats in the election of 1832 when they were replaced by Lalor Shiel (the playwright) and Cornelius O'Callaghan.

When he succeeded to the title of Lord Donoughmore, in 1832, he moved into the House of Lords. From that time on the Donoughmores represented Tipperary and Ireland as Peers in the House. John was married twice and had two sons and four daughters. His eldest son Richard John became the 4th Earl and his other son went into military service.

In April 1838 two land agents, Austin Cooper and Francis Wayland, were shot at Ballinaclough on their way to the Tipperary fair. Subsequently thirty two Tipperary magistrates, headed by the Earls of Donoughmore and Glengall and by Viscount Lismore, signed a petition to the Chief Secretary, Drummond, asking for more stringent legislation to suppress such crimes. The reply they got was scathing of their stewardship and included a paragraph on the duties of men of property.

'Property has its duties as well as its rights; to the neglect of those duties in times past is mainly to be ascribed that diseased state of society in which such crimes take their rise; and it is not in the enactment or enforcement of statutes of extraordinary severity, but chiefly in the better and more faithful performance of those duties, that a permanent remedy for such disorders is to be sought'.

Richard John was Colonel of the south Tipperary militia in 1849 and was made President of the Board of Trade in 1859. He had succeeded his father as Lord Donoughmore eight years earlier when the 3rd Earl died in 1851. Richard John had four sons and two daughters.

Only the Earl's third son, Patrick Maurice, went into the military service where he served with distinction. He fought in the Zulu war of 1877 and in the Egyptian war of 1882. He received medals for bravery in both wars.

His second son, Walter Francis, an Oxford educated lawyer, had a brilliant career in the colonial service. His career, which spanned three decades, took him around the world. He was colonial secretary of the Barbados, chief secretary to the Governor of Malta, Lieutenant Governor of Malta, Governor and Commander-in-Chief of the Windward Islands, Governor and Commander-in-Chief of Natal and Zululand, Governor of the Cape of Good Hope and High Commander for South Africa.

Unlike, Patrick Maurice who died unmarried, Walter Francis wed and had three sons and two daughters all of whom were living at the turn of the 20th century.

The Earl's fourth son lived in Tipperary for a time where he was a J.P. but later married a widow and moved to England.

John Luke George, the eldest son, who succeeded as the 5th Earl in 1866 was an Oxford graduate and a J.P. in Tipperary. He had one son and four daughters.

His son, Richard Walter John, the 6th Earl of Donoughmore, had a distinguished career in the government and became Under Secretary of State for War in 1903 and Deputy Speaker of the House of Lords from 1911. He succeeded his father as Earl in 1900. He married a New Yorker, Elena Grace, and had two sons and one daughter. His eldest son, John Michael Henry, was given the title of Viscount Suirdale during the lifetime of his father.

Fishing Party at Knock lofty (courtesy I.A.A.)

The Langley Family

Cromwell's siege of Clonmel in May 1650 lingers on in Tipperary folk memory, not least because it was where Cromwell met his only real repulse in Ireland, and where Irish resistance finally collapsed. Looming large in the folklore is one Henry Charles Langley, a lieutenant in one of Cromwell's cavalry regiments, Colonel Sankey's Regiment of Horse. He is on record as being one of the first to volunteer to storm the breach made in a wall of the town, after an earlier assault on the breach had left about a thousand Cromwellian infantry trapped inside and slaughtered.[170] When the infantry refused to advance a second time the General appealed to his cavalry. Folklore embellishes the moment, telling that Cromwell called out that whoever would be first through the breach would get his pick of Tipperary land, and that it was Langley who was that first brave man. Folklore also has it that Cromwell had earlier declared that Tipperary was indeed a countryside worth fighting for.

It is on record that Langley, who was strikingly tall, put himself at the head of the dismounted cavalry, and that, with Colonel Sankey in charge, the second assault was so fierce that the assailants managed to force their way through to an opposite wall, in the face of muskets, pikes, scythes and cannon. When Langley tried to mount the wall his left hand was swept off by the blow from a scythe wielded by one of the town's defenders. Fierce fighting went on for some four hours, by which time most of the

---

[170] P. O'Connell and W. C. Darmody, eds., 1650-1950 Siege of Clonmel Commemoration Tercentenary Souvenir Record, 1950, pp. 16-33; Rev. D. Murphy, *Cromwell in Ireland*, pp. 334-337

assailants were killed or wounded. The much-bloodied Langley, who had distinguished himself in the fray, managed to escape when the survivors were forced to retreat.

The weary defenders had a respite to congratulate themselves, attend to their own wounded, and mourn their dead, among them the scythe-man, the 'mower', who swiped off Langley's uplifted hand. The story of that brief, vicious encounter of defender and tall, daring Langley was later immortalized in ballad form. The pun-laden ballad gives a Cromwellian viewpoint, and is titled *Langley of the Iron Hand*:

> When Erin before Cromwell fell,
> A man of whom I'll tell ye,
> As they advanced to storm Clonmel,
> Was foremost in the melee.
>
> Charles Langley, high, a man of power,
> Of all the troops the best,
> For when they stormed the western tower,
> He towered above the rest.
>
> A mower standing in the breach,
> With scythe to guard the pass,
> His hand cut off, as if to teach
> That flesh is still but grass....
>
> The furious foe, in joyous glee,
> The bleeding hero scanned,
> And bade him then in irony
> To get an iron hand.
>
> But Langley with his sabre bright,
> Struck at the boasting clown,
> To crown the labours of the fight,
> He cut him through the crown.
>
> His iron hand he henceforth wore,
> His various works to settle,
> Thus proving then, just as before,
> Himself a man of mettle.[171]

---

[171] Gortnahoe-Glengoole, A Guide, undated, pp. 39-40; Prendergast, op. cit. pp. 424-425

While the ballad tells something of the fury and savagery of the siege, it nonetheless belies the fact that it was the bloodiest and costliest victory achieved by Cromwell in Ireland. He lost thousands of the best of his army in trying to assault the town. When he saw he could not take it by force, he decided to change the siege to a blockade and try what famine could do. After two months shortage of food and ammunition finally forced Colonel Hugh "Duff" O'Neill, the wily Irish Commander, to slip secretly out of the town with a chosen band to try and organize another stand. He instructed the mayor of the town to treat for a surrender on acceptable terms, which saved Clonmel, and its surviving garrison and townspeople.

After the surrender of Clonmel most of the land of Ireland was available for sharing out among the victorious soldiers and their backers, the Adventurers. Whatever folklore says about Langley winning the pick of Tipperary's land, his allotment was in the hilly, "thin-skinned" barony of Slieveardagh and Comsey, the barony, which together with the barony of Kilnamanagh in west Tipperary, was allocated to Cromwell's soldiers.

Henry Charles Langley, generally known as Charles, was about 36 years of age when he took up his grant of almost a thousand acres in Lisnamrock and Killeheen in Ballingarry parish, which had been in the ownership of Edmund Marnell and Pierce Butler, who were dispossessed. Langley probably took up residence in Marnell's small castle of Lisnamrock, which was still in good condition, and which had a large bawn attached in which there were a few thatched houses. Nearby was a watermill on a little stream, a tributary of the King's River.[172]

Henry Charles was not the only Langley involved in the storming of Clonmel. Another was John Langley, who is thought to have been a relative. He too was injured, getting shot in one of his legs. He got a grant of about three hundred acres also in the Slieveardagh area, and he called his farm "Blackkettle" for some reason. He is best known for his will, made in 1674, in which he left his farm to his son, "commonly called Stubborn Jack,......provided he married a Protestant, but not Alice Kendrick, who called me 'Oliver's whelp' ".

---

[172] Richard C. Simington, ed., The Civil Survey 1654, Co Tipperary, Vol. 1., p. 114

He also instructed that his body "be laid out on the oak table in the brown room, and fifty Irishmen shall be invited to my wake, and everyone shall have two quarts of the best aquavitae, and also a skein, dirk or knife laid before him."   When some friends asked him why he wanted to treat the Irish so liberally with whiskey at his wake, a people he had little time for, he is said to have replied that they would get so drunk that they will kill one another with the conveniently placed knives, "and so we shall get rid of the breed. And if every one would follow my example in their wills, in time we should get rid of them all"[173].

Henry Charles, who settled in Lisnamrock, was known as 'Langley of the Iron Hand', and "Iron Hand Charlie", as he had his lost hand replaced with an iron one, made by the farrier of his cavalry regiment. He belonged to the Langleys of Prestwick in Lancashire, a family founded by Richard de Langley, who lived in the 14th century.

"Iron Hand" married Anne, daughter of Edward Cooke of Kiltinan Castle, near Fethard, one of the Cromwellian adventurers, who got that prestigious manor formerly belonging to James Butler, baron of Dunboyne.[174]   Charles was only around 49 years of age when he died in 1667, leaving three sons and two daughters. His eldest son, Charles of Lisnamrock and Coalbrook, married Margaret Clutterbuck, a descendant of another adventurer who got a grant of Bannixtown near Cloneen.

His second son, John, described as a Gentleman of Ballynonty, married a Lloyd of Co Limerick. He first rented land in Ballynonty, and then in 1705 bought the lands of Lickfin and Tulloquane, to the east of Ballynonty, from the Duke of Ormonde, when changes in land ownership were brought in to enable the duke to dispose of some of his immense estates by long leases or sale to reduce his enormous debts. Many of the descendants of the Cromwellian grantees used the opportunity to take leases of or buy Butler lands, and so consolidate and expand their holdings.

The Lickfin branch of the family built Knockanure House in Lickfin townland. The family built another house in Clonoura, a townland south of Boulick, which they also acquired. A later inheritor of this Lickfin branch

---

[173] Prendergast, op. cit., p. 425
[174] Burke's Irish Family Records, pp. 688-689

in the 19th century was known as "Yellow Seán", and became notorious for the numerous evictions he was responsible for, which served to intensify local agitation leading finally to the division of the land by the Land Commission in the early 20th century. Local legend has it that he was once fired on coming from Clonoura, but only his horse was injured.[175]

The main branch of the Langleys, the Lisnamrock branch, became known as the Langleys of Coalbrook, as it was in Coalbrook townland that they built their principal residence. This upland townland to the north of Lisnamrock, formerly known as Glais an Ghial, was probably purchased by them as they advanced their land interests. They renamed it Coalbrook on account of the coal seams discovered there, and they built their principal residence, Coalbrook House, in a pleasant setting within a sheltered and fertile valley in the townland. The present-day house, now owned by the Cantwell family, is a two-storied L-shaped, early Victorian house, with a basement. This is an early 19th century remodelling of the original house, which had three storeys above the basement. The large enclosed yard, with its lofted out-houses and sunken well is part of the original building. It is attached to the house, and the driveway enters through a deep archway. No doubt this well-designed farmyard provided extra security for the house, which stands at an altitude of around 500 feet, one of the few landlord residences built in Tipperary at that level. The Langleys of Coalbrook formed part of the "close coterie of resourceful families" in the Slieveardagh area, made up also of Hunts of Glengoole, Cookes of Poynstown, Lanes of Lanespark, Poes of Harley Park, and Barkers of Kilcooley.[176]

The family was proud of their Iron Hand founder, "the man of mettle", and the farrier-crafted hand came to rest above the original entrance door at Coalbrook.[177] More folklore grew up around the family, and a headless coachman was said to be seen driving down the avenue. Langley descendants must have been grateful to Iron Hand too for the lands he drew by lot in Slieveardagh which turned out not only to be great

---

[175] Gortnahoe-Glengoole, A Guide, p. 34

[176] William Nolan and Thomas G. McGrath, eds., Tipperary History and Society, p. 300

[177] The iron hand is now preserved in the museum in Taunton, Somerset

grazing land but also to contain coal seams where were discovered between 1730 and 1740.

Coalbrook 2003 (courtesy Mr. Cantwell)

Coal mining operations involved the family in considerable risks, and were not always successful. Other landlords of the area to become involved in the coalmining industry were the Barkers of Kilcooley, Ambrose Going of Ballyphillip, and Sir Vere Hunt of New Birmingham. Slieveardagh area also produced culm (coal dust) and limestone, which were widely valued and distributed among farmers, who used culm to burn the limestone in their limekilns, which was then spread on the land.

In general the eldest of the sons of the Lisnamrock and Coalbrook Langleys stayed on to manage the estates, while many other sons went in for military and legal careers. The Christian names Henry and Charles were passed on to successive generations of inheriting sons. The Charles who succeeded to Lisnamrock and Coalbrook around the time of the 1798 rebellion was part of the yeoman troop of cavalry captained by Chum (Chambré) Ponsonby-Barker of Kilcooley. W. G. Neely, in his *Kilcooley: Land and People* describes him as being traumatized by all the disturbances taking place, adding that after the rising he 'was deeply disturbed and even

114

twenty years after was reporting to Dublin Castle every whisper of rebellion, with the certainty that once more the country would be in arms'[178].

In all that period the Palatines, who formed a numerous tenantry on the nearby Kilcooley estate, felt like a community under siege, being Protestant, and both racially and culturally distinct from the majority inhabitants of the region. In 1815 Charles was very concerned about the situation in the Kilcooley area where the Palatine tenants 'had for their protection a good many stand of arms'. He wrote to Sir Robert Peel, then Chief Secretary, to enquire what he wanted done with the armed farmers, and recommended that a small detachment of police be put among them 'as it would be impossible to leave them unprotected'.

In the late 1820s he himself became a prominent member of the Slieveardagh Brunswick Club, set up by Chum Barker-Ponsonby, which was part of a movement founded by the gentry who opposed Daniel O'Connell's campaign for Catholic Emancipation. The Palatines formed the main body of the members of the club. At the first meeting of the club held in the courthouse in Ballynonty in 1828, a group of Palatines, led by Barker Ponsonby and Langley was confronted by a large hostile Catholic crowd. Only the intervention of Fr Michael Meehan, parish priest of Gortnahoe, prevented an attack on the Brunswickers.

One descendant (great-grandson) of Henry and Anne (nee Clutterbuck) Langley of Lisnamrock, John Langley, CBE, had the distinction of being the man who supervised the building of the First Aswan Dam in Egypt. He was also director general of the State Domains in Egypt from 1916 to 1922, and Under-Secretary of State for Agriculture there in the same period. He died in 1945. His son, Brigadier Charles Ardagh, CBE, served with distinction in World War One and Two.[179]

Two other branches of the Langley family sprung from the Lisnamrock and Coalbrook Langleys, namely the Brittas branch and the Archerstown branch. Henry Langley, a great-grandson of Iron Hand, and the second son of Charles of Lisnamrock (died 1791), founded the Brittas branch, and his younger brother, Thomas, founded the Archerstown branch.

---

[178] W. G. Neely, Kilcooley: Land and People, 1983, pp. 91-92
[179] Burke's Irish Family Records, p. 690

Henry was the proprietor of Priesttown House and its estate, close to Drangan village, which was also then known as Langley Lodge.

In 1754 he married Margaret Grace, the daughter and heiress of Oliver Grace of Brittas, near Thurles. Oliver was descended from John Grace, to whom Brittas, a former Anglo-Norman manor, owned by the Dunboyne Butlers up to the Cromwellian period, was granted in 1667, after the restoration of Charles 11 to the throne in England[180]. It is not clear if Henry and Margaret lived at Brittas or Langley Lodge in Priesttown. The fact that they were both buried in the small graveyard of Brittas would seem to indicate that they lived in Brittas for some period at least.

The medieval castle of Brittas, with its attached bawn, recorded to be in a good state of repair in 1654,[181] had some additions added on to it by both the Graces and the early Langleys at different stages to make it more habitable. The eldest son of Henry and Margaret, born in 1757 and named Henry Grace Langley, certainly lived in Brittas from the time he inherited it, and managed the estate for around forty years. He was a magistrate and member of the Grand Jury, and used his influence to get the section of the Thurles-Templemore road that went through the townland of Brittas diverted away from the castle, and along its present-day straighter line. He also was responsible for many improvements on the estate, including tree landscaping, and probably additions to the house, which was erected against the old bawn walls of the castle.

He was a man of many ambitions, one notable one being the creation of an English-styled village in Cooleeney townland in Moyne parish, a townland which was also part of his landed estate. He was progressing that ambition around the mid-1810s, and it is said that he intended calling his village Wellington, in honour of the victor of Waterloo. The first building taken in hands was a Protestant church, complete with bell-tower and steeple, and then two single-storied Georgian houses, one named Cooleeney Lodge, and the other Cooleeney Glebe House, serving as a rectory. The field margins and roadsides were planted with trees, but apart from those main buildings, the landscaping, and a few small cottages, Henry's Utopian village never really materialized.

---

[180] Brittas Castle, Manuscripts Notes, undated, Langley Papers, Brittas Castle.
[181] Civil Survey 1654, Co Tipperary, Vol. 1., p. 55

Brittas Castle from the 1823 etching

The major loss, which Henry had to contend with, was the burning of Brittas Castle about a year before his own death, which occurred in 1821. An etching, printed in 1823, shows the castle as consisting of three towers, two of which are square, the third a rounded one, and an attached three-storied house along the western side of the old bawn wall. Although Henry was married twice, (his second wife being the youngest daughter of John Bagwell, MP, of Marlfield near Clonmel), he had no family. The inscription to his memory over the family vault he had constructed in Brittas graveyard records that he was "the improver of Brittas estate…laudably expending his income on the employment of the surrounding poor…" He was succeeded by his nephew, Major Henry, the son of his brother Oliver, who lived in Parkstown House, Horse and Jockey.

The extent of the damage done to the castle and residence by the fire in not known, but Major Henry, who was captain in the 2nd Regiment of Life Guards, apparently found the place uninhabitable, and sold it and part of the lands to his first cousin, Henry Augustus of Priesttown, another military man, a captain of Dragoon Guards. As an apparent replacement of the old castle and attached house, Henry Augustus embarked on the building of what has been described as "the first 'archaeological' 19ᵗʰ century castle in Ireland", a full-scale replica of Warwick Castle itself. The architect he engaged for this immense project was William Vitruvius Morrison, who is best known for his designs for Fota House, near Cobh, and Thomastown Castle, near Golden. Morrison based his drawings for Brittas Castle on medieval originals, which included an authentic moat, surrounding the entire castle. If the project had been completed it would have been a closer copy of a medieval castle than any of the revival castles then being built by gentry in various parts of the country.

When the building operations got under way it is said that two carts were constantly employed bringing the cut limestone to the site from the quarries, and that one cart was drawn by a horse and the other by a jennet. It is also said that such was the amount of stone required that it covered seven acres of ground.[182]

But only the gate-tower of massive proportions was built, which incorporates the gateway set beneath a series of tall arches, flanked by polygonal turrets. The bases of four corner turrets were also put in place, and much of the moat. The entire building operation, however, came to an abrupt end. Family lore relates that one day a stone fell on Henry Augustus as he was inspecting the work and killed him. It was sometime in late August 1834. There is a rectangular tablet to his memory on a wall of the ruined chapel in the little graveyard on the estate, and it records that he "…lived much beloved and died sincerely and deeply regretted after a few days illness on the 24ᵗʰ of Aug. 1854 in the 36ᵗʰ year of his age". So it seems that he lived for a few days after the tragic accident. The castle project was brought to a halt, and family lore relates that when word of the death of Henry Augustus was brought to the stone carters, they upended their loads of stone into the roadside ditch and hurried back to Brittas.

---

[182] Family folklore related by Miss Langley of Brittas Castle

The massive Gate Tower of Henry Augustus Langley's Castle was the only section built when his tragic death in August 1854 brought the ambitious project to an abrupt end (photo courtesy Miss Mabel Langley).

Remarkably Major Henry, who had sold Brittas to Henry Augustus, died some six weeks later, and the inscription on the side of his tomb records that Henry Augustus bequeathed him the lands of Brittas, thereby making him "2nd time possessor of the estate". He was 49 years of age. Henry Augustus apparently had no children, and was probably unmarried. His enormous undertaking shows every sign of having been suddenly abandoned, with the working staff simply walking away. The massive gate-tower looms up over the green level fields, dwarfing the house, now reduced to a single storey, and the farmyards. If it had been completed and had survived to the present time it would be the most remarkable and impressive revivalist castle to be built in Ireland in the 19th century.

By the time the two Henrys had died the estate was probably heavily in debt as a result of the castle project. The Great Famine of the following decade would have had its impact as well, a period when income from rents was greatly reduced. In 1853 Captain Henry's eldest son, yet another Henry, sold Brittas in the Encumbered Estates Court. The purchaser was Colonel William Knox from Mayo, who was said to be passing through Thurles when he happened to hear that the property was for sale. The total estate, including Priesttown, was 2509 acres.

In that immediate post-Famine period there were 21 tenants on the lands. According to family lore one of the first things Colonel Knox did was to sell all the stone, which was lying in the fields around the castle site, much of which was purchased by the Great Southern and Western Railway Company for the building of railway bridges.[183]

The connection between the Langleys and Brittas remained broken until modern times. Most of the children of Henry, who sold the property in 1853, and who was also a major of Life Guards, resided in England. Gerard Charles, his second son, was a Vice-Admiral in the British navy, and his grandson, Henry Desmond Allen, MBE, born in 1930, and educated in Eton and Sandhurst, is the present-day representative of the Langley of Brittas line. He lives in Lithook in Hampshire. He was formerly one of Queen Elizabeth's bodyguard, and Governor General of Bermuda. He was also Lieutenant-Colonel of Household Cavalry and Life Guards. He has two children, Henry Fitzroy John, born 1958, and Charlotte Maria Grace, born 1962.

Brittas remained in the Knox ownership for some generations, and the extensive, roadside woodland of the estate became known locally as Knox's Wood. It has now returned into the ownership of a Langley again through a bequest from Captain J.F.Knox, who was unmarried. Anna Mabel, daughter of Thomas Finlow Langley, became the beneficiary of that bequest, and she resides in the single-storied house of Brittas, beneath the shadow of the Henry Augustus' great castle gate-tower, and manages the farm now reduced to around 500 acres.

---

[183] Miss Langley stated that after the sale of the stone Knox had only to pay £500 for the entire estate!

Miss Anna Mabel Langley, daughter of Thomas Findlow and Alice neé
Wallace Langley the present proprietor of Brittas Castle

The third main branch of the Langleys, the Langleys of
Archerstown, was founded, as mentioned, by Thomas, brother of Henry
who founded the Brittas branch. Thomas acquired the Archerstown

property in the parish of Thurles, and in 1780 married Catherine, daughter of John Nicholson, who was renting Turtulla House, now the Clubhouse of Thurles Golf club. Archerstown was formerly the property of the Archer family, (hence its name), who were dispossessed in the Cromwellian times. They resided in a tower-house type of castle which had a bawn attached and a water mill nearby. By 1654 the castle was "out of repair", and apparently never used afterwards as a residence. The former status of the Archer family can be gauged from the finely sculpted table tomb in St Mary's churchyard in Thurles.

The Archerstown Langleys built a modest two-storey Georgian house abutting the old bawn walls of the castle, a section of which survives, overlooking the yard. They also built a deer park, the high walls of which still remain. The Christian name Henry was favoured also by this branch of the Langleys. Thomas's eldest son and successor was so named, and he was a captain of the Tipperary Yeomanry, which was very active in the Thurles area in the year of rebellion, 1798. He had a family of eight children, five of whom died young, including his eldest son Thomas. He was succeeded by his second son, Henry (1817-1899), who was a magistrate, and who married Catherine Maria, daughter of Dr John Toler, of Dublin. The extent of the estate was then 2,808 acres.

His eldest son, Henry Oliver, an army officer and a JP, who succeeded to Archerstown, married Ethel Maud, daughter of John Max of Maxfort, Thurles. On his death in 1927 his only son Henry Richard (Harry) succeeded. He became a veterinary surgeon, and married Sheila Hinds, from Canterbury, New Zealand. They had two children, Oliver Henry, who succeeded and also became a vet, and Ann Catherine, who married Peter William Walsh-Kemmis, of Garrans, Stradbally. Oliver, who was also a veterinary surgeon, died a few years ago and his widow Diana and family now manage the farm.

The Extended Langley Family in North Tipperary

Thomas Finlow and Alice (nee Wallace) of Newbrook House, mentioned above, had seven children. Four sons came first—Henry Charles, William Hector, Thomas George (never married), and John Frederick. Henry Charles (Charlie) married Anna Maria (Ciss) Smith, Bullock Park, Cashel, and they lived in Bullock Park and Cabra Castle. Their youngest son, Oliver, continues to farm Bullock Park. Another son, Keith, married to

Catherine O'Connor from Waterford, recently built a house in Bullock Park. The eldest son, Aidan, is a veterinary surgeon in Enniscorthy, and is married to Jane Gardiner. They have two sons.

William Hector, (Willie), married Maude Smith, Mountmellick, and they lived in the former rectory in Holycross. They had three children, twin girls at first, one of whom died young, and the second of whom, named Beryl, resides with her family in Australia. Their third child, a son named Hector, lives in England and is unmarried. Maude, now a widow, lives in St Mary's Avenue, Thurles.

John Frederick, the fourth son of Thomas Finlow and Alice nee Wallace, married Marjorie Gamble, Piltown, and they live in Otway House, Templederry, the former parish rectory. They have two sons and three daughters. Their eldest son, Finlow, inherited Newbrook from his uncle and namesake. He is married to Dorothy Johnston, Ballinaslow. George, their second son, takes care of Otway House on behalf of his father. He married Rose Moorehead of Silvermines, and they have three children. The three daughters of John and Marjorie are Amy, who is married to Sidric Howry, Margaret, who is married to Peter Parlon, and Pamela, a teacher, who is unmarried and lives in Dublin.

The three daughters in the Thomas Finlow-Alice (nee Wallace) family are Catherine Elizabeth, who married William Gilbert Stanley, Douglas, Cork, Anna Maria Mabel, mentioned above, who inherited Brittas, and is unmarried, and Amelia Annie, who was also unmarried and is now deceased. William and Catherine Elizabeth Stanley have two sons, John Thomas Gilbert and George Raymond, both of whom live in Brittas townland, and help to run Brittas Castle farm with their aunt Mabel. Gilbert lives with his wife, Linda Catherine Pallin of Roscrea, in Woodview, Brittas, and Raymond and his wife, Lila Frances Mooney of Templederry, live in Brittas Lodge. Raymond and Lila have four children, Cheryl Elizabeth, Dwayne Ambrose, Ian William, and Roy Gilbert.

Brittas and Archerstown now are the two main old properties in continuous Langley ownership, while Newbrook, now in the ownership of Finlow Langley, has been in Langley ownership since the end of the 19th century.

Mansergh of Grenane

The Mansergh family, whose principal residence is Grenane House, in the townland of Grenane,[184] near Tipperary Town, has been much researched, thanks mainly to Senator Martin Mansergh, the most high-profiled member of the present generation, and to his grandmother, Ethel Marguerite Mansergh.[185] She was herself a Mansergh, belonging to the Cork branch of the family. She was born in 1876, and was partly educated at Bowenscourt, the home of the novelist Elizabeth Bowen, with whom the Cork Manserghs were connected by marriage. Ethel Marguerite married her second cousin Philip St George Mansergh of Grenane in 1907. It was not the first time that a Mansergh married a Mansergh cousin.

Philip St George Mansergh, born in 1864, was sent to Australia at the age of 18, with only £40 in his pocket and his passage. That was in the 1880s, at a time when Grenane estate, consisting of 2,086 acres, was heavily mortgaged. Family settlements had to be made out of the estate, and there was a general downswing in the estate income, as there was in the case of estates throughout the country at the time, due to land agitation and the consequent difficulty in collecting rent. Grenane was let. Philip's elder brother, Richard Southcote Mansergh, a confirmed bachelor, who had succeeded to Grenane, went to live in Friarsfield House in a neighbouring townland, built by the family as a dower house around 1860.

---

[184] The placename is given as Grenane in the Ordnance Survey maps, but the Mansergh family have always used the form Grenane, which is the form used in the Civil Survey of 1654

[185] Mansergh Family History by Ethel Marguerite Mansergh, undated manuscript, and A Brief History of the Mansergh Family and Grenane, typescript by Martin Mansergh, 1996. I have relied heavily on both scripts in preparing this article.

Philip had trained as an engineer, and is said to have paid for his education by his success at poker. He became a surveyor, and was involved in the construction of railway lines in Queensland and New Zealand. Then in 1892 he sailed to South Africa, got an introduction to Cecil Rhodes, and offered his services as an engineer for six months without pay. On being asked when he would be ready to start, his "Now" reply so impressed Rhodes that he sent him to Beira in Mozambique as surveyor on the Cape to Cairo railway, then being planned. During the following fourteen years he pegged and constructed 1200 miles of railway from Beira to the Kafue River, which flows through Zambia (formerly Northern Rhodesia), and is a major tributary of the Zambesi. His work was described as a 'triumph of construction'.[186]

Friarsfield House, the home of Senator Martin Mansergh and his family.
The house dates from the early 1860s and was built as a dower house.

Following his brother's death in 1906 Philip returned, married cousin Ethel Marguerite Mansergh, and took over the management of the estate, then in the process of being reduced to its demesne under the Land Purchase Acts. Among the tenants of Grenane who had already bought out

[186] M. Mansergh, op. cit., pp. 12,13

their farms was Dan Breen's father. The 'Troubles', as the War of Independence is often referred to, was sparked off by an event which occurred only about three miles west of Grenane on 21 January 1919. That event was the shooting dead by Dan Breen and Séan Treacy of two armed policemen escorting gelignite to Sologheadbeg Quarry. But Grenane survived the Troubles, even though the grounds were billeted. Philip Mansergh would not allow politics to be discussed in the house, although a contingency plan was drawn up to evacuate it, if it were going to be burned. In the event of that happening, it was arranged that everybody in the house would be given ten minutes to collect precious possessions. The only casualty of Grenane House, however, was Philip's son's pet dog, shot outside the entrance gates by the Black and Tans in 1921.

Reflecting on that callous event and many much more serious ones on the part of the Black and Tans, Senator Martin Mansergh stated that, "Most Southern Protestants decided that if the Black and Tans were the price they had to pay for the protection of the Union and their privileged status the price was much too high". [187] His grandfather Philip settled into the life ushered in by the Free State. He donated the Mansergh Cup to the Clanwilliam Rugby Football Club in 1927, for the most successful County Tipperary Team, a trophy, which is still competed for. He never bought a motorcar, and generally walked into town each day. He did that even in the 'Trouble Times', and knew his neighbours and townspeople well, including Denis Lacey, Commanding Officer of the Third Tipperary Brigade. He died in October 1928.

Philip and Ethel had two sons, Charles Ogilvy, born in 1908, who succeeded to Grenane, and Philip Nicholas, born in 1910, who inherited Friarsfield. The latter, who used Nicholas as his first name, was Martin's father. He studied at Oxford, became a professor, eminent as a political scientist and historian. He wrote sympathetically about Irish institutions and Anglo-Irish relations, his first book *The Irish Free State: its government and politics,* appearing in 1934. He has written studies of Eoin McNeill and John Redmond, and among his other numerous works are *The Irish Question 1840-1921* (1966), and *The Government of Ireland Act 1920,* (1974). His last work appeared in 1991.

---

[187] Ibid. p.33

The full name of Charles, the elder of the two brothers, was Charles Ogilvy Martin Southcote, and that of Nicholas was Philip Nicholas Seton. These names, taken from both remote and recent family lineages, show the wide spread of marriage connections over the ten generations, spanning the three and a half centuries that the Manserghs have been in Ireland. They stem from three brothers, Brian, James, and Robert Mansergh who came to Ireland from Westmoreland, in northwest England, with their uncle, Daniel Redman, sometime just before the Cromwellian times of the late 1640s and the early 1650s.[188] They became involved in the Cromwellian campaign, Daniel as a major and his nephews as officers. In 1659, after Cromwell's death, Daniel entered into secret negotiations with the restored Charles 11, was formally pardoned for his support of the Parliamentarians, and by 1688 was owner of nearly 13,000 acres in Kilkenny. By then his nephews found themselves favourably circumstanced as well, by the land settlement of 1661. James got a grant of Macrony Castle in Cork, which is still lived in, and Brian and Robert settled near their uncle in Kilkenny. Virtually the whole Mansergh family is descended from James and Brian.[189]

At the time Redman and the three Mansergh brothers came to Ireland, Grenane, like so much of Tipperary's land, was in the ownership of James Butler, Duke of Ormonde, and was on long lease to Sir Hardresse Waller. Waller was a prominent Englishman who was encouraged to settle in Ireland, where he acquired extensive lands through marriage, and took up the lease of Grenane. He was one of the 69 regicides who signed the death warrant of Charles 1, played a prominent role on the Parliamentary side in the civil war of the 1640s, and in the 1650s was among the handful of military commanders implementing the Commonwealth policies, including the transplantation of the heads of the native population to Connaught and Clare.[190] His daughter, Elizabeth, married Sir William

---

[188] The family name Mansergh, is considered to be of Hiberno-Norse origin, and was originally the name of a manor or townland. The –ergh ending means a hill pasture. The name in the form Manzerge is first mentioned in the Doomsday Book of 1085-86, and Adam de Mansergh, whose name appears on a record of 1187, is considered to be the founder of the family. The village of Mansergh in Westmoreland is now little more than a farmhouse and outbuildings. Ibid. p. 4; E. M. Mansergh, op. cit., pp. 2-5

[189] Burke's Landed Gentry of Ireland, pp. 382-83

[190] E. M. Mansergh, op. cit., p. 92

Petty, author of the Civil Survey of 1654. In the Survey the Grenane property in the parish of Templenoe is recorded as consisting of "the castle and town of Grenane and Ballyhosty" (Ballyhusty) and 660 plantation acres. The castle is described as a garrisoned castle, with thirty thatched cabins and houses nearby, forming the "town".[191]

For his services to the Commonwealth Waller was allowed to hold on to his Grenane lands in the Cromwellian confiscations, even though the barony of Clanwilliam, in which Grenane is situated, was earmarked for division among the Cromwellian soldiers and adventurers. On the restoration of Charles 11, however, he could expect little mercy. He was arrested, sentenced to death and ended his days in a Jersey Island fortress.

The next to occupy Grenane was Nicholas Southcote, a royalist from Devon, who is alleged to have married, as a second wife, another of Hardresse Waller's daughters, whose name is not known. He is recorded as paying Hearth Tax for four hearths at Grenane in 1664.[192] Presumably he was then living in the castle. His son, also named Nicholas, married Eleanor, daughter of Captain James Mansergh of Macrony Castle in 1684, thus initiating the Mansergh link with Grenane, and the tradition of using the name Southcote as an added Christian name in future generations of Manserghs. The Mansergh link with Grenane was cemented a generation later when Mary, the daughter and heiress of Nicholas and Eleanor, married Daniel Mansergh, JP, her first cousin once removed, who was the nephew and successor of the above Captain James Mansergh of Macrony Castle.

It was probably in the first decade of the 1700s, in time of Daniel and Mary Mansergh that the oldest portion of Grenane House was built from the stones of the castle. The main house, a three-bay Georgian house of middle size, dates from around 1730, and remained detached from that first old portion.[193] The second son of Daniel and Mary, Nicholas Southcote Mansergh, inherited Grenane in 1735. One of their daughters, Mary, married Edward Pennefather of Marlow, Cloneyharp.

The Mansergh owners of Grenane were relatively long-livers. Nicholas Southcote Mansergh owned Grenane for 33 years, but not much is

---

[191] R. S. Simington, ed., Civil Survey of Ireland, Co Tipperary, Vol. 2, p. 42, 1934

[192] Thomas Laffan, ed., Tipperary Families, being the Hearth Money Records, 1665-1667, 1911

[193] E. M. Mansergh, op. cit., p. 95; M. Mansergh, op. cit., p. 13

known about him. He married Elizabeth, daughter of Richard Lockwood of Castle Leake, (Castlelake), Cashel, in 1750. His two eldest sons, Nicholas Southcote, the second, and Daniel, continued the Tipperary branches of the family. In 1770 Nicholas married Elizabeth, daughter of John Carden of Templemore, and sister of Sir John Craven Carden. In their time Grenane House was lowered by a storey, and the south wing, a long two-storey structure, built. They had seven sons and two daughters. Their daughter Ellen is mentioned in Dorothea Herbert's Diary in her entry for the day of the Cashel races in the summer of 1789. She was probably 16 or 17 at the time. Dorothea describes her as "one of the head beauties" who distracted John Roe, for whom Dorothea had an unrequited love, at the dance in the Assembly Room following the race meeting. [194] In 1805 Ellen married William Kemmis, crown solicitor, and owner of a handsome house in the Wicklow hills, called Ballinacor.

Nicholas Southcote, the 2nd, owned Grenane for around fifty years, outliving his eldest son John Southcote, who was to be his heir. Grenane passed to his grandson, Richard Martin Southcote, the second son of John Southcote, whose wife was Mary, daughter of Richard Martin of Clifford, Co Cork. It was through that marriage that the Christian name Martin came to be used subsequently in the Mansergh line.

Richard Martin Southcote, born in 1800, the year the Act of Union was passed, inherited Grenane at the age of 18, and had to cut short his legal studies at King's Inns. He married Jane Rosetta, daughter of Robert Bomford of Rahinstown, Co. Meath. He owned the house and estate for about 60 years, years which saw some of the most turbulent times in Ireland, beginning with the disturbances which arose from the economic downturn following the ending of the Napoleonic Wars, the growing poverty of the smaller tenants and labouring class, the escalation of the population almost up to eight million, the Great Famine of the 1840s, which gave rise to the Young Ireland Rebellion of 1848 in Ballingarry, and the land agitation of the 1850s and '60s.

Richard, known to subsequent generations as "The Old Man", has been described by Senator Martin Mansergh as "a benevolent, but

---

[194] Dorothea Herbert, Retrospections, 1789-1806, 1930

somewhat gruff and practical paternalist".[195] He was a magistrate, and in that capacity he was sometimes called on to investigate outbreaks of faction fighting which peaked again in the 1820s in a particularly virulent manner in the Tipperary Town area, especially between the Shanavests and Caravats, and the Three Year Olds and Four Year Olds.

There were faction fights of a more local character as well, such as that between the Hogans and the Hickeys, which erupted at the fair of Kilfeakle on 11 July 1826, and which went on for more than two hours, leaving many participants wounded and even some killed. A man named Martin Hogan, who was armed with a "long gun", was arrested after the fight had ended. As one of the magistrates of the area, Richard Mansergh was called on to investigate the "dreadful riot", as that vicious faction fight was called in the police report. Members of the Hogan family were among his tenants, and Richard wrote to the Lord Lieutenant to try and prevent the transportation to Australia of some of that family arrested for their involvement in the fight at Kilfeakle fair that day.[196]

Richard Mansergh was also involved in the trial of William Smith O'Brien after O'Brien was arrested at Thurles railway station shortly after his abortive Young Ireland rising which fizzled out at the Widow McCormack's farmhouse at Ballingarry in July 1848. At the subsequent trail before a jury, O'Brien was found guilty of high treason. Richard Mansergh was chairman of the jury, and as such had to announce the verdict. In association with the jury he made a plea for O'Brien's life in the following terms:" We earnestly recommend the prisoner to the merciful consideration of the Government, being unanimous of the opinion that, for many reasons, his life should be spared".

The jury also included Southcote Mansergh of Grallagh Castle, near Horse and Jockey, a former property of a junior branch of the Butlers. Smith O'Brien, whom Mansergh regarded as a good friend, was transported to Tasmania, and pardoned six years later.

At the time of the Fenian Rising of 1867, when the largest assembly of rebels gathered at Ballyhurst, which was part of the Grenane estate,

---

[195] M. Mansergh, op. cit., p. 25
[196] Denis G. Marnane, Land and Violence, A History of West Tipperary from 1660, 1985, p. 48; M. Mansergh, op. cit., p. 25

Richard Mansergh locked up certain of his tenants for a few hours in the turf-house to ensure they would not get involved.

Richard Mansergh was a member of the Select Vestry of Tipperary Church of Ireland parish, which approved of the building of the new parish church in the town in 1829. He paid £300 for the family box pew. He always drove by himself to church, and according to a family tradition, after going into his family pew he spread a handkerchief over his face and went to sleep. On other outings as magistrate he drove in a coach and four with two postillions dressed in the family livery of buff with scarlet edgings.

He did not employ a land agent. On the occasions of the Spring and Autumn gale days, the days on which the rents were due, it was his custom to site at a table under a lime tree at the corner of the avenue, receiving the rent from his seventy or so tenants, listening to whatever complaints they were brave enough to voice, and "dispensing justice as he thought fit". His eldest son and heir, John Southcote, popularly called Colonel Johnny, stood beside him, "and sometimes helped to soften the decision". [197]

During the years of the Great Famine, Colonel Johnny was chairman of the Tipperary Town Relief Committee, the function of which was to submit orders for Indian meal, raise subscriptions, apply for matching government grants and supervise public works. The main works undertaken were whitewashing the poorer houses, putting in sewers and footpaths to try and reduce the risk of fever, and leveling and draining a number of roads leading out of the town. Despite hopes that the 1846 potato crop would be free of blight, he wrote in mid-August to the secretary of Relief Board in Dublin stating "…. I have to inform the Board through you that the present potato crop is much worse than at a corresponding date last year and fears are entertained that there will not be a potato in the district by December". As he intimated, the worst was yet to come.[198]

Colonel Johnny also gave practical help by allowing a sewing project for women on the estate in the late 1840s. Sir William Wilde, the famous physician and eye specialist, commented favourably on this project. The walled garden was also built in the famine period as a means of

---

[197] M. Mansergh, ibid. p. 30
[198] M. Mansergh, op. cit., p. 27

providing much needed work for distressed people. Colonel Johnny has been described as "a softhearted man". He had an expensive life-style, some failed marriage matches, a bit of gambling and some experiences of army life. In one of his earlier letters to his father he wrote: *"…I never played with dice except with my own officers, and I never played higher than one shilling. I was also very foolish on the way. Women, they are a bad lot, the most expensive thing a young man can make a fool of himself about, which I am sorry to say I did. Had I remained in Glasgow I think I would have picked up as nice a woman as I ever met…."[199]*

He eventually married Sissy Wyatt of Flintstone, but only about six months after his father's death in 1876 he and Sissy moved to London, where they continued to live until their death. It was at that stage that Grenane became heavily mortgaged and was let, as was mentioned above. Grenane was not lived in again by a Mansergh until Johnny's grandnephew, Philip St George Mansergh, returned from his railway engineering in Africa in 1906, by which time the estate was reduced to its demesne lands.

Grenane House, which remains essentially unchanged since the 18th century, is one of Tipperary's important surviving Georgian houses of middle size, and is one of the county's longest lived-in houses. Among its main features are the windows after the design of James Wyatt, the brilliant architect in much demand in the Ireland of the 1780s. Other fine features are its mantelpieces by Bossi and Adam. It is one of the county's listed buildings, open to the public during the months of April, May and September. Its carefully maintained originality and intactness impress as one enters the lime-fringed driveway, at the end of which the house reveals itself in mature landscaped grounds. There is intactness and a sense of continuity all round—the fine yard houses, the walled garden with unique hazel walk, the woodlands complete with beech walk, all set among the fertile fields of the Golden Vale.

The most important aspect of Grenane's continuity is the long link between family and house, which goes back to 1684. The present proprietors of Grenane are Philippa Mansergh and her husband, John Wallace, whose family hails from Mayo. Philippa is the daughter, and only

---

[199] ibid. p. 31

child, of Charles Ogilvy Mansergh, who was popularly known as Gregor, and was the son of Philip, mentioned above. Philippa and John have four children, Adrian, Serena, Esme and Avena. Also maintained is the family link with Friarsfield, sited near the entrance gates to Grenane. It is the home of Senator Martin Mansergh[200] and his wife Elizabeth Young, who have five children, Fiona, Lucy, Daniel, Alice and Harriet.

The Tipperary Mansergh line continues strongly through Philippa and her family, and through Martin's family and his siblings. His brother Philip, who lives in England, has two daughters, and his sister Daphne, a university lecturer who lives in Dublin, has four children. His other brother, Nicholas, a county planner, is unmarried, as is also Jane, a social worker in London.

Grenane House, showing the three-by Georgian house, built in the 1730s and its later south wing addition.

---

[200] Senator Mansergh, a former civil servant has been a special advisor to successive Fianna Fail Taoisigh on Northern matters and continues to play a substantial roles as such and as head of the party's research division.

Mathew

Perhaps the most famous of all the Mathew family was the priest whose name became synonymous with the Temperance Movement, Fr. Theobald Mathew.

Lady Elisha Mathew, sister of 2nd Lord Llandaff, survived him dying in 1840. She left, in her will, all her estates to the Duke of Leinster, James Daly and Rev. Theobald Mathew with remainders to Viscount Chabot, his son Viscount Jarnac, Captain Mathew reputed to be her son by George IV, and James Daly.

Father Theobald Mathew was the godson of Elizabeth Mathew and she was very caring towards him. He was descended from Theobald Mathew and Anne Salle, the founders of the Thurles and Annfield lines, through his father, a second cousin of Francis the 1st Earl. Fr. Mathew was therefore a third cousin of Elizabeth Mathew.

Fr. Mathew became very famous because of his campaign against the abuse of drink. He was ordained as a Capuchin monk in 1814 and worked tirelessly for the benefit of the poor of Cork city. It was there he saw the dreadful effects of the abuse of alcohol at first hand. He founded the Temperance Movement, which became a national body. Its success can be gauged by the fact that the production of spirits in Ireland more than halved in the early 1840s. He was also provincial of the Order from 1828 to 1851. When the Famine struck in the mid 1800s Fr. Theobald worked tirelessly to relieve the sufferings of the stricken. He was sent to America in 1849 and returned in 1851. Due to his ill health he had to refuse the offer of a bishopric. He became a chronic invalid and died in 1856.

Dean Swift planned to stay a month at the seat of George Mathew, in Thomastown (between Tipperary and Cashel) but was so smitten with the hospitality he stayed three months! Guests were encouraged to treat Mathew's house as a hotel, taking advantage of the forty bedrooms, the large coffee room and bar and the detached tavern. Newspapers were provided, billiard tables, games, fishing tackle, rods, buckhounds, foxhounds and harriers, a bowling green and twenty hunters in the stables.[201] It was stated that the Lord of Thomastown greeted every guest by saying "This is your castle; here you are to command as in your own house; you may breakfast, dine, and sup here whenever you please, and invite any of the company as are most agreeable to you, or you may dine in the common parlour, where a daily ordinary is kept; but from this moment you are never to consider *me* the master of the house, but only as one of the guests."

Viscount Thurles was Thomas Butler the eldest son of Walter the 11th Earl of Ormonde. Thomas's wife was Elizabeth the daughter of Sir John Poyntz of Acton, Gloucester and she was a Catholic. Thomas died tragically in a drowning accident as he was travelling to Ireland from England in 1619.[202] His widow, Elizabeth had three sons and four daughters. Elizabeth's eldest son became the 12th Earl and the 1st Duke of Ormonde. She did not remain a widow for long. She married George Mathew of Llandaff, Glamorgan, in 1620.

George and the widow, Elizabeth,[203] had two sons, Theobald, who founded the Thurles and Annfield dynasties of Mathew and George Reihill, later of Thomastown, who managed the estates of the Ormondes in Tipperary.[204] In the process George succeeded in acquiring substantial properties himself. The fact that George Reihill married Eleanor Butler, the

---

[201] Peter Somerville-Large *The Irish Country House*

[202] The ship was called the *Skerries*

[203] This enterprising lady managed to save Thurles during the Cromwellian wars by telling Cromwell that she had refused to allow a Royalist company under Colonel Brian O'Neill to occupy the town and sought Cromwell's help. This action saved the town of Thurles from being despoiled and saved the Mathew family from being dispossessed.

[204] In the late decades of the 18th century there were three branches of the family, at Thomastown, Annfield (near Thurles) and Thurles. They managed to survive as Catholic landowners because of the patronage of the Duke of Ormonde, their relation.

daughter of Lord Dunboyne and widow of Lord Cahir (another Butler) helped considerably. George raised her young son the 4th Lord Cahir and when he was of age married him off to his niece, Elizabeth. George Reihill was the ancestor of the Thomastown Mathews.[205]

Thurles Castle 2003

When the Duke and Duchess of Ormonde were away in England or in Dublin the maintenance of Kilkenny Castle was the provenance of Captain George Reihill Mathew, their relation. The Duchess bombarded him with orders ' my Lord and I doe so much apprehend the danger to the roof of the old hall of the castle of Kilkenny and he desires it may be

---

[205] George surrendered Cahir Castle to Cromwell in 1649. Apparently he had been warned by his mother, Elizabeth, to follow that course of action as she had done in Thurles.

secured, repaired and mended with as much speed as may be'-' I desire you will furnish the castle of Kilkenny to be in readiness to receive me, my son and his family in the middle of next month'[206]

When Lady Cahir died George married another widow, who brought with her a dowry of £10,000. She was the widow of the last Earl of Tyrone. She had no children and when George died in 1689 she became somewhat isolated at Thomastown.[207] She fled to London in 1690 where she petitioned the government for help, stating that she, a Protestant, had been driven out of Ireland by her in-laws who were Catholics.[208]

George Reihill was succeeded by his second son[209] Theobald, who was also twice married. He died in 1711. Theobald's son, George, known as "Grand" George, inherited the estate of Thomastown. In his will[210] Theobald left several bequests including monies to be put in trust and managed for his three daughters until they got married or reached the age of twenty-one.[211] He expected a return of eight per cent on the money. He left money to the youngest son Bartholomew and to 'his dear cousin' Major George Mathew of Thurles. Four convents in Clonmel[212] benefited from his largesse as he left them £50 each. He was quite fussy about his funeral arrangements and insisted that he be interred at Thurles where his father and grandmother, Lady Thurles, were interred. He asked his son to remember his desire to have a monument erected in Thurles.

The problem of succession in the Catholic Mathew families contrasts with the almost smooth successions achieved by the families of the Butlers of Cahir and the Ryans of Inch.

---

[206] Ibid

[207] Thomastown was built around 1670 by George Reihill. Prior to that he had lived in Cahir Castle.

[208] Marnane *Land and Violence in West Tipperary*

[209] The eldest son, George, was educated in England and died on the way home from England in 1666.

[210] None of the Mathew wills is remarkable and they were all predictable. There are two other Mathew wills to be seen in the *Inch Papers*.

[211] The ladies in question were (1) Elizabeth who married Christopher O'Brien of Co. Clare, (2) Frances who married John Butler of Co. Tipperary and (3) Elinor who married Kean O'Hara of Co. Sligo.

[212] What is significant about this is that, in what we perceived as a time of persecution of the Catholics, four convents were in existence in Clonmel.

The Thurles Mathews were fortunate in that there were three single male heirs following the death of Theobald Mathew in 1699. This meant that no stratagem had to be used to avoid carving up the estate. However a failsafe plan was put in place in the event that the male heirs were not forthcoming. In 1713 a settlement was put in place, which ensured that in default of male heirs the estate would go to the Annfield and Thomastown branches successively. Similar plans must have been put in place in the other Mathew properties because in 1738 the Thurles and Thomastown estates were joined because of the failure of direct heirs in Thomastown. It should be noted that 'Grand' George Mathew who died in 1738 had converted in the early years of the 18th century. This inheritance did put a strain on the Thurles owner, George Mathew, who felt it incumbent to change his religion in 1740.

Theobald of Thurles (who died in 1699) did in fact have several sons and daughters himself. He was married three times. By his first wife, Margaret the daughter of Sir Valentine Browne he had three sons, George, known as Major George who inherited in 1699, Edmund who died young and James who married Elizabeth Bourke, daughter of the 3rd Baron Brittas[213]. James had no family. He also had two daughters – Elizabeth who married the 4th Lord Cahir and Anne who married Viscount Galmoy. By his second marriage to the heiress, Anne Salle of Killough Castle, Co.Tipperary, he had one son, Thomas who succeeded to the estates. By his third wife, Catherine Neville, an Englishwoman he had two sons and two daughters – Mary who was Maid of Honour to Queen Mary, the wife of James II and Catherine who died unmarried. The sons were Francis, who entered Military Service in France and Peter, who became a priest and ministered in England.

The Annfield branch of the family found life a little more complicated in that Theobald of Annfield, [214] who inherited in 1714 had two brothers. However there is no record on any legal pressure being applied to compel the family to comply with the penal laws of inheritance.

---

[213] He is acknowledged to be the father of James Mathew of Thomastown and later of Rathclogheen, who was adopted by his cousin and guardian the 1st Earl of Llandaff. James of Rathclogheen is the ancestor of the modern day Mathews.

[214] In 1713 Theobald of Annfield appointed Edward Fitzgerald, a merchant of Waterford, to recover rents, debts etc.

When Theobald died in 1745 the estate went to his son Thomas Mathew.[215] Again there does not seem to have been any pressure put on Thomas to divide the estate. However, in 1755 just prior to Parliament considering framing anti-Catholic laws Thomas decided to convert. The fact that his relation, George Mathew of Thurles, who had inherited Thomastown, was now elderly and had no male heir may have been a contributory factor also. George died in 1760 and Thomas Mathew of Annfield now became the sole owner of all the Mathew properties.[216]

Thomastown Castle

---

[215] Thomas had three sons and two daughters, one of whom, Mary, married John Ryan of Inch. The sons were Theobald, who inherited in 1714, Edmund who died in 1772 and James of Borris who married the heiress Anne Morres. They had one daughter who married her cousin Charles Mathew.
[216] Ibid.

Gateway to Thomastown Castle

Thomastown had been repaired and reconstruction began in 1711.[217] It was reported that "Grand" George Mathew and his family lived 'frugally' on the continent for seven years on £600 a year in order to devote his £8,000 rental to the laying out of his 1500 acre demesne and the fitting out of the house with forty bedrooms.[218] Fifty years later it was visited by Thomas Campbell, who, although quite enraptured with the natural setting of the house against the backdrop of the Galtees, was less than overjoyed with the neo classicism of the garden and park layout. He had this to say 'every violence that she is capable of suffering has been done to nature'. He raged against 'the square parterres of flowers, terraces thickly studded with busts and blind avenues' and regretted that the whole park had been 'thrown into squares and parallelograms with numerous avenues fenced and planted'.

"Grand" George of Thomastown turned Protestant in the early decades of the 18th century and was elected an M.P. for Co. Tipperary. George sat as a Tory and a supporter of the 2nd Duke of Ormonde. He was also elected M.P. for the period 1727-1736. He died two years later. This was the same George Mathew who was visited by Dean Swift in 1719. In 1704 he was one of nine Catholics in the county who were given licenses to carry arms. However this situation changed after 1715 when the government ordered the seizure of Catholic horses and arms. At some stage in the following years George and his son were apprehended and searched for arms.

The other two branches of the family remained Catholic. When Lady Thurles died she left her second son Theobald the town and manor of Thurles and an estate of four thousand acres. He was married three times and his second wife was Anne Sall, an heiress. Theobald gave her estate to his second son Thomas and so began the Annfield family. The changes in land ownership, which was effected by the necessity of the Ormonde Duke to reduce his overwhelming debts, benefited many landowners in Tipperary, including the Mathew family. They used the opportunity to consolidate and expand their holdings.[219]

---

[217] W.Nolan in *Tipperary History and Society*
[218] T. Power in *Land, Politics and Society in 18th century Tipperary*.
[219] Other families to benefit were Sadleir, Coote, Langley, Baker, Cleere, Dawson, Dancer and Harrison – T. Power in *Land, Politics and Society in 18th century Tipperary*.

The Mathew family owned Thurles town and because of their patronage the Catholic Butler bishop was allowed to live there.[220] In addition the Mathew family of Annfield built Inch and Thurles Chapels. A plaque on the wall of the chapel, which was built in 1730 in Thurles, stated that it was built by 'Big' George Mathew. He was the George Mathew of Thurles who married his stepsister Martha Eaton. He was also the son of the Major[221] mentioned above. The Tabernacle of the well-built chapel was bought in Paris for £50 and donated to the church by the Mathew family. In the climate of the times, which was hostile to Catholicism, the family took what steps they deemed necessary to protect their property. For example an oath of allegiance to the British monarchy was framed which would be sworn by Catholic subjects in Ireland as an indication of their loyalty. Catholics were divided on the issue but in Tipperary it would seem that the majority of the prominent Catholics favoured the idea. This acceptance was spearheaded by Archbishop James Butler II and George Mathew.

The Thomastown dynasty came to an abrupt end with the death of "Grand" George and his grandson who both died in 1738. "Grand" George's son, Theobald, had died two years earlier in 1736. He was married to a cousin from Thurles, Mary Ann Mathew. Her brother, George of Thurles inherited Thomastown at this time. As George of Thurles had no sons the Thomastown and Thurles estates passed into the ownership of Thomas of Annfield in 1760. The will, transferring the ownership, was contested unsuccessfully by Margaret the daughter of George of Thurles.

Thomas had converted to the Church of Ireland in 1755 and he was returned an M.P. for Tipperary in 1761. In the turbulent political climate of the times, his election was seen as a triumph for the pro Catholic interest in the county. Thomas was perceived as being of dubious conformity himself.[222] He conformed again in 1762.[223] He was elected M.P. again in

---

[220] Whelan in *Tipperary History & Society*

[221] The Major was given a D.C.L. at Oxford and was later an emissary to the courts of Versailles and Madrid. He was a Major in the Dragoon Guards. After the battle of the Boyne he was twice arrested as a Jacobite but later released. He died in 1725.

[222] Bric in *Tipperary History & Society*

[223] There were six Mathew conversions in the 18th century – George of Thomastown in 1711, Thomas of Thomastown and Annfield in 1740 and 1762, James of Cashel 1761, Francis (1st Earl of Llandaff) 1762 and Charles of Thurles 1768.

1768 but by a very small margin of 25 votes. On petition the result was overturned. Unlike the Pritties who were very widely connected with the Protestant landowning classes, Thomas Mathew had to rely on his own voters and whatever support he could muster from among the more liberal gentry.

That particular election was fought in a very bitter manner. In the early part of the 18th century one of the Mathew ladies had married Sir James Cotter, the chief advocate of the Stuart cause in Ireland. Cotter was executed for his pains in 1720. This alliance was alluded to some forty years later, when his opponent, Sir Thomas Maude of Dundrum, made this fact public and indeed objected to Mathew on the grounds that 'he had professed the popish religion many years after the age of twelve and had not conformed to the Protestant religion or educated his children as required by several acts of Parliament'.

The Mathews were no strangers to political controversy. In the by-election of 1735 Joseph Damer was elected as an M.P. for the county. He had been advanced in the Mathew interest (Tory). The defeated candidate, John Dawson, attributed his failure to certain irregularities, chief of which was the delayed opening of the poll by Theobald Mathew of Annfield, the Sheriff. This delay facilitated the creation of freeholders who voted for Damer.

Thomas Mathew's son, Francis, was also perceived as being a closet Catholic. However, Francis was fortunate in that he had John Scott (later Lord Clonmell) as his brother-in-law. Scott became solicitor-general and was very influential in Government circles. Through his influence, Francis, formerly an opposition M.P., became a government supporter and this led to his elevation to the peerage as Lord Llandaff in 1784. Though he had, to some extent, changed his allegiance, he still championed the Catholic cause right up to the end of the century and beyond.

The Act of 1778, which gave an enormous measure of relief to the Catholics, was widely welcomed by the Catholics in Tipperary. The men most associated with the carriage of the Act were Francis Mathew of Thomastown, Lord Clonmel (John Scott – a brother in law of Francis

Mathew), Sir William Osborne and John Hely-Hutchinson.[224] The main features of the Act were (1) the removal of the requirement that Catholic property had to be divided among the surviving sons. (2) Leases could now be given for more than 31 years. (3) The removal of the decree that a son who converted would get immediate possession making his parent a tenant for life only. The Act would only apply to people who took the oath of allegiance. In Tipperary county over 900 people took the oath. This number probably represented the vast majority of Catholic landowners in the county and included Archbishop Butler and many of his clergy.

That is not to say that Francis favoured any change in the status quo with regard to property rights. During the heyday of Whiteboyism he stood four square with the landlords. After the murder of Ambrose Power, a landlord, in 1775, over sixty of the leading figures in Tipperary including Francis Mathew and Thomas Maude, pledged their lives and fortunes to suppress Whiteboyism.[225]

With the re-emergence of considerable agrarian unrest, the American war of Independence and threatened French invasions Volunteer Corps were founded all over Ireland. In Tipperary, by 1782, there were eighteen functioning Volunteer corps. In the north of the county the leading gentry all had their own corps including Peter Holmes, Henry Prittie and Carden of Templemore.[226] The corps on the Cahir estate was composed of Catholics and was commanded by Pierce Butler, Lord Cahir's brother. Cornelius O'Callaghan had his own corps. Each corps was comprised of about forty rank and file members drawn from the head tenantry or from friends or associates of the colonel. Francis Matthew had three corps, one in each of his main holdings at Thomastown, Annfield and Thurles.

Thomas died in 1777 and was succeeded by his son Francis who sought election as an M.P. for the county in 1790. However on petition the seat went to John Bagwell who had been sponsored by Henry Prittie who did not stand. The other M.P. who topped the poll was Daniel Toler. Later, in 1796, Francis Mathew was elected without opposition to the seat when

---

[224] This close association between Lord Clonmell and Francis Mathew wasn't always harmonious. According Barrington, in his *Reminiscences*, Lord Clonmell fought duels with Lord Llandaff, Lord Tyrawley and others.
[225] Bric in *Tipperary History & Society*
[226] Stoney, Jocelyn, Toler and Parsons were also part of this group.

Daniel Toler died in that year. In the election of the following year Bagwell and Mathew were returned unopposed.

Francis was made Baron Llandaff of Thomastown in 1783 and he was later made Earl of Llandaff in 1797. The Earl lived the life of a Lord and entertained and was entertained royally. Jonah Barrington the famous barrister, hosted a dinner in Dublin which was attended by many of the great nobles including the Duke of Wellington, Sir John Parnell, Lords Dillon, Yelverton, Clonmell, Buckinghamshire, Blacquirie and Llandaff. The latter loaned him two cooks. Barrington stated that the 'the evening passed amidst that glow of well-bred, witty and cordial vinous conviviality which was, I perceive, peculiar to high society in Ireland.'

During the precarious year of 1798 Hon. Francis Mathew now known as Lord Mathew administered the oath of allegiance to over 1000 people at Golden chapel. His father, the Earl, died in 1806.

In 1812 Francis the 2nd Earl, employed the architect Richard Morrison to 'throw a Gothic cloak over the earlier house' (at Thomastown) as Nolan so aptly put it.[227] 'Towers, battlements, parapets, a Gothic hall and Gothic library gave the mansion its much admired castellated appearance which is present to this day in the ruins' Quoting the field surveyors he goes on to say ' surrounding scenery and richness of the soil, the age and antiquity of the timber, entitle this demesne to rank with the first in the kingdom.'

The Mathew finances had begun to creak somewhat, even when Thomas died, despite the income from rents on the Thomastown estate, which had grown substantially in the hundred years from 1718 (£8,000) to 1808 (£28,000). The family also benefited from urban rents collected in Thurles.

Another source of income was the dowry. Fortuitous marriages brought additional wealth to the Mathew family starting with George the first Mathew to arrive in Tipperary, who married the widow of Viscount Thurles. His son George Reihill married the widow of Lord Cahir who was also the daughter of Lord Dunboyne. "Grand" George Mathew, a grandson

---

[227] Nolan in *Tipperary History & Society* - The architect he engaged for this immense project was William Vitruvius Morrison, who is best known for his designs for Fota House, near Cobh, and Brittas Castle, near Thurles, which was to have been "the first 'archaeological' 19th century castle in Ireland", a full-scale replica of Warwick Castle.

of George Reihill, married as his second wife Lady Ann Hume who brought him an estate worth £10,000 in the 1680s. He converted the title to his own use and that of his heirs and used the money to make further land purchases. Francis Mathew, the 1st Earl received £10,000 with Ellis Smyth of Co. Wicklow when they married in 1764.

These were the most illustrious and beneficial marriages entered into by the members of the family. They brought advancement in terms of social standing, wealth and land.[228]

Mathews were British landowners also.[229] This did not prevent the estate going into debt.

Francis was in serious debt when he inherited in 1777 due largely to marriage payments and unpaid debts from previous generations.[230] Trustees were appointed by Parliament to unravel his affairs and lands had to be disposed of.

When he died in 1806 the estate was still very much in debt for a variety of reasons one of which was his sponsoring a bill to bring a water supply to Thomastown Castle. By 1810 most of the debt had been paid off but new debts had arisen due to the personal borrowings of Francis the 1st Earl and his sons Francis (who became the second Earl) and Montague. They borrowed from James Scully their head tenant (£12,000) and David La Touche the Dublin banker (£2,400) and others. In the period of 1809 – 1814 sales of land on the Thomastown estate realized £149,950. Two of the principal purchasers were Nicholas Maher (£26,000) and James Scully (£33,200). Maher and Scully now entered the landowning class where up to

---

[228] After 1710 the pattern of Mathew marriages continues to exhibit social ambition. In the male line the Thurles branch made alliances with the Butlers of Kilcash and the Brownlows of Lurgan. The Thomastown men married into the Butlers of Ballyragget and the widow of the last Earl of Tyrone, while the Annfield members married women from the families of Shelly, Morris and an Indian nabob.

[229] T. Power in *Land, Politics and Society in 18th century Tipperary.*

[230] Thomas Mathew also gave away lands. John Scott, a solicitor who later became Viscount Clonmell, was made trustee of lands, which Thomas Mathew settled on his mistress. In 1768 Scott was married to Mathew's widowed daughter. In the same year that Scott's wife died (1771) he got possession of the lands of Thomas Mathew's mistress and he laid claim to monies in right of his wife. -T. Power in *Land, Politics and Society in 18th century Tipperary.*

this they had only been tenants. Another purchaser was Thomas Ryan who spent £8,000.

Francis the 2nd Earl died in 1833. He had been predeceased by his brother Montague in 1819. His second brother George was insane and had died in 1832, so the estates passed to Elizabeth his sister. She too died unmarried in 1841.

Francis in his youth had been a very close friend of the Prince Regent and his wife was a daughter of John la Touche of Harristown, Co. Kildare.

While the main branch of the family disappeared the Mathew name was kept alive by brothers of Fr. Mathew. For example, Francis Mathew of Rockview House who was mentioned in the will of Elizabeth was married twice and had four sons and two daughters. His descendants became judges, lawyers, surgeons, engineers, clergymen, Army Officers, businessmen, nuns and some of them were prolific authors. Many were educated at Eton and went on to universities such as Oxford, Trinity and Cambridge. One of the authors was a Bishop in various parts of the world, David James Mathew. He published more than eighteen books dealing with a variety of historical subjects including one entitled *Sir Tobias Mathew*. That branch of the family is represented today by Michael Mathew,[231] an international banking consultant of Camberley, Surrey.

Another brother of Fr. Mathew was Charles and his numerous descendants likewise went into the professions and the service. One of his grandsons was knighted as Sir Charles Mathew. They are represented today by Robert, a Barrister who lives in London, Thomas, a businessman who married a Russian Princess, Francis Anthony a stockbroker and Anne who married the 6th Earl of Norbury.

The modern Mathew descendants are too numerous to detail in this book but interested persons can see the details in Burkes Peerage.

---

[231] His father, also Michael, an R.A.F. officer was killed during the Second World War in 1943.

Maude

Dundrum House, the seat of the Maude Lords Hawarden, is now one of Ireland's premier Hotels. Dundrum House, a magnificent building designed by Sir Edward Lovett Pearce in the middle of the 18th century, was bought by Mr. Austin and Mrs. Mary Crowe about twenty years ago. Much of the old building has been retained and is carefully maintained.

A general election was held in 1761. One of the candidates was the very right wing Protestant, Sir Thomas Maude. The other was the converted Catholic, Thomas Mathew. Thomas Mathew was perceived as being of dubious conformity.[232] He conformed again in 1762.[233] During the course of polling, Maude's election agent, Daniel Gahan, questioned the qualifications of freeholders, whether they were born of Catholic parents, educated as Catholics, or if converts, to produce their certificates of conversion. Gahan challenged Mathew's election agent, Thomas Prendergast, with the assertion that his wife was Catholic and that therefore he was disqualified from voting. A duel ensued resulting in Prendergast's death.

The fact that three candidates, Maude, Mathew, and Henry Prittie of Kilboy, went forward in the election meant that a contest was inevitable. When polling closed on 8 May 1761 the poll stood thus: Prittie 924 votes, Mathew 532, and Maude 486, with Prittie being elected (marking the successful entry of that family to the county representation) and a double return made in respect of the other two, because of which both candidates

---

[232] Bric in *Tipperary History & Society*
[233] There were six Mathew conversions in the 18th century – George of Thomastown in 1711, Thomas of Thomastown and Annfield in 1740 and 1762, James of Cashel 1761, Francis (1st Earl of Llandaff) 1762 and Charles of Thurles 1768.

were obliged to petition. The result of the petition went in Maude's favour and he was deemed elected.

The Maudes owned Dundrum and several townlands in the neighbourhood of Mokarky, Cooleky, Parkestowne and part of Curragheen.

They were descended from Robert Maude of West Riddlesden, Yorkshire, who bought lands in Kilkenny and Tipperary in the latter half of the 17th century. His wife was Frances Wandesforde, the sister of Christopher Wandesforde, the 1st Lord Castlecomer. Robert was the father of Anthony who was an M.P. for Cashel in 1686 and High Sheriff of the county in 1695. Anthony's son, Sir Robert, also an M.P., was created a baronet of Ireland in 1705 and died in 1750. These men were only sons. Sir Robert had several children but he left his estates to his eldest son, Sir Thomas, who was created Baron in 1776.

Dundrum House now a Hotel (courtesy Mr.& Mrs. Crowe)

Sir Robert was the man responsible for building Dundrum House. It is said that the house was built adjacent to the O'Dwyer castle, which was knocked down and the castle stones were used for building the house. In the course of time the demesne was enclosed and contained 2,400 acres of which almost a thousand acres were planted. The original house consisted of a two-storey block over a basement. It would seem that Dundrum House, designed by Sir William Lovett Pearce, was built sometime between 1730 and 1750.

At the Clonmel assizes of June 1762 a reward of £20 was offered by 27 leading landowners including Maude and Henry Prittie (Dunalley) for the discovery and prosecution of "each of the first three Papists guilty of carrying arms in said county".[234] Three years later Sir Thomas Maude was elected High Sheriff. He was considered to be an extreme right wing Protestant at the time.

As High Sheriff in 1766, he was intimately involved in the Fr. Sheehy affair, which has been dealt with in the notice about the Bagwell family. Fr. Sheehy's trial was not conducted in a manner conducive to his obtaining justice. Prosecution witnesses perjured themselves and in addition, on the day of the trial, the streets outside were patrolled by a party of horse, led by Thomas Maude of Dundrum, who was said to have 'menaced Sheehy's friends and encouraged his enemies'. This involvement by Sir Thomas was to have serious repercussions almost a hundred years later when one of his lateral descendants was standing for election.

Sir Thomas Maude and Sir William Barker, who were closely involved in the events of that decade, were subsequently associated with schemes to promote Protestant settlement on their estates. As early as February 1767 Maude was seeking Protestant manufacturers for settlement on his estate at Ballintemple, and in the 1770s he promoted the linen industry. This led to a period of sustained employment in the general area. In 1766 there were just forty-four on the estate but by 1831 there were almost one hundred and sixty. This occurred as a result of the Whiteboy activity of the 1760s.

Between 1755 and 1775 Sir Thomas Maude accumulated debts of £27,000, which passed to his brother Cornwallis Maude, Viscount Hawarden (d. 1803), after 1777. A successful marriage by Thomas Ralph, second Viscount (d. 1807), to the daughter of the archbishop of Cashel (later earl of Normanton) may have served to reduce the debt, for the

---

[234] This was in response to an outbreak of Whiteboy activity.

Hawarden estate survived intact to be one of the largest in the county in the nineteenth century[235].

Most of the money spent by Sir Thomas was used to improve his estates. He sponsored large-scale remodelling of the landscape, drainage schemes, an estate village at Dundrum, new tenants, and resettlement. He developed a Deerpark in which he built three houses in which the estate workers lived (and protected his deer). Such endeavors could entail substantial capital investment the scale of which is indicated by the fact that in 1775 the principal debt owed by Sir Thomas Maude stood at £27,000 at a time when his improvement schemes were most intense.

Following the murder of Ambrose Power, a landlord, in 1775 over sixty of Tipperary's leading figures, including Thomas Maude and Francis Mathew, pledged their lives and fortunes to suppress Whiteboyism. In the following months two developments strengthened the resolve of the gentry. First, a revised and extended Whiteboy act was passed which added to the list of felonies incurring the death penalty and increased the powers of the magistrates. In the following year 1776 a number of Volunteer Corps were formed and one of these was founded by Sir Cornwallis Maude, the brother of Baron de Montalt. By May two corps under Benjamin Bunbury and Sir Cornwallis Maude were formed, in July another at Nenagh under Peter Holmes, and by the end of the year another 28. These corps, coupled with the determination of the gentry following Power's murder, served to quell Whiteboy agitation at this time.

Maude was a staunch government supporter and he was rewarded for his support by being elevated to the peerage in 1776 as Lord De Montalt.[236] He was one of twenty-two new peers created in that year as part of the government's winning of support for delicate measures, notably the despatching of 4,000 troops to America.[237]

---

[235] The lands owned by the Maudes exceeded 15,000 acres by the mid 1800s.

[236] At that period most of the Tipperary M.P.s were generally, though not always, government supporters including Pennefather, John Damer, Peter Holmes and John Hely-Hutchinson, with only four in opposition – O'Callaghan, Prittie, Osborne and Mathew.

[237] T. Power *Land, Politics & Society in 18th century Tipperary*.

Following the 1768 election Maude came in as a government supporter having been made a privy councillor by Townshend[238]. Maude's advancement as a privy councillor was an expression of the new policy enunciated by Townshend of creating a strong 'Castle' party, dependent on the lord-lieutenant, and rendering him a majority in parliament in return for patronage. But most Tipperary gentlemen, entering parliament in 1768, opposed government, with Maude and Guy Moore Coote (MP for Clonmel, 1761-82) the only committed government supporters.

Sir Thomas Maude, Baron de Montalt, died in 1777 and his estate and honour of Baron de Montalt passed to his brother Cornwallis who was forty-seven years old at the time. Cornwallis was later given the title of 1st Viscount Hawarden in 1793.

Cornwallis was married three times. Unlike many of his peers who were married a number of times, Cornwallis did not rush into his second marriage. He waited nine years after his first wife's death in 1757. The three wives were from mainland Britain and this would suggest that Cornwallis spent some considerable time in England. The fact that seven of his eight daughters married English gentlemen would support that assumption. In addition to the four daughters he had six sons, and while they too may have spent considerable time in England, the two who succeeded to the title must have spent a reasonable time in Ireland. They were Thomas Ralph, the only son of the second marriage, who became the 2nd Viscount, and Cornwallis the eldest son of the third marriage, who became the 3rd Viscount.

While his son, Thomas Ralph, the 2nd Viscount, by his first marriage, had no children and his son Cornwallis, the 3rd Viscount had only one son and four daughters, the remaining sons of the 1st Viscount were remarkably prolific and details of their descendants can be seen in Burkes Irish Family Record. They were quite amazing people who achieved high office and served in far-flung lands.

Sir Cornwallis seems to have steered clear of politics in the county and in fact represented the borough of Roscommon in parliament. It is not surprising that he was somewhat less active politically than his brother with

---

[238] George Townshend, 1st Marquess Townshend, was a Privy Councillor in England and held office in Ireland.

the burden of a very large family to be settled. He simplified his position even further by employing the professional estate agents Coopers in the 1780s.[239]

He lived to see the 1798 rebellion and the Union and he died in 1803. Despite the fact that he managed to escape becoming embroiled in any way during those controversial periods, his son Thomas Ralph did not.

In July 1798 the Hon. Thomas Maude, the son of the 1st Viscount Hawarden, gave evidence against two Dundrum men, Ryan and Coffey, who had been arrested on the charge of breaking the curfew. They were tried by court martial at Cashel. Maude gave evidence that his men, residents of Maudemount, had discovered the accused men absent from their homes on that night. This evidence was collaborated by three of Maude's tenants, a farmer, a cooper and a weaver. The prisoners pleaded not guilty and stated that they were out looking after their cows. Several witnesses spoke on their behalf including one of the Manserghs. Despite this, both men were found guilty and sentenced to be shot and then beheaded and their remains to be buried near the 'other traitors' in the street adjacent the jail at Cashel.[240]

Thomas Ralph died in 1807 and the honours and lands passed to his half brother, Cornelius Maude, who became the 3rd Viscount Hawarden. In 1815 Viscount Hawarden sent a series of letters to William Gregory, the Under Secretary at Dublin Castle concerning renewed agrarian disturbances. Sometime before May of that year he wrote as follows:- "I have learned of the meetings (of Whiteboys, to use this generic term) which take place nightly and the strength of their assemblies ... Notices have been served upon many of my tenants for the purpose of fixing the price at which they were to let their lands for potatoes. ... The tenants who are in the new village (built by me) have also received threatening notice… such being the state of the country, allow me to again suggest the necessity of having troops or assistance afforded me."

---

[239] The family originally settled at Killenure near Cashel in the 1740s as part of the household of Archbishop Price. They later rose to prominence in the Treasury Office in Dublin. As well as being agents for the Damer estate they were agents for the Maudes, Cashel See, Erasmus Smith and Lloyd estates.- T. Power in *Land, Politics and Society in 18th century Tipperary*

[240] D. Marnane A *history of West Tipperary from 1660*

Sometime later he wrote to the Under Secretary again saying:-
"I regret to say outrages have increased. On the night of the 2nd (May) I armed my steward, gardeners and bailiffs, together with two other men.... remained out till daylight.. most of the threatening notices which have been posted up were against strangers (warning against taking land) ..... I have this minute returned from Cashel, where I saw Mr. Wilicocks, Chief Constable who has promised to send me four dismounted men to accompany me out this night, as I consider it neither prudent to go without a stronger party (to search for Whiteboys) or to leave Lady Hawarden unprotected."

Yet another letter complains that :-
"Further outrages were last night committed.....and the following houses were (attacked).....Daniel Heffernan's was the last they attacked. They fired three or four shots into his house and afterwards brought him out for the purpose of shooting him but allowed him to return on his swearing to quit his farm by Thursday. ..... They (the people attacked) all agree in stating the force of the party (of attackers) to have been from forty to fifty people…"

Despite the unrest on his estate the Viscount's attitude hardened if anything as in 1816 he was said to have embarked on a religious crusade against Catholic labourers of Clonoulty, Knockavilla and Anacarty when he sacked everyone who refused to work on Church holydays.[241]

Despite his troubles at home Cornwallis was not one to miss a good party. It was noted by a diarist, Emma Sophia Sherwill, the fiancé of Sir William Parker Carrol, a Tipperaryman, that she had been introduced to Viscount Hawarden at Court in London, at a Grand Ball in 1817.[242] A great friendship existed between the Prittie, Carrol and Maude families. A story is told that this arose because Parker's father deputized for the very young Henry Prittie (the second Lord Dunalley) in a duel with an English officer.[243]

In 1831 the son of the Rev. Carew Armstrong was shot inside the demesne of Lord Hawarden. Carew Armstrong was in a state of constant warfare with his parishioners. He obtained hundreds of decrees against

[241] Marnane
[242] D. Murphy *The Two Tipperarys*
[243] See the Prittie article for this detail.

them but he was unable to serve them. In the same year Carew Armstong's proctor, Denis O'Shaughnessy, was murdered and robbed of his tithe valuation book while valuing a field of wheat at Kilpatrick.[244]

To his credit, Cornwallis, the 3rd Viscount, made a determined and successful effort to solve the tithe problem in his area. Whatever the reason it is definitely the case that both Maude and his neighbour Carrol introduced revolutionary thinking with regard to the collection of tithes in their areas. They simply by-passed the hated proctors altogether and increased their own share of the tithes, being large landowners. Many of the tenants were Catholic. This move led to a period of relative peace and harmony on the estates in the north of the county.[245]

Seventy-five years after his granduncle Sir Thomas Maude had become embroiled in the judicial murder of Fr. Sheehy, Cornwallis the son of the 3rd Viscount stood for election for the county. He was a conservative candidate and his running mate was Ponsonby Barker in the 1841 election. They were opposed by the liberal candidates Valentine Meagher and Robert Otway Cave.

Cornwallis was to find out that the Tipperary Catholics had long memories. While canvassing in Newport someone scrawled a message on his carriage. It read 'who hung the priest?'

In the subsequent name and shame game both Catholics and Protestants blamed each other for writing the message.

However on the day in question a large congregation came out of Mass in Newport and saw the message scrawled on the carriage. Some of the people became so incensed that they answered the question by dispatching the carriage over the bridge into the river Mulcair where it smashed on the rocks disgorging champagne, cheroots and cold meats.[246] To add insult to injury the servants of the young lord were attacked by a crowd, which was batoned, by the police as the local Temperance Band tried to quell the tumult.

On the hustings in Clonmel the conservative candidates met with a torrent of abuse from the supporters of the liberal candidates. Cornwallis

---

[244] McGrath in *Tipperary History & Society*
[245] D. Murphy *The Two Tipperarys*
[246] McGrath in *Tipperary History & Society* pg. 278

Maude was jeered with the shouts of 'who hung the priest' but Michael Laffan, the Catholic Archdeacon from Fethard, attributed Maude's unpopularity to the evictions that were being carried out on the Maude estate at Dundrum.

In 1842 the Viscount evicted 200 Catholic families, 1300 people in all, from his estate at Dundrum. In 1843 Fr. O'Brien Davern reminded the Viscount that he was descended from a Cromwellian settler whose usurpation of the estate (of the O'Dwyers of Kilnamanagh) was made legal.[247]

Cornwallis was married to an English lady in 1811 and they had one son and four daughters. Predictably two of the daughters married English noblemen and one died unmarried. The other, Isabella, married Lt. Colonel Charles Tottenham[248] of Woodstock, Co. Wicklow. Cornwallis died in 1856 and was succeeded by his son, Cornwallis, the 4th Viscount.

The 4th Viscount had the distinction of being a lord-in-waiting to Queen Victoria from 1866-68. He was created Earl de Montalt in 1886. An Army man, he was a Captain of the 2nd Life Guards. He was also an honorary Colonel of the Tipperary militia. He was a Justice of the Peace and a Magistrate. In addition he was a Custos Rotulorum and Lieutenant for the county. It was during the 4th Viscount's tenancy of the estates that the Land Acts came into force compelling landlords to sell their farms to the tenants. Prior to these events he built an extra storey on to Dundrum House in 1860 and carefully maintained the gardens and lands. The Maude family was responsible for bringing the Great Southern and Western Railway through Dundrum.

The 4th Viscount was married to Clementina, the daughter of Admiral the Right Hon. Charles Fleeming. They had two sons (the second of whom died in infancy) and seven daughters. Five of them married, two to Irish gentlemen and the other three to English men. The fourth daughter, Kathleen, married to Gerald Brooke of Sommerton, Co. Dublin and the seventh lady married Major William Adam of Kinnea, Co. Cavan.[249]

---

[247] This may not have been true as there is no mention of the Maudes in Prendergast's *Cromwellian Settlement of Ireland*.

[248] For notices of this family see *The Wexford Gentry II* by Art Kavanagh & Rory Murphy.

[249] Isabella the eldest married the last Baron Colchester and they had no family. Elphinstone Agnes the 5th daughter married the Hon. Walter James Sugden and they had a

Cornwallis, the eldest son of the 4th Viscount, an Army Officer, was killed in the Boer War in 1881. He had married Eva Brooke, a sister of Gerald of Sommerton, and he left two daughters.[250]

When Cornwallis the 4th Viscount died in 1905 the earldom became extinct but the other honours passed to his cousin Robert Henry, a retired Colonel who was the eldest son of Very Rev. Robert Maude, the Dean of Clogher.[251]

Robert Henry, the 5th Viscount Hawarden, died in 1908 and his son Sir Robert Cornwallis Maude became the 6th Viscount at the age of eighteen. This young man, a Lieutenant in the Coldstream Guards, was killed in action in 1914. His brother Eustace Wyndham Maude became the 7th Viscount.

Eustace Wyndham Maude the 7th Viscount was born 1877 and also joined the Army. He served in World War I and was mentioned in despatches. He survived the War and in 1920 he married Marion Wright of Derby and they had two sons[252] and one daughter.[253]

The 7th Viscount died in 1958 and was succeeded by his eldest son Robert Leslie Eustace Maude, the 8th Viscount Hawarden. Robert was born in 1926. He was educated at Winchester and Oxford and later joined the

---

family. The 6th lady, Leucha Diana married Sir Thomas Courtenay Warner and they had children.

[250] His eldest daughter, Clementina, became heir to the possessions of several families – Lords Elphinstones, the Flemings (Earls of Wigtoun), the Keiths (Earls Marischal) and the Drummonds (Earls of Perth). She married William Frederick Loftus Tottenham in 1909. She died in 1961.

[251] Very Rev. Robert William Henry, Dean of Clogher, was the 3rd son of Sir Cornwallis Maude the 3rd Viscount. For an account of the descendants of the other sons of the 1st Viscount see Burkes Peerage.

[252] The younger son was the Hon. Henry Maude who lived in Kent and was High Sheriff of that county. He served in World War II and was married to Elizabeth Lockie of France. They have two sons Francis Hugh and Anthony Eustace and one daughter Elizabeth. Elizabeth married Andrei Majidian of Tehran and they have a son Daniel Martin who was born in 1996.

[253] She married Peter Baxter of Dorset and they had one son, Charles and three daughters – Joanna, Margaretta and Victoria who were all born in the 1950s.

Army. He served with distinction in World War II. He married Susannah Gardner and they had two sons and one daughter, Sophia Rose.[254]

His younger son is the Hon. Thomas Maude who lives in Kent and who is married to Christine Stowe.

The eldest son is Robert Connan Wyndham Leslie Maude who became the 9th Viscount when his father died in 1991. Sir Robert was born in 1961 and now lives in Kent. He is married to Judith Bates of Kent and has one son, Varian John.

Sir Stanley Maude was a cousin of Captain Anthony Maude of Belgard Castle in Co. Dublin. Sir Stanley was a General in the Great War and he commanded the expedition to Mesopotamia. General Maude expelled the Turks from Iraq and was killed in Baghdad in 1917.

Captain Anthony spent Easter at Knocklofty with the Donoughmores. It was a bit of a picnic as the house was mostly under dustsheets, but they enjoyed the fishing and the peace and quiet of the Suir valley. All three, with another guest, Maurice Headlam, an English Civil Servant, left on Easter Monday taking the Dublin train from Clonmel. At Thurles the train stopped for longer than usual. They whiled away the time playing bridge. Then someone came and told them that there was a rebellion in Dublin and that the train would go no further. Nobody seemed to know what had happened. The Donoughmores, who were intent on returning to England, decided to take the next train south hoping to catch the boat from Rosslare.

Captain Maude, anxious to join his wife and children at his home in Dublin, hired a car and set off with Headlam, stopping to buy provisions in case his family was without food. By the time they reached the Curragh it was eleven at night so he decided to knock up Captain Harry Greer, the manager of the National Stud, and ask him for a bed for the night. They found the house locked and barricaded, but Greer, looking out, recognised Captain Maude and let them in.

Early on the Tuesday morning Captain Maude and Headlam set off from the Curragh. They reached Maude's home, Belgard Castle, without incident. As they drove up the avenue they saw, standing behind the closed

---

[254] Sophia Rose married Michael Steel from Hantshire and they have one son, Anthony (b. 1988) and three daughters Isabella (b. 1984), Emily (b. 1992) and Oriel Sophia (b. 1995)

gates of the courtyard, Maude's two schoolboy sons and his fourteen year old daughter, each holding one of their father's guns and ready to defend the house against the rebels.

O'Callaghan of Shanbally

In what must have been one of the most traumatic events in the history of this famous Tipperary family, Cornelius O'Callaghan, Lord Lismore, divorced his wife in 1826. This was no quietly hidden divorce but was the subject of a Bill in the House of Lords. The Bill was entitled "An Act to dissolve the Marriage of the Right Honorable Cornelius Viscount Lismore, of the Kingdom of Ireland, with Eleanor Viscountess Lismore his now Wife, and to enable him to marry again; and for other purposes therein mentioned".

In the course of the proceedings many witnesses were called who told of the events leading up to the separation and subsequent divorce of the couple. The witnesses included the Hon. & Rev. Richard Ponsonby, the Dean of St. Patricks, who officiated at the wedding, William Edmund Tugwell, a clerk who served Lady Lismore with a copy of the Divorce Bill, Sarah Bean, a servant, Miss Patey,[255] a companion to Lady Lismore, the Rt. Hon. the Dowager Viscountess Lismore, Lieutenant General Sir R.W. O'Callaghan, the Duke of Ormonde, the Marchioness of Ormonde, George O'Callaghan, Doctors and other officials.

It would seem from the evidence that the marriage ran into trouble shortly after the fourth child was born when Lady Lismore began the habit of chastising her husband, both verbally and physically. According to her brother, the Duke of Ormonde she was a lady who frequently lost her temper.[256] George O'Callaghan gave evidence that he had seen her strike her husband on more than one occasion. In addition she frequently taunted

---

[255] Later Mrs. Ann Cutbush

[256] He said 'her conduct and temper was such towards her husband that no man could live with her'.

him by stating that Shanbally might be fit for the wife of Lord Lismore but was not fit for Eleanor the sister of the Duke of Ormonde.

They had four children and the two youngest were about twelve and eight years of age at the time of the divorce.

One of the most startling facts to emerge was that, at the time of the separation, Lord Lismore was in extreme financial difficulty. Although he owned over forty thousand acres of land and despite having received almost £40,000 as a dowry with Eleanor he was reduced to dire straits in the period from 1816 to 1825. His brother stated that he had only one servant in Shanbally and owned only one carriage and no carriage horse. He also said that in 1817 Lord Lismore was so financially embarrassed that he could not travel over to London to see his wife. In further evidence he said that there were over three thousand acres of land untenanted at the time. He himself was Sheriff of the county in 1824 and there were three executions issued against his brother's property. Lord Lismore was unable to pay his mother her annuity on a regular basis and money owed to George had not been paid either.

The couple was separated in 1819 and Lady Lismore,[257] on the advice of her doctors, decided to travel to a southern country where the climate might be good for her asthma. She took a manservant, Sarah Bean, Miss Patey and her two children to Italy. They returned briefly to Ireland in 1821[258] but went back to Italy again. While she was away a member of her family wrote to Lord Lismore looking for money to be sent to her. He told his agent to send her money but the agent said there was none. A few days later an English gentleman sent him £300 he was owed and he immediately sent that money to Lady Lismore.

While Lady Lismore was in Italy for the second time she took a lover, a young man called the Hon. Richard Bingham and in evidence it was proved that they had slept together and therefore she had committed

---

[257] It would seem that Lord Lismore kept the fact of the separation secret from his wife. She was informed of the separation by Miss Patey and was so emotionally distressed by the news that she became physically ill.

[258] She got news that her eldest son was seriously ill and went to England as fast as was possible. He had recovered by the time she arrived. Her two youngest children were taken from her at that time.

adultery. It was on the grounds of this adultery that Lord Lismore sought the divorce.

Lady Lismore, too, felt the cold pangs of penury abroad and was forced to reduce her staff. At one stage she had to pawn her jewels, to Torriano the banker, and on another occasion she had to borrow from Miss Patey. Despite this she was able to travel to Florence, Naples and Rome.

After this Lady Lismore moved to Paris and generally stayed on the continent. She did not contest the divorce. The children were reared by their father.

The seat of the O'Callaghans (later Lords Lismore) was at Shanbally Castle, near Clogheen village, where they built a mansion about 1735. There was over 1200 acres of land in the demesne. After the peerage was obtained in 1785 their house was renewed as a castle in 1812.[259] The new neo-classical house was designed by John Nash. Round and octagonal towers, battlements and machicolations were featured in the new design.[260]

Shanbally Castle had a beautiful woodland setting with an artificial lake amid the fabulous mountain scenery of the Knockmealdowns and the Galtees. The castle had twenty bedrooms and the entire complement of

---

[259] The Castle was, unfortunately, demolished in 1957.
[260] Nolan in *Tipperary History & Society*

rooms was embellished with stucco ceilings with elegant marble fireplaces throughout.

Cornelius O'Callaghan (the elder) was a small Co. Cork landowner and successful Dublin lawyer. He was Sir Redmond Everard's solicitor and facilitated him in getting mortgages. Like Redmond he was a convert. In 1713 he and Redmond represented Fethard in Parliament. It is probable that O'Callaghan's political advancement was paid for by a reduction in Everard's debts. In 1721 Everard sold his property in Iffa & Offa and centred on Clogheen to O'Callaghan for £11,500. The O'Callaghan family built upon this base and extended their holdings during the next one hundred and fifty years so that by the mid-nineteenth century they were the county's largest landowners. In 1883 the Lismore estates totalled a staggering 42,000 acres. In Tipperary they owned almost 35,000 acres, while they also owned 6,000 acres in Cork and over 1000 acres in Limerick. The rent roll was valued at over £16,000 per annum.[261]

As can be inferred from the above the O'Callaghans had a voracious appetite for land acquisition. Lord Lismore in his will of 1787 stipulated that his younger son lay out £9,999 in the purchase of lands, and in 1803 his heir bought an estate in Co. Laois for £43,620.[262]

Cornelius had a son Thomas who married Sarah the daughter of John Davis of Carrickfergus, Co. Antrim as his first wife. They had a son Cornelius who was born in 1740. He was known as Cornelius the younger.

In the 1740s the O'Callaghans began to introduce Protestant tenants into their estate. Some Catholics converted such as the head tenants Prendergast and McGrath, but there were still Catholic head tenants there such as Woulfe and Sheehy. In September and October 1747 twenty-two individuals including eight couples converted on the estate. This number included six farmers, the rest being tradesmen or merchants in Clogheen. Of these farmers the surnames of Curtin, Fennessy, Murphy, and Walsh imply Catholic status, while those of Bradshaw and Burnet would point to those families being Protestant. Despite this show of conformity the

---

[261] The income from rents on the estate grew substantially in the eighty years from 1743 (£477) to 1823 (£17,120)
[262] T. Power in *Land, Politics and Society in Tipperary*

O'Callaghans were noted for their sympathetic approach to the Catholic Relief movement.[263]

The O'Callaghans spent considerable sums over the decades of the 18th century improving their estates, building Clogheen village (where Protestant artisans and craftsmen were brought in), drainage schemes and large scale remodelling of the landscape. These works were facilitated by the appointment of agents. One of the first on the O'Callaghan properties was Daniel Lenihan who was appointed in the early 1740s.

Specific instructions were given by the O'Callaghans about the type of house to be built for Daniel Lenihan. He was to have a two-lofted slated house with stabling for six horses. Such a house was considered a mansion in those times.

In 1754 there was a by-election and Robert O'Callaghan was elected M.P. for Fethard. Robert must have been a son of Cornelius the elder. The O'Callaghans had built up an influence in the corporation by virtue of their association with Everard in 1713, and because they had acquired part of the encumbered Everard estate in the 1720s. As with Pennefather at Cashel and Moore at Clonmel, O'Callaghan's emergence at Fethard was aided by the creation of ninety-eight new freemen in 1754.

Already a rival to the O'Callaghan claims had arisen following the purchase by Thomas Barton of the remnant of the Everard estate in 1751. Yet the Bartons found it difficult initially to achieve any solid influence in the borough. The final agreement on the division of the corporation and the borough representation came only in 1787.

In the period of the mid 1760s Cornelius junior was appointed a magistrate in the area, as the number of magistrates was considered insufficient at the time to deal with the agrarian unrest. Two of his head tenants were also appointed, John Miles of Rochestown and William Bagnall of Marlhill.

During the Fr. Sheehy affair, Fr. Sheehy offered to surrender to Cornelius O'Callaghan.[264] This was agreed by the Dublin authorities and when Fr. Sheehy met Cornelius (whose grandfather was Catholic) the latter

---

[263] Ibid.

[264] Fr. Sheehy was related to a namesake of his own, one of the head tenants on the O'Callaghan estate.

offered him one hundred guineas and told him to make his way out of the country at once. O'Callaghan knew the feeling of the Tipperary gentlemen and that going to Dublin would not protect Sheehy from their vengeance.[265]

In 1775 Cornelius O'Callaghan the younger of Shanbally was a representative for Fethard. He was married to a daughter of the Speaker Ponsonby, the Right Hon. John Ponsonby, who was the 2nd son of the First Earl of Bessborough. They were married a year before he was elected as M.P. for Fethard.

With the re-emergence of considerable agrarian unrest, the American war of Independence and threatened French invasions Volunteer Corps were founded all over Ireland. Cornelius O'Callaghan had his own corps. Like the rest his corps was comprised of about forty rank and file members drawn from the head tenantry or from friends or associates.

In advance of the election of 1783 a body known as 'The Constitutional Associating Freeholders' was formed in Clonmel to promote parliamentary reform. Their main aims were to reduce the influence of the crown on parliament, to make representatives more responsive to the views of their constituents and to make voting more equitable by a reduction in the influence of the great interests. Those conspicuous by their absence were people who controlled 'pocket boroughs'. These included Cornelius O'Callaghan, Henry Prittie, Thomas Barton, the Moores of Clonmel, Peter Holmes and the Pennefathers of Cashel.

In 1787 there was an agreement with the Bartons about equal representation in the borough of Fethard. The O'Callaghans were to nominate one candidate and Bartons the other. An equal division was agreed on, whereby the nomination of one of the MPs was to lie with O'Callaghan, the other with Barton. To complement this it was proposed to reduce the number of freemen so that the influence of both parties could be exercised more effectively. Thus the 900 freemen of 1783 had by 1790 been reduced to 300, and by the 1830s to a nominal 13 or 14. This pattern of a reduction in the number of freemen, once a dominant interest had become established, accords with that at Cashel and Clonmel.

In 1785, in a placatory gesture to the Ponsonby/Bessborough interest, which was opposed to a trade bill, the government decided to offer

---

[265] W.P. Burke *Clonmel*

a peerage to Cornelius O'Callaghan, the Ponsonby's Tipperary ally and in-law. He was created Baron Lismore of Shanbally. Cornelius died in 1797 at a comparatively young age. His widow moved to Tunbridge Wells where she remained for the rest of her life until her death in 1827. They had at least two sons, Cornelius and Robert William.

Cornelius was succeeded in his titles and estates by his son, also called Cornelius. He was born in 1775 and was only twenty-two at the time of his father's death. He took his seat in the House of Lords and voted against the Act of Union in 1800.

The second son, Robert William who was born in 1777 was a much more interesting character. He was a career Army Officer who attained the rank of General. He joined the Army in 1794 as an ensign and was promoted to Lieutenant to the 30th Light Dragoons in the same year. In the following year he was made a Captain. In 1803 he was promoted as Major of the 40th Regiment of foot and later the same year he was made Lieutenant Colonel of the 39th Foot. He saw action in Europe in 1806 when he commanded a grenadier battalion at the battle of Maida in Italy. He was given a gold medal for his valorous behaviour on the battlefield. In 1811 he went to the Peninsula where he was given the post of Colonel. He was placed in command of a brigade at the battle of Vittoria and was noted by Wellington in his despatches. He continued in command of his brigade during the following three years and was present at many of the important battles then fought against Napoleon. He was promoted to the rank of Major General. He was given a knighthood in 1815. General Sir Robert William saw action all over Europe in the succeeding decades and also fought in India. He died unmarried in London in 1840.

In 1806 Cornelius was created Viscount Lismore of Shanbally and in 1838 he was created Baron Lismore of Shanbally Castle. This was one of the Coronation Peerages of Queen Victoria. Cornelius got married in 1808 to Eleanor the sister of Walter, the 1st Marquess of Ormonde, and daughter of John Butler, Earl of Ormonde and Ossory. Her mother was Susan Wandesforde the daughter of the Earl of Wandesforde (of Castlecomer, Co. Kilkenny). After eighteen years of marriage they got divorced.[266] Baron Lismore was Lord Lieutenant for Tipperary from 1851 until his death.

---

[266] This lady lived until 1859 and died at Sorrento in Italy.

During the famine the Lismores worked extremely hard to alleviate the sufferings of the poor. Lord Lismore reduced their rents and provided a soup kitchen at the gates of his castle. He was described as one of Ireland's benevolent landlords and the town of Clogheen grew and prospered after the Famine.

The Baron and his wife had three sons but only one of them survived his father who died in 1857. He was George Ponsonby O'Callaghan. The eldest son was Hon. Cornelius O'Callaghan and he was very active in 1847 working on Relief Committees with people such as Samuel Barton and William Perry of Woodrooff. He died, unmarried in London in 1849. The other son was William Frederick O'Callaghan, a Captain in the 44th Foot. He died in India in 1836.

George was an Officer in the 17th Lancers and was Sheriff for Tipperary in 1853. He was Lord Lieutenant for the county from 1857 until 1885. He married Mary Norbury in 1839. They had two sons, George Cornelius Gerald and William Frederick. George outlived both his sons and died in 1898. According to a note in the *Complete Peerage* he 'showed a very keen appreciation of the pleasures of the table'. He died in Folkestone in Kent and was buried at Shanrahan.

In the election of 1874 the Hon. W.F. O'Callaghan, who supported Home Rule, topped the poll in Tipperary with his running mate the Hon. C.W. White. They won easily with the support of the clergy. He died in 1877.

The eldest son, George Cornelius Gerald, was married in India to Rosina Follett. They had no children. He predeceased his father and died in 1885.

The Mausoleum of Cornelius O'Callaghan
(courtesy I.A.A.)

Otway of Templederry

John Otway, a lieutenant in Cromwell's army, and formerly of Ingham Hall in Westmoreland, found himself at least in a geographically prominent position around 1655 when he took possession of the old Morris stronghold in Latteragh, up about 700feet on the south-west shoulder of the Devil's Bit range.[267] Across the valley of the little Nenagh River, then known as the River Geagh, the shapely Templederry Hills looping along the skyline presented a most pleasing view. Towards the west the straight-topped bulk of the Silvermine Mountain, with the summit of Keeper Hill showing above it, added to the picturesque scene. Despite its commanding situation Latteragh Castle, a 13th century circular keep on a rocky hillock, had one major drawback for Lieutenant Otway: it was hopelessly dilapidated, due probably to the Cromwellian campaign. By 1654 only the bare walls were left of the main structure, and the only usable part was the barbican or outer tower, which was still intact.[268]

Latteragh Castle, in the barony of Upper Ormond, had been the chief seat of the Morrises, descendants of Geoffrey De Marisco, the Norman knight who acquired it around 1200. Sir John Morris, recorded as the proprietor in 1641, had died in 1647 before the Cromwellian confiscations took place. It was his widow, Dame Katherine, who had been dispossessed by the Cromwellian settlement, and who was the recipient of a transplanters' certificate for land set out to her in Connaught. She had set

---

[267] William Smyth, The mid Seventeenth Century, in Tipperary: History and Society, ed. William Nolan and Thomas G. McGrath, 1985, p. 137
[268] Civil Survey, Co Tipperary, Vol. 11, p. 225

out for Connaught sometime after 1654 with 35 followers, including her son, John, 10 cows, 16 garrans (colts), 19 goats and 2 swine. [269]

John Otway added to his original grant by purchasing debentures for land from Cromwellian soldiers who had got small grants of land in Upper Ormond. In August 1660 he purchased 73 extra acres in Latteragh from John Stafford, yeoman.[270] But he was among the Cromwellian grantees in an unsure position after the restoration of Charles 11 to the throne in 1660. James Butler, the duke of Ormonde, and then Lord Lieutenant, one of the king's most loyal supporters, was at once put into possession of his confiscated estate. Not only did the agile duke increase his share of Tipperary land, but ensured that his relatives and allies would also be restored to their lands. Among his distant relatives was Dame Katherine Morris, who was enabled to return and obtain recovery of Latteragh for her son, another Sir John, who was married to a daughter of Purcell, the baron of Loughmore.

John Otway, however, played his cards well. Knowing that he had to give up his lands in Latteragh, he had, as early as January 1661, secured a certificate from the Court of Claims for a new grant of lands as yet undisposed of in Templederry parish, among the lovely hills he often viewed, and lands which no doubt he well inspected. In 1684, to make doubly sure of his title, he used the good services of the earl of Mountrath, a former Cromwellian leader who still wielded much influence, to obtain the king's patent under the Commission of Grace for his new estate, comprising the old lands of the O'Kennedys of Cloghonan, nestling among the Templederry hills.[271]

John Otway was now at last able to "sit down" on his landed estate in Cloghonan in the heartland of former 'O'Kennedy country'. He had got a huge tract of land in Templederry parish, as well as portions more in the neighbouring baronies of Kilnamanagh and Ileagh, with entitlement to establish 'the Manor of Ottway with power to appoint Seneschals (court officials) and other officers, to keep a prison, to have jurisdiction to the

[269] John P. Prendergast, The Cromwellian Settlement of Ireland, 2nd Edition, 1875, p. 105
[270] Miriam Lambe, A Tipperary Landed Estate, Castle Otway, 1750-1853, 1998, p. 12
[271] Dermot F. Gleeson, The Last Lords of Ormond, Revised edition 2001, Relay Press, p. 115; Miriam Lambe, A Tipperary Landed Estate, Castle Otway 1750-1853, 1998, p. 58, n. 5

extent of £5 in all actions of debt, covenant and trespass, and also a Saturday weekly market in the town of Ottway als (alias) Cloghonan and two fairs on 25th March and 29th September'. [272] His descendant, Cooke Otway, was to interpret these 'petty baron powers' to his own advantage in dealing with suspected United Irishmen among his tenants in 1798.

John Otway also had the advantage that the Cloghonan Castle, a former O'Kennedy stronghold, was in fairly good shape, having been 'partly repaired at the Common Wealth's charge' prior to 1654.[273] He accordingly had a well defended residence at his disposal, which was later to be renamed Castle Otway. It was only about 2kms distant from the old Morres stronghold of Latteragh. He had the shapely Templederry hills all round—Knockadigeen to the north-west, with Knockacraheen behind it, Ballinacurra to the south-west, and across to the west Cooneen Hill. As early as 1650 John had married Phoebe Loftus, a daughter of Nicholas Loftus of Fethard, Co Wexford, who was a son of Sir Dudley Loftus of Rathfarnham Castle, near Dublin.[274] Accordingly he was already linked with the ascendancy, and was soon playing a prominent role among the new elite of Tipperary, by getting elected High Sheriff of the county for 1680.

John's eldest son, also named John, died in 1722 without a male heir, and it was Henry, the eldest son of his third son, Thomas, who inherited Castle Otway. Thomas had established himself at Lissenhall, near Nenagh, only about 3kms south-west of the town. He probably built a small residence there at first, where around the mid-18th century an elegant middle-sized Georgian house, a 'delectable abode', was built where some members of the Otways lived for some generations.[275] Through his wife, Christian, daughter and co-heir of Richard Lock, Tullagory, MP. and his daughters, Thomas established early marriage and political alliances with other newly emerging ascendancy families in north Tipperary, and elsewhere, such as the Bloomfields of Newport, the Tolers of Grange, the

---

[272] Patent 36, Charles 11, 5 Dec 1684

[273] Civil Survey, Co Tipperary, Vol. 11, p. 230

[274] He was a descendant of Adam Loftus, appointed Protestant archbishop of Dublin by Queen Elizabeth

[275] E.H. Sheehan, M.B., Nenagh and its Neighbourhood, p. 57. Lissenhall House is now ruinous.

Peppers of Mota, and the Craven-Cardens of Templemore. The Pritties of Kilboy (Dunalleys), the Lloyds of Lloydsboro, and the Wallers of Castlewaller, Newport, and many others were also taken into that kin network.

Castle Otway (courtesy Irish Architectural Archive)

Henry, who inherited Castle Otway, married Mary, daughter of Phanuel Cooke of Clonamiklon, near Urlingford. His eldest son and successor, Thomas, married Martha Prittie, a sister of Henry Prittie of Kilboy, 1st Lord Dunalley. Cooke Otway, Henry's younger brother, who became a captain in the Life Guards, was called after his mother's maiden name. He married Elizabeth, a daughter of Samuel Waller of Lisbrien. Both Henry and Thomas were educated at Trinity College, and in their time Otway House was built, incorporating the 16th/17th century O'Kennedy tower house, with its slit windows and gun loops.[276] It was a fine two-storey, mid-Georgian house, with a Doric pedimented doorcase, and had all

---

[276] Jean Farrelly and Caimin O'Brien, Archaeological Inventory of County Tipperary, 2002, Vol. 1, p.365

the elegance of Lissenhall   Indeed there was such striking similarity between the two houses that it is thought that the same architect was engaged for both.[277]   The new Otway House demonstrated that the Otways were fully emerging from any siege mentality which may have characterized their earlier generations.   Cooke Otway, who had succeeded to Castle Otway by the time of the disturbed 1790s, when the hill country around was seething with rumours of rebellion, showed himself more than competent to deal with any incipient insurgency.

The new house faced southeast towards the undulating countryside, which dips down to the Nenagh River. The elegant building seemed to grow out of the old tower house, which loomed over it. The landscaped grounds were embellished with trees, paths, shrubs and gardens, and woodlands at a remove from the house and yards were providing a lovely, sylvan setting. These woodlands came to be named Cobb's Wood, Holly Wood, Felix Wood, and The Shrubbery.   A lake was dug out in lower ground at the end of the extensive lawn fronting the house, and a deer park put in place. The avenue had its lodge entrance, and just a kilometer or so from the entrance gate was the landlord-sponsored Established Church, serving as the parish church of Templederry. This was still the medieval parish church, which had been kept in repair, surrounded by its ancient graveyard. Later, in 1828, a new church, with a fine limestone tower, was built as a replacement, and the stones from the medieval building were used in its construction. It contains the burial vault of the Otway family, and the walls are decorated with finely crafted memorials that record Otways' shared loyalty to Empire and the family home in Templederry. [278]   Also to come on the scene was the constabulary barracks at the village crossroads, conveniently sited near the perimeter demesne walls, as in the case of many other landlord demesnes. Castle Otway was among the most picturesque of the landlord residences in Tipperary, an "oasis of gentility, respectability and refinement".[279]

---

[277] Knight of Glin, David J. Cuffe, Nicholas K. Robinson, Vanishing Houses of Ireland, p. 133; Maurice Craig, Classic Irish houses of the middle size, 1976, p. 122
[278] Philip Dwyer, A.B., The Diocese of Killaloe, 1898, p. 515; Templederry, My Home, A Parish Story, 1980, p. 49
[279] Lambe, op. cit., p. 14

In the 1780s the Otways, like other landlords in the region, set up a volunteer corps, with Thomas Otway, nominated a colonel, in command. At that time Ireland's undefended condition due to the American War of Independence led to the formation of the Irish volunteers all over the country, and the barony of Upper Ormond was well to the fore in the call to come to the country's defence. Besides the Castle Otway volunteer corp, which had a scarlet uniform with green facings, there were Colonel Henry Prittie's Ormond Union Cavalry, Nenagh town's Nenagh Volunteers, and Colonel Daniel Toler's Ormond Independents. The great parade of volunteers in College Green in Dublin in 1782 in support of Grattan's parliament had wrestled a greater measure of national independence from the reluctant English Government. The economy had improved considerably towards the end of the 1780s, and the Otways were leasing out more of their estate lands to tenants, about sixty per cent of whom were Catholics who were benefiting from the Relief Act of 1778 enabling them to take leases for 999 years or five lives, provided they took the oath of allegiance. A good proportion were Protestant tenants, noted for being hard-working and industrious farmers, shopkeepers and millers, and for being zealous members of the volunteer corp. Some of the Protestant tenants, such as Baskervilles and Shouldices, may have been Palatines.

Thomas Otway has been portrayed as "a harsh and stern landlord". One entry in the estate ledger for the 1780s noted that a 'spalpeen' (journeyman labourer) ran away even though he had money due to him. Thomas sternness was also shown in the notice he issued to his tenants and workmen, a sizeable number, proclaiming that those who did not come to work on the holy days observed by the Catholic Church would be fined a shilling each for the first offence. The only days the workmen were allowed off work were Sunday and Christmas Day. Thomas added on his notice that anyone who was not satisfied with this regulation 'may provide for himself another place'.[280] Besides the Sundays there were then eighteen holy days in the year with obligation to attend Mass. How hard this regulation impinged on the mostly Catholic working staff of Castle Otway estate is debatable, as the obligation to attend Mass and abstain from servile work on such days was not as fully observed as it became in the post-

---

[280] Lambe, op. cit., p 14

Famine period. Thomas Otway also seemed to have an intolerance towards the native language. In 1772 Silo Magher was fined for speaking Irish in his presence.

Thomas Otway received recognition as an 'improving landlord' from the Dublin Society, which presented him with a silver medal in 1767. The estate improvements mentioned were draining, ditching and planting of his lands.[281] He was also elected as a member of the Society. He died in 1786, and as he was childless, he was succeeded by his brother Cooke Otway.

Around 1775 the yearly income from rents on the well-populated Castle Otway estate was between £2000 and £3000.[282] Despite that the estate was getting into a state of indebtedness towards the end of the 1780s and in the early'90s. The living conditions for much of the rural population was then on a downturn due to the economic conditions prevailing. On top of that, high rents to the landlords or middlemen, tithes to the Established Church and other cesses, low wages and the rapid increase in population--- all these were bringing their own pressures on the ordinary people and giving rise to growing agitation and unrest. The secret societies, such as the Whiteboys, had grown in strength, and by the mid-1790s were given the umbrella name of the Defenders. The Orange Society had recently emerged as well, with the aim of maintaining Protestant ascendancy, and was spreading throughout the land.

Another more significant society to be founded in that decade, the United Irishmen, sought a union of Catholics, Protestants and Dissenters under a truly democratic government of all the people of the country. It was getting strong support from the Presbyterians, or Dissenters, in the North. When the government, nervous of any form of radicalism, especially in the wake of the recent French Revolution, suppressed the United Irish Society, it went underground to become a secret, revolutionary organization bent on establishing a republic with military support from France. The movement became meshed with the Defenders in many parts. Militant loyalism and revolutionary republicanism were heading towards a confrontation.

---

[281] ibid. p. 16
[282] William Nolan, Patterns of Living, in Tipperary: History and Society, p. 297

Nenagh had become one of the most important United Irish centres in Tipperary, its chief secret organizer being Hervey or Harvey Montmorency Morres, of the family which formerly owned Latteragh fortress and lands, who was a close friend of Lord Edward Fitzgerald. Cooke Otway reorganized the Castle Otway volunteers as the Castle Otway Yeomen Cavalry, composed now mainly of his Protestant tenantry. The corp captured a local United Irish organizer named Daniel Darcy, who was transferred to Clonmel gaol to await trial. If convicted of administering the United oath he faced execution.

Organising in the hill country, nonetheless, continued. In May 1797 it was reported to Dublin Castle that "in the Tipperary hills the mountaineers think the northern Protestants are coming to help the Munster Catholics, that the French are going to land, that the land would be equally divided..." [283]. Peter Holmes of Johnstown House, Puckane, who was the proprietor of Nenagh, formerly owned by the dukes of Ormonde, became so alarmed that he urged John Carden of Barnane, the High Sheriff for that year, to call a county meeting of the grand jury, including all the magistrates, among whom was Cooke Otway. Holmes was married to Elizabeth Prittie, a sister of Dunalley of Kilboy, and hence linked by marriage with the Otway family. Like Holmes, Dunalley belonged to the conservative wing of North Tipperary's landed gentry opposed to any further concessions to Catholics, and determined that there should be no change in the status quo for Church or State.

After some local 'big houses' in the Templemore area were robbed of their arms in early 1798, Sir John Carden, who was married to Cooke Otway's first cousin, reported to the Lord Lieutenant that the countryside around should be declared to be in a state of rebellion. Dublin Castle declared martial law on the whole county in April. The High Sheriff, the notorious Thomas Judkin Fitzgerald, later dubbed "The Flogger Fitzgerald", now came onto central stage in the county with his own repressive campaign, savagely aimed at all suspects. As rumours of rebellion grew, panic set among many of the gentry in the county who quitted their residences and went into the towns. The High Sheriff then ordered every gentleman, under "such penalties as he should be empowered

---

[283] William J. Hayes, Tipperary in the Year of Rebellion 1798, 1998, p. 16

to inflict and the circumstances of the time justify", to return and remain at his country seat, to help restore law and order. [284]

Cooke Otway was not the sort of "timid" landlord the High Sheriff railed against. He proved himself a ruthless rebel-hunter. He got to hear of a local man, Kennedy by name, who was a sworn member of the United Irishmen, and had him rounded up and threatened that unless he confessed all he knew of the organization he would be flogged. When the man repeatedly affirmed his innocence, Otway, availing of his inherited "petty baronial powers", ordered him to be tied up, probably to the dreaded triangle, and given twenty five lashes in the presence of Sir James Duff, the county commander. When that failed to elicit any information, Otway had him tied up again next day and was about to order the same treatment on the man's lacerated back, when he gave in and confessed his own involvement, and also revealed that the parish was well organized and well armed with pikes. [285] That was the earliest recorded instance of the use of torture in the county to elicit information, which offers of bribery had up to then failed to do.

Word went quickly around about all that the tortured man had revealed. The people involved in the United organisation were now in fear of their lives that they had been named, and decided on the more attractive option of surrendering their arms and voluntarily confessing. According to reports within a few hours seventeen hundred pikes were handed in. The parish priest, Fr John Kennedy, who was living in Killeen beside the Catholic chapel, also came forward and acknowledged that he had been sworn in by Fr William O'Meara, parish priest of Nenagh. Fr Kennedy was first interrogated by Cooke Otway, then tried, and sentenced to transportation and eventually pardoned.[286] Presumably all his parishioners who confessed were let off after taking oaths of allegiance.

But Fr William O'Meara did not escape so lightly. He and Fr James Talbot, parish priest of Portroe, were arrested, together with Rev Henry

---

[284] Freeman's Journal, 8 May 1798

[285] Sir Richard Musgrave, Memoirs of the different rebellions in Ireland, 1801, Appendix, No XI, 49

[286] Richard Hayes, Priests in the Independence Movement of '98, in Irish Ecclesiastical Record, Vol. LXVI (Oct. 1945), pp. 265-6. Fr John Kennedy became known as 'Daddy Jack'. He died as PP of Shinrone in 1825

Fulton, vicar of the Church of Ireland parish of Nenagh. They were tried by justices of the peace in Nenagh, with Cooke Otway no doubt on the bench, on the charge of administering the United oath, and as the Ennis Chronicle of 28 May 1798 reported, "in consequence (they) are to be sent to serve His Majesty abroad, agreeable to the Insurrection Act". The three were sent first to Duncannon Fort, near Waterford harbour, and then transported to Cobh where they were confined in a prison hulk awaiting transportation to Botany Bay. Of the three only Henry Fulton, one of the few Church of Ireland clergyman to become involved in the United Irish movement, survived to see Australia's penitential shores. The two Catholic priests, who were older, died on the prison hulk in Cobh.

In 1799, the year after the fated year of rebellion, when all abortive insurrectionary plans in Tipperary were repressed, two Templederry men were charged with treasonable practices in assembling at Ormond Stile, just above Templederry village, and conspiring to murder Cooke Otway, captain of the Castle Otway yeomanry. They were James Flannery and Matthew Gleeson. Flannery was sentenced to transportation for life, and Gleeson, who was not found guilty of the conspiracy, was sentenced to seven years penal servitude.[287] It has been said that Cooke Otway was the most effective ally the 'Flogger' Fitzgerald had in suppressing insurgency in Tipperary in 1798.

Cooke's sixth son, Loftus William, rose to the rank of Lieutenant General in the British army. He was the colonel of the 84th Regiment, and became Knight Commander of Charles 111 of Spain.[288] Cooke Otway died in December 1800, the year the Act of Union was passed. He was succeeded by his second surviving son, Henry 1768-1815, who married Sarah, daughter of Sir Thomas Cave of Stanford Hall, Leicester. She became heir to her family property, and she and Henry resided at Stanford Hall, and in Grosvenor Square, London. This marked the beginning of the absentee landlord phase of the Templederry Otways. The Otway estate then consisted of 6,667 statute acres.

---

[287] Sheehan, op. cit., p. 57
[288] Burke's Peerage and Baronetcy. Loftus William, son Loftus Charles, C.B., became His Majesty's Minister Plenipotentiary in Mexico, and Consul General in Milan

Henry's younger brother, Admiral   Robert Waller Otway, 1770-1851, became a distinguished naval officer, and on the occasion of the coronation of William IV in 1831 was created a baronet for his services. In the immediate aftermath of Catholic Emancipation Admiral Otway displayed an ecumenical gesture by presenting in 1832 'an Illuminated drawing of the Crucifixion of Our Blessed Redeemer' to Killeen chapel, then still serving as the Catholic parish church for Templederry. The picture contained a view of 'the ancient city of Jerusalem' in the background. [289] Such large pictures, hung on the wall behind and above the altar, were a feature in Catholic chapels of the 19th and early 20th centuries.

Stanford Hall

The baronetcy descended through this Robert Waller branch of the family, first to his eldest son, Admiral Sir George Graham Otway (1816-1881), and then to George Graham's brother, Arthur John Otway, 1816-1891, 3rd Bart. who lived in Brighton.

---

[289] Ignatius Murphy, The Diocese of Killaloe, 1800-1850, 1992, p. 298. Around the 1820s and '30s Rev Caesar Otway, who resided in Dublin, was publishing a number of books, including Sketches in Ireland, 1827, and A Tour of Connaught, 1839. He was a journalist and short story writer, who edited The Christian Examiner, a prominent proselytizing journal. He also co-authored the Dublin Penny Journal, and patronized William Carlton. I have not been able to establish where he fitted into the Otway family tree.

To return to Henry, who assumed the additional name of Cave, and lived at Stanford Hall, it was through him that the Castle Otway branch of the family continued. He was succeeded by his second son, Robert Otway Cave, who became heir to Castle Otway, Robert was a man of much more liberal bent of mind than his grandfather Cooke, or his granduncle Thomas. He embarked on a political career as a young man, serving as MP for Leicester in 1826-30, and supporting Catholic Emancipation.

In 1835 he ran as a liberal candidate in the Tipperary election of 1835. As it happened there was there was no poll in that election and he was joined as one of the two Tipperary MPs by the well-known Richard Lalor Sheil. Despite his ascendancy background, one of Otway's policies was opposition to the tithe system, the major and most controversial issue of the time. He was also on the side of O'Connell's repeal of the Union campaign. He resided when convenient at Lissenhall and held his Tipperary seat until 1844. He died the following year, which saw the beginning of the Great Famine. His wife Sophia was a daughter of Sir Francis Burdett, of Foremark. They had no family.

Sophia Otway, although an absentee landlord, continued to take a keen interest in her Castle Otway estate and its people. She headed the Borrisoleigh Poor Relief Fund with her £30 donation in 1846, and financially helped some families to emigrate to America.

Most of the labourers' and small tenants' families were then living in single-roomed or two-roomed cabins. It is notable that she had a cordial relationship with the volatile and revolutionary-minded parish priest of Templederry, Fr John Kenyon, a close friend of John Mitchell, and an assertive supporter of the Young Ireland Movement. He and 'his zealous French friends' were entertained at Castle Otway by Sophia on one occasion, and she was all in favour of a 'proper habitation' for him in Templederry among his parishioners. [290] Fr Kenyon wrote a characteristic note in his Baptismal Register for 27th July 1848: "This evening I heard of a rebellion in South Tipperary under the leadership of William Smith O'Brien—may God speed it".

When Sophia died in 1849, Castle Otway was inherited by Vice Admiral Robert Jocelyn Otway, JP, second son of her husband's brother,

---

[290] Lambe, op. cit., p. 19

Rev Samuel Jocelyn Otway. In 1836 Robert Jocelyn married Anne Digby, daughter of Sir Hugh Crofton, of Mohill House, Co. Leitrim, and his only offspring, Frances Margaret, married William Clifford Bermingham Ruthven of Queensboro, Co Galway. Through that marriage the surname became Otway-Ruthven. The eldest son and heir of William and Frances, Captain Robert Mervyn Birmingham, married Margaret, daughter of Julius Casement, of Cronroe, Co Wicklow, in 1900. They had seven children, all of whom were given Bermingham as the last of their Christian names apart from their eldest son, Robert Jocelyn Oliver, born in 1901. [291] He was last Otway owner of Castle Otway. At least as far as the 19th century is concerned, the Otways were looked upon as good landlords.

Castle Otway was burnt down in the time of the Civil War, 1922. The remnant of the estate was divided following the 1926 Land Act. The roofless house and its old attached fortress, that 'oasis of gentility and refinement', now stands gaunt and empty in its picturesque setting. Some solitary trees stand there as reminders of the well-tended and lavishly landscaped demesne. The other former Otway residence, the 'delectable' Lissenhall, another of Tipperary's architecturally important houses, is also a sad ruin.

---

[291] Burke's The Landed Gentry, Ireland, 1904, p. 526. One member of the Otway-Ruthvens, Dr A. J. Otway-Ruthven, became a noted historian and lecturer. She was educated at Trinity and Cambridge, and was appointed lecturer in history in Trinity College in 1938. In 1957 she became Lecky Professor of History in Trinity. Her major work, A History of Medieval Ireland, was published in 1968. She published a translation of Liber Primus Kilkenniensis, and was a regular contributor to Irish Historical Studies, and the Journal of the Royal Society of Antiquaries.

Ponsonby/Barker of Kilcooley

When Captain Chambré Ponsonby brought his wife back to Kilcooley in 1873 the happy couple were greeted with illuminations and a triumphal arch in the neighbouring town and a bonfire at the entrance to the demesne. Cheering tenants pulled their carriage and there was music and dancing all night.

Whiskey and beer were provided for all comers by the bridegroom's uncle, Sir William Ponsonby-Barker, the then owner of Kilcooley. Though a stern Evangelical he did not object to the country people enjoying themselves.

This was the same William Ponsonby-Barker who, on occasion, took a maidservant to bed with him as a human hot water bottle. He justified himself on the spiritual precedent of the Biblical King David. It seems that after family prayers he would line up the maids to make his choice.[292] Bence Jones goes on to say that on one occasion the maid of his choice *'offended his olfactory sensibilities, so he sprinkled her liberally from a bottle which he took in the dark to contain eau de cologne but which in fact contained ink!'*

Kilcooley in the foothills of the Slieveardagh Hills, on the Tipperary-Kilkenny border, was first granted to the Cistercians in 1182 A.D. by Donough Mor O'Brien who gave them what land he could encircle in a day's ride. There they built an Abbey and the monks lived and worked there until the Reformation in the time of Henry VIII. After that it came into the possession of the Earls of Ormonde.

---

[292] Bence-Jones – *The Twilight of the Ascendancy*

The Abbey and lands of Kilcooley were purchased in 1636 by an Englishman, Sir Jerome Alexander for £4,200, from the then Duke of Ormonde. Known as the Hanging Judge, Jerome was much feared in post Cromwellian Ireland. At the time a phrase was coined *"to be alexandered"*. It meant to be executed without mercy. Jerome is best remembered for the fact that he gave a very substantial bequest of £600, and his own large collection of books to Trinity College with a brief that a library be founded there.

He also left a few strange bequests in his will – *'my pocket tweezers which I bought in Brussels'* to Dr. Jones, Bishop of Kildare, gold spectacles to the Bishop's wife, and to his daughter Elizabeth *'my great dyamonde ringe, gold and silver watches and my case of silver instruments which I bought at Brussels and I verily believe cost me three score pounds'*. The provost of Trinity College was left his *'gold headed stick with tweezers on top'*.[293]

He left the great bulk of his property to Elizabeth, including Kilcooley and his other lands, but she was to forfeit all if she *'at any time after my decease marry and take as husband any Lord of Ireland by what name or title soever he bears or the son of any such Lord, nobleman or Nobleman Baronet, Knight, Esquire, gentleman, Archbishop, Prelate or any Irishman that comes of an Irish extraction and descent or that hath been born or bred in the Kingdom of Ireland'*. She was likewise forbidden to marry any papist.[294]

Jerome was born in Norfolk and after his schooling became a barrister in 1617. Within a short period he was imprisoned for 'sharp practices' and debarred. Upon his release he decided to try his fortunes in Ireland. He set up a legal practice in Dublin in 1627 and soon found employment with important noblemen. He was very ambitious and tried unsuccessfully to become Clerk of the Crown. His debarring in England was a serious obstacle and he decided to go there to have the orders of debarment lifted. Instead of that happening he made the King (Charles) furious by his persistence and was again imprisoned. However his powerful friends soon arranged his release and he was pardoned.

---

[293] One of the watches is in the National Museum
[294] Neely – *Kilcooley: Land and People in Tipperary*

183

Upon his return to Ireland in 1634 he was elected as a member for the Borough of Lifford in Donegal where he was expected to forward the Ulster Plantation. It was at this period that he met the Duke of Ormonde and persuaded him to sell Kilcooley. Jerome never saw Kilcooley until the 1660s and he never lived there.

Jerome Alexander

He was an enemy of Strafford, the Lord Deputy, and a ruthless judge who had received a spell of imprisonment from the Lord Deputy. In 1641 he fled from Ireland with his wife and children – *'escaping in their night clothes'*. After the rebellion of 1641 he made claims against the

Government for losses as Kilcooley had been restored to the Cistercians. He did not recover Kilcooley until after the Restoration. It would appear that Jerome Alexander had risked his life for the King (Charles II) by taking part in the secret negotiations that brought about his restoration.[295]

Jerome died in 1670 and was predeceased by his wife who died in 1667. Both are buried in St. Patrick's Cathedral in Dublin.

Elizabeth Alexander married Sir William Barker of Essex in 1676 and thus began the unbroken succession of Barkers and Ponsonbys who have held onto Kilcooley until the present day.

Neither Sir William nor Elizabeth ever lived in Kilcooley and regarded the estate just as a source of revenue managed by various agents. In the 1670s the estate netted about £250 per annum.

When Elizabeth died in 1702 Sir William married a girl of twenty, Letitia Motham, but they do not appear to have had any children.

The second Sir William did not spend much time in Ireland either but his son the third Sir William was educated and brought up in Ireland. The second Sir William inherited the estates in Ireland in 1719 upon the death of his father.

Sir William III was educated at Kilkenny College and in 1720 was sent to Trinity College in Dublin. While his father lived mainly in England Sir William III was sent to Kilcooley to manage affairs there. He had to live in the old Abbey, which would have been considered a miserable residence by any gentleman of the time.[296]

Not only did his spendthrift father keep William III short of money but he also sent his two brothers to Kilcooley to live with him. They did not get on very well and when William complained to his father he wrote saying to tell his brother *'he would come to Ireland, make him his boot black and teach him with a whip to have manners'*.

In 1733 Sir William III married Mary Quin from Adare, Co. Limerick[297] and in 1737 a son was born, also christened William. He was to be the last Barker baronet. His father died in 1746 and Sir William III became heir to all the Irish estates, which were valued at the time at £5000.

---

[295] Carte Papers Vol. 34.
[296] Neely
[297] Her portrait was sold in the Dunraven sale of Adare in 1982.

He had a town house in Rutland Square in Dublin and spent his winters there. His careful way of life laid the foundation of the considerable prosperity of his son.

The fine Palladian residence, in which the subsequent Barker descendants lived, was built around 1762 by the last Sir William though his father was alive at the time. Sir William IV had a sister, Mary, who married Chambré Brabazon Ponsonby. Chambré's father was the Hon. Henry Ponsonby, the younger son of the Earl of Bessborough.

Kilcooley (courtesy I.A.A.)

In the later 18th century Sir William Barker IV incurred the displeasure of his tenants and of the country people in general when he began enclosing his lands. An article in the Irish Historical Journal cited Sir William as an example of the type of landlord who helped produce the Whiteboy movement of agrarian crime by enclosing land that had formerly been commonage. Despite this W.G. Neely, in his in-depth study of the owners of Kilcooley, insists that there is no evidence of Whiteboyism in the Kilcooley area in those years. However this may not have been the case.[298]

The Whiteboys were so called because they chose to wear a white smock (something akin to that of the Ku Klux Klan). They began their activities in Co. Tipperary at Clogheen. It was a protest movement against the imposing of tithes on potatoes and corn. The tithe on potatoes was what hit the poorest hardest. The outrages, such as houghing of cattle, etc., began about 1761 and were aimed at the tithe proctors and those who took over the lands of tenants evicted for non-payment of the tithes. Fethard, Thurles and Cashel were areas of major unrest (as well as Co. Kilkenny), but Kilcooley was somewhat removed being in the hilly country of Slieveardagh.

In 1772 Sir William granted leases to Palatine families that he brought to Kilcooley from Adare, on condition that they never employed anyone professing the popish religion.[299]

Sir William who married Catherine Lane, an heiress, had no family so when Chambré Ponsonby died in 1762, Sir William invited Mary Ponsonby, his sister, to stay in Kilcooley with her children Chambré and Mary.

During the last decades of the eighteenth century life at Kilcooley seemed to be idyllic if one is to judge from the letters of the family members. While Sir William might have been something of a bigot[300] the same cannot be said of young Mary Ponsonby Barker's half sister, Sarah Ponsonby. Sarah wrote with advice to her friend Susan Tighe of

---

[298] In January1786, a tithe proctor living on the estate of Sir William was forcibly brought to Urlingford and there cropped and buried.- T. Power in *Land, Politics and Society in 18th century Tipperary*.

[299] One of the families was named Switzer – Christie Switzer from Kilcooley established the famous Switzers of Grafton St., Dublin and James Switzer, his brother, built the Kilkenny Alms house, which he called St. James. The Alms House was to accommodate twenty widows or unmarried women of good family, eight Roman Catholic and twelve Protestant. He provided an annuity of £20 for each woman and the porter and the chaplain. Another famous Palatine was Richard Sutcliffe who became one of the world's foremost mining engineers.

[300] Sir William was elected as High Sheriff in 1764 and was considered to be part of the extreme right wing of Protestantism.- T. Power in *Land, Politics and Society in 18th century Tipperary*

Woodstock in Co. Kilkenny. Susan was contemplating the gift of a cow and a bible to her married Protestant tenants and Sarah recommended that she 'extend a little comfort to Roman Catholics also, such as a little Pig or Cock or Hen or possibly a few trees to plant around their cottages – as they will feel being totally excluded from it.'

This was the Sarah Ponsonby who ran away with Eleanor Butler, a daughter of the Ormond heir. Sarah was the object of unwanted affection from her godmother's husband, Sir William Fownes. Eleanor Butler, a Protestant, was persecuted by her Catholic stepmother. Sir William, when told of the sad situation of the two young ladies gave Sarah £580 which set them up for many years. The two ladies intended going to France but en route they arrived in Llangollen, in Wales, and fell in love with it. They lived there for the rest of their lives. When Mr. Butler became the Earl of Ormond Sir William Barker persuaded him to help his daughter, now Lady Eleanor Butler. This he did and in time they became famous as 'The Old Ladies of Llangollen'. Celebrities such as Sir Walter Scott, the Duke of Leinster and the Duke of Wellington 'could not visit Wales without calling on them'.[301]

Despite being avowedly non-political Sir William took the lead in forming two companies of Volunteers – the Kilcooley True Blues and the Slieveardagh Light Dragoons. According to some commentators the Volunteers in Tipperary were formed in direct response to the growing threat of agrarian violence and not to support Grattan, as it was perceived. Sir William was a delegate to the National Convention held in Dublin in 1783.

It was during this period of his life that Sir William undertook improvements to the estate such as the construction of a lake in 1789 with a Gothic Boat House.

Chambré Ponsonby the heir apparent and nephew of Sir William married Lady Harriet Taylor, the daughter of Lord Bective. Chambré had been a Lieutenant in the Army but resigned his commission after his marriage. He went to live in Belmont Lodge, near Durrow. He had a small estate of his own at Galmoy, but seems to have been somewhat

---

[301] Bence-Jones The *Twilight of the Ascendancy*

impecunious until he inherited Kilcooley in 1818. He and Harriet had three sons and one daughter, Catherine.[302]

Chambré seems to have been a spendthrift and in 1791 the Earl of Bective and Sir William discharged a debt of £4000 owed by Chambré. Later in 1814 he owed over £3000 to the Bishop of Waterford and this too had to be discharged.

In 1798 Chambré became Captain of the local Yeomanry, who were on full time duty patrolling the Urlingford-Mullinahone-Killenaule district. According to Neely there was no incident at all in the area at the time other than the attacks on the game in the district by the restless bored young men themselves.

When the 1798 rebellion broke out Sir William fled with his family to England, where they had a large property at Bath. Neely states that he went to England for his health.

By 1799 the danger had passed but the Slieveardagh Yeomen were reluctant to be stood down. They sent a petition to Chambré stating that for the security of the country, troubled as it was by numerous bandits, they should be kept in arms.

Rumours of rebel bands marauding near the towns of Naas and Kildare deterred Sir William from returning to Ireland. Whenever he did it was only to see that the estate was being maintained in good order.

Sir William died in 1818 and Chambré Ponsonby inherited the estate. In accordance with the wishes of his uncle he changed his name to Ponsonby-Barker.

In 1821 as High Sheriff of the county he presided over a meeting of Magistrates in Cashel who petitioned the Lord Lieutenant to have the Insurrection Act enforced, to put the district under military law and return the Yeomen to full time duty. This they claimed had restored order in the serious troubles of 1815.[303]

In 1828 at the first meeting of the Slieveardagh Brunswickers, held in the courthouse of Ballynonty, the magistrate, Ponsonby Barker, and Charles Langley leading a group of Palatines of Kilcooley, were met by a large hostile Catholic crowd. The Brunswickers were founded by the gentry

---

[302] Catherine married Thomas Connolly of Castletown
[303] Neely

who opposed Daniel O'Connell's move for Catholic Emancipation. Only the intervention of Fr. Michael Meighen of Gortnahoe prevented an attack on the Brunswickers.[304]

Chambré Ponsonby-Barker died in 1834 and was succeeded by his son William, who dropped the Ponsonby and was known simply as Mr. William Barker. He inherited estates of over 8000 acres in a very troubled time with grave unrest in every area due mainly to the 'Tithe War'.

Mr. William Barker was considered to be somewhat rigid in his views and ways, bordering on the eccentric. He was separated from his wife shortly after his marriage and there were no children. He was implacably opposed to Daniel O'Connell and to Emancipation and Repeal. He preserved a letter from his friend Mrs. Hely Hutchinson describing a visit to Derrynane, in which she said of O'Connell – *"He is like the very Devil himself, arrogant, self opinionated and will brook no contradictions."*[305]

One of his first acts upon taking over the estate was to establish an Orange Lodge there. The Orange Lodge was, in essence, a Protestant defence association in the face of constant rumours of rebellion and Protestant massacres, following the bitterness of the Tithe War. It had 112 members drawn mainly from the Palatine tenants of the Kilcooley estate and from the tenants of Balief and Woodsgift owned by the St. George family.

The Lodge came to an abrupt end when William Barker and the St. Georges were warned from Dublin about the illegality of the Order. William subsequently joined the Free Masons, became a Knight Templar and a Knight of St. John of Malta.

William was reputed to be a good landlord and he was also one of the main shareholders in the local Coalmining Company. He tried to expand the coalmines during the 1840s and it is to his credit that during the worst of the famine years none of the coalminers was made redundant, despite the fact that the demand for coal almost dwindled away to nothing.

The mansion at Kilcooley was seriously damaged by fire in 1839 in most unusual circumstances. It would appear that a woman carrying a child

---

[304] McGrath in *Tipperary History & Society*
[305] *The Irish County House* – Peter Somerville Large

had presented herself at the front door demanding to see the butler, Mr. Ashby. William Barker, himself had come to the door to inform her that it was no place for her to knock, as the servant's entrance was elsewhere. When he heard her story he was so incensed that he sacked the butler on the spot. Ashby packed his bags determining to go abroad but he also packed the chimney with all the paper he could find and before leaving lit the fire. As a result the chimney went on fire and all but one of the wings of the house was burnt.

The house was rebuilt but was not finished until 1843 and the expense made serious inroads into the family finances, which became depleted thereafter.

When the scourge of the famine hit the area William Barker did much to help the poor by undertaking the building a demesne wall of about five miles. He was compelled to sell the family jewels to pay for it.

Just prior to the famine, in 1841, William had aspirations to become an M.P. Thomas Maude of Dundrum and William were the Tory candidates. The liberals, Robert Otway Cave and Valentine Maher, who won convincingly, opposed them.

Interference with voters was almost a commonplace occurrence. Such interference occurred in 1841. Sir William's Protestant tenants marched in a body with the intention of going to Clonmel to vote but were confronted at Clonamiclon by a hastily thrown up stonewall which they easily surmounted. At New Birmingham it was different. There the way was blocked by carts filled with culm – coal dust – and a 300 strong crowd. In the fracas which followed the tenants were forced to find sanctuary inside the walls of the estate.

Again in 1857 he offered himself for election and according to Neely he stood for *"Justice for Ireland, civil and religious liberties and the Maynooth grant. He did not see the need for any radical change but rather fair play and justice for all within the existing order."* He was again defeated.

When he died in 1877 he was succeeded by his huntin', shootin', fishin' brother Thomas, a sprightly septuagenarian who rejoiced in the nickname of "Damnation Tom" as every sentence he uttered was prefaced with the word "Damn". It fell to the lot of "Damnation Tom" to sell off a considerable portion of the Barker lands in such far-flung places as

Ashgrove in Co. Waterford and Callan in Co. Kilkenny, to reduce the burden of debt. However he managed to hold on to the very valuable Clarina estate in Limerick, which at the time brought in more rent than the Kilcooley estate.

"Damnation" Tom's son was Chambré Ponsonby. He was the man mentioned at the start of this article. Such was the state of Ireland at the time that Chambre despaired of the future. His brother-in-law, Horace Plunkett,[306] who was in ill health, had gone to Wyoming where he worked on ranches and later bought himself a ranch on the Powder River. He declared that the future was in America. Chambré went out to visit Horace and decided to sell out his estates and move to America. On his way home, in 1884, he took ill and died suddenly on the voyage. As his eldest son and heir Thomas was only six years old at the time his mother had to take the responsibility for running the estate. She was helped by her brother Horace, who from the distant Rocky Mountains and the occasional visit to Kilcooley fought a kind of rearguard action in the land wars of the last decades of the nineteenth century.

Mary Ponsonby had further troubles when her brother, Lord Dunsany, died and she undertook the task of rearing his two sons, the eldest of whom was the Lord Dunsany of literary fame. As soon as the children were old enough to be sent to boarding school Mrs. Ponsonby retired to England and remained there until her death in 1921.

In the 1920s Tom Ponsonby, a grandson of "Damnation Tom" was the owner of the estate, which he had inherited in 1884. He had been educated at Eton and Oxford and had entered the army with a commission in the 10th. Hussars. He fought in the Boer War in South Africa and then spent three years in America managing his uncle Horace Plunkett's ranch.

When living at Kilcooley and expecting guests from England he would arrange for them to be given a hamper by the stationmaster in Dublin to sustain them on their journey south to Kilcooley. The station master used insist on the Kilcooley guests going first class even if they had only bought third class tickets, and he would select a compartment for them with care.

---

[306] The 2nd son of the 16th Baron of Dunsany.

192

'No, not that one Ma'am, poor Lord Ashtown, too much of the drink, you know.'[307]

His wife, Mary Paynter, whom he married in 1909, spent considerable money in renovating and refurbishing the house. They had four children, Chambré, George, Henry, and Noreen.

During the 1916 rebellion, Tom was in Dublin with Sir Horace Plunkett when he was shot and seriously wounded by 'friendly' fire. It would seem that the car they were travelling in was mistaken for a car carrying rebels and was shot at by British soldiers. Tom eventually recovered.[308]

Kilcooley was raided during the Civil War, when a gang of men broke into the house. Tom managed to pull the fuse and left the house in darkness. Then he put on rubber-soled shoes and began walking about the house opening doors. The raiders who had only one flash lamp were non-plussed by this strategy and left after some time. The only other person in the house was young George, who was asleep in his nursery. On another occasion, the butler, who heard the raiders coming, got out on the roof and began blowing *The Last Post* on a trumpet. Again the raiders left in a hurry.

Tom Ponsonby was an astute manager and farmed what was left of his estate in a most profitable way until the advent of the Economic War with Britain, which ruined Irish farming. Tom was wealthy enough to survive but he was obliged to lease most of his lands to the Forestry Department.

He was a much-travelled man who expanded not only his own horizons with his innovative interest in farming methods and forestry, but by his writings he educated others also.[309] In 1919 he was appointed as one of the five commissioners with the newly established Forestry Commission with responsibility for the entire British Isles.

He was married to Frances Paynter the daughter of a wealthy member of the English gentry. They had three sons. The two eldest sons found careers in the Services and Chambré was a Military Attaché in

---

[307] Neely – Kilcooley: Land & People of Tipperary
[308] Bence-Jones in *Twilight of the Ascendancy*
[309] He wrote an important Pamphlet entitled *Agricultural Labour* for the Co-Operative Reference Society in 1917 and he wrote a scientific treatise for the Scottish Forestry in 1931.

Norway while George, a Major, served with the 1st. Army in North Africa and Italy during the Second World War. George was wounded four times but was fortunate in that he was able to recover and return to Kilcooley. The third son, Henry Jeffrey inherited the house and lands of Grove from his Barton cousin, Charles Robert in 1955. Henry Jeffrey married Rosemary Wells of Sussex and they have one son, Julian, and two daughters, Jane and Rosanna.

Lt. Col. Chambré, the eldest son, felt unable to accept the responsibility of Kilcooley and when Thomas Ponsonby died in 1943 the estate was left in the capable hands of George his second son.

Chambre was married twice and had two sons and one daughter, Merelina Karen. His sons are Richard Chambre and Miles Brabazon.

George married Elizabeth Melville of Somerset and they have three sons, Thomas Charles, Henry Brabazon and Peter Douglas. All three were educated in Eton and Thomas went on to study music in London.

Peter Douglas is the last of the Ponsonbys to occupy Kilcooley House.

Prittie of Kilboy

Kilboy House, the home of the Prittie family, who later became Lords Dunalley, was designed by William Leeson around 1780. Described in *The Vanishing Houses of Ireland*[310] as the most important house that Leeson designed, the author went on to say 'Kilboy had a superb entrance front with engaged Doric portico. It had a very fine interior with good plasterwork and imperial main staircase. The house was burnt in 1922 and well restored but without the attic storey. In the mid 1950s it was demolished and a single storey house was built on top of the basement storey; reached by the original steps.'

Kilboy has now come into the possession of Mr. Shane Ryan, son of Mr. Tony Ryan of G.P.A. fame who has developed the demesne, capturing much of the former glory of the old Kilboy.

The Prittie dynasty in Kilboy began with Colonel Henry Prittie, one of Cromwell's more trusted commanders. He was a Captain in Cromwell's New Regiment of Horse. During the war in Ireland he was made Sheriff of Carlow (1650) and later Governor of Carlow. After the successful campaign Prittie was given about 1000 acres in the area in lieu of pay. Like many of his brother officers he immediately began buying up the lands that had been awarded to his fellow soldiers who had no wish to remain in Ireland. This, combined with his descendants fortuitous marriages to heiresses, meant that the estate grew over the next two hundred years, so that by the middle of the 19th century the Pritties owned about 16,000 acres

---

[310] Knight of Glin, David Griffin and Nicholas Robinson.

of land in county Tipperary most of which was centred around Kilboy[311]. Henry was married to Honor Foley of Stourbridge and he had one son, also called Henry. The Captain died in 1671. He was succeeded by his son Henry.

Henry was besieged for twenty-one days in his castle of Dunalley by the Jacobites after the Battle of the Boyne. They eventually gained entrance and seized Henry and threw him from the battlements. Henry, quite extraordinarily, survived the fall unhurt and managed to escape. Henry was married to an Alcock and they had two sons and five daughters. The second son, Richard, married an heiress, Barbara Bourchier from Wexford in 1714. One of the daughters was married to Captain John Bayly of Ballynaclogh, another Cromwellian grantee.

Kilboy (courtesy I.A.A.)

---

[311] The Pritties also owned Corville, near Roscrea, during the 18th and 19th centuries.

It was through marriages to heiresses that estates were extended. The outstanding example of this at the outset of the century is the marriage in 1702 of Henry Prittie (the Colonel's grandson) to Elizabeth daughter and heiress to James Harrison of Cloghjordan. This alliance added to the sizeable Prittie estate of 3,600 acres a further 900 acres centering on Cloghjordan which had the advantage of being in the same region as the home estate. The joining of the estates brought the Prittie family important political benefits, since by the extension of its landed interest it gained in freeholder strength in an area where rural Protestants were more numerous than elsewhere in the county. In this way the displacement of one landed family consolidated the interest of another and enhanced its political prospects, which for the Pritties were largely built on a family interest.

In the next two generations each of the heirs to the Prittie estate married heiresses: Deborah Bayly in 1736 and Catherine Sadleir in 1766, thereby further consolidating the family's interests, landed and political.

While the Prittie men were lucky in their matrimonial choices, by a strange quirk of fate the number of male children in each generation was generally one and seldom exceeded two, while the number of females was very great. This meant, of course that husbands (and dowries) had to be found but equally it meant that extensive and expensive lands did not have to be found on which to house younger sons.

Though numerically small in number the Prittie heirs proved to be able men who left their mark on the evolving political, social and economic entity that became modern Tipperary.

Colonel Henry's grandson, Henry, who was born in 1682, became a High Sheriff for the county in 1706. As already alluded to, he was married to an heiress, Elizabeth, the daughter of Colonel James Harrison of Cloughjordan. On the death of Colonel Harrison the estates of Cloughjordan came into the possession of the Pritties of Kilboy. Henry and Elizabeth had one son, Henry, and three daughters who married Croker of Limerick, Meade (later Lords Clanwilliam) and Clutterbuck[312] of Derryluskan.

---

[312] Richard Clutterbuck, an Adventurer, received over 3000 acres in Middlethird Barony in 1654

The son, Henry (born 1708) was active politically and was an M.P. for Tipperary from 1761- 8. A magistrate, he was firmly in the forefront of promoting law and order[313]. He was married to an heiress, the daughter of Venerable Benjamin Neale of Leighlin and widow of John Bayly of Debsborough.[314] This Henry was the man who successfully launched the family into mainstream politics.

In the 1761 contest there were three candidates, Maude, Mathew, and Henry Prittie of Kilboy. When polling closed on 8 May 1761 the poll stood thus: Prittie 924 votes, Mathew 532, and Maude 486, with Prittie being elected.

He also made attempts to use the natural resources on his lands. In the 1720s and 30s the Pritties revived interest in mining in the Silvermines. Lead was the mineral being mined at this time. After 1730 the mining was left in abeyance until 1802 when the Dunalley Mining Company was formed with the intention of exploiting the ore there and also at a number of other locations.

Henry Prittie who died in 1768 had one son and six daughters who married various local landowners such as Peter Holmes, Matthew Bunbury of Kilfeacle, Thomas Otway and Michael Head. His son, Henry, became the 1st Lord Dunalley.

In order to avoid confusion this Henry who did not become a Lord until 1800, will generally be referred to as 1st Lord Dunalley. He was married to Catherine Sadleir in 1766. Their eldest son Henry Sadleir married in 1802, Maria Trent, a niece of John Fitzgibbon, first Earl of Clare,[315] and in 1826 he married Emily Maude, daughter of their nearest neighbour and fellow Cromwellian, Cornwallis Maude (Viscount Hawarden).

Francis was the second son of Henry Prittie and Catherine Sadleir and he married Martha Otway of the Templederry family. Their daughters married as follows – Catherine to Henry Cole Bowen of Bowenscourt,

---

[313] At Clonmel assizes of June 1762 a reward of £20 was offered by 27 leading landowners including Maude and Henry Prittie (Dunalley) for the discovery and prosecution of "each of the first three Papists guilty of carrying arms in said county".
[314] She had three children at least by John Bayly. She was somewhat older than Henry and she was about 36 years old when they married.
[315] Henry got a dowry of £5,000 from the Earl.

Cork; Deborah to Samuel Perry of Woodrooff; Mary to Michael Cox of Castletown; Martha to Lorenzo Jephson of Wilmar and Elizabeth to Colonel Bernard of Castle Bernard, an M.P. for Co. Offaly.

There was a general election called in 1768 sometime prior to the death of Henry Prittie.[316] In the 1768 contest Henry promised his surplus votes to Thomas Mathew, of Thomastown and Annfield, conditional on a bond of £1,000. However, Henry did not demand payment on the bond after the election. When the next election occurred in 1776, Mathew assumed the understanding with Prittie would be binding on his son the 1st Lord Dunalley, but when approached the 1st Lord declared that he wished to stand singly and unconnected. At this stage Mathew promised to honour the bond. Prittie declined the offer, but conceded that Mathew would get half his surplus, the other half going to Daniel Toler. Prittie then contended that he was now freed from the bond. The result of the election was that both Prittie and Mathew were elected for the county with Prittie heading the poll. His success came about as a result of the widespread marriage alliances that were forged with the leading landowners of North Tipperary.[317] He represented the county from 1776-90 and was High Sheriff in 1770. He was decidedly not in favour of granting any relief to Catholics and like his father he was an ardent supporter of the rule of law.

With the re-emergence of considerable agrarian unrest, the American war of Independence and threatened French invasions Volunteer Corps were founded all over Ireland. In Tipperary, by 1782, there were eighteen functioning Volunteer corps. In the north of the county the leading gentry all had their own corps including Peter Holmes, Henry Prittie and Carden of Templemore.[318] Each corps was comprised of about forty rank and file members drawn from the head tenantry or from friends or associates of the colonel.

On the question of Catholic Relief, Prittie and Toler the M.P.s in the later decades of the century, took a hard line and when there was a movement for Catholic Relief in the early 1790s. Prittie, Toler and others

---

[316] From 1768-76 Henry Prittie of Kilboy, 1st Lord Dunalley was M.P. for Gowran.

[317] His brothers-in-law were Thomas Otway, Peter Holmes, Michael Head and Matthew Bunbury. His father-in-law, Francis Sadleir of Sopwell Hall and he had the support of the very influential Earl of Clanwilliam, one of the county's leading landowners.

[318] Stoney, Jocelyn, Toler and Parsons were also part of this group.

from the north of the county were reported to have been forcing their Catholic tenants to sign the Nenagh Address.[319]

However, the opposition was in vain as a major Catholic Relief Act was passed in 1793, which gave very many concessions to the Catholics. The passage of the Act was marked by celebrations in Tipperary and by expressions of thanks from local delegates and towns.

In contrast to his public stance Prittie got on well with his Catholic neighbours and a great friendship existed between the Catholic Carrol family of Lissenhall in North Tipperary and the Pritties. A story is told that this arose because Sir William, Carrol's father, deputized for the very young Henry Prittie (the second Lord Dunalley) in a duel with an English officer. In the course of the fight, which was fought with swords the tip of Carrol's sword was heard to hit metal, indicating that the Englishman was wearing armour under his clothes. Carrol's second muttered in Irish "Don't you know, sir, where Daly sticks the sheep in Tulla?" Carrol took the hint and stabbed his opponent in the neck, thus winning the duel.[320]

The Pritties were good neighbours to the Catholic Daltons of Grenanstown, near Nenagh. The Daltons had distinguished military service in the Austrian and German armies. Peter Dalton received the title of Count from the German Emperor. While they were absent from Ireland their landed interests appear to have been attended to by the Pritties. In 1796 Dalton wrote to Prittie of that 'mutual friendship that has so long existed between our families'.[321]

---

[319] In the last decade of the 18th century there was a nation-wide movement, in the form of the Catholic Committee, in which Tipperary played a significant role. There were representatives from Carrick, Clonmel, Cashel, Nenagh and Thurles on the county committee. The county delegates were Laurence Smith, a merchant from Carrick, James Scully of Kilfeacle and John Lalor of Long Orchard. In direct response to this and only a day after the delegates were selected the Protestant diaspora of the county held a meeting, in Nenagh, of gentry, freeholders and clergy that was very well attended. The meeting formulated an address to the two county M.P.s, John Bagwell and Daniel Toler instructing them to 'vigorously oppose all attempts at innovation or alteration in Church and State' and to support the constitution. – T. Power in *Land, Politics & Society in 18th century Tipperary*

[320] D. Murphy *The Two Tipperarys*
[321] T. Power Land, *Politics and Society in 18th century Tipperary.*

Traditionally the Pritties stood for the established order in church and state; a fact reflected in marriage patterns. However the marriage in 1802 of Henry Prittie (2nd Lord Dunalley) and Maria Trant, a family supportive of Catholic relief, was contemporaneous with a shift in the political stance of the family. The marriage of his brother, Francis A. Prittie, to Elizabeth Ponsonby consolidated this for the Ponsonbys were already married into the O'Callaghans, Lords Lismore, who also favoured relief. Given the position of prominence already established by the Pritties as political leaders of the northern gentry, this transition was a highly significant one for the landed class in the county as a whole.[322]

In the course of the 18th century the Pritties established direct marriage links with nine leading families: Sadlier, Harrison, Bunbury, Holmes, Otway, Head, Bayly, Meade, and Clutterbuck. Through them the Pritties became linked to about thirty other major and minor families in the north. These alliances formed the basis of a unified gentry and cohesive landed class in the northern part of the county. They served to elevate the Prittie family to a leadership position based on family ties and, by extension, command of freeholders, which were most numerous in the north before 1793. The marriage with the Meades, future earls of Clanwilliam, in 1736, was an important factor in extending this power base outside the north as it brought further freeholder support from a large estate in the south, a dimension consolidated by links with the Armstrong, Bradshaw, Chadwick, and Smithwick families via the Sadlier marriage.[323]

A Volunteer Bill in the House of Commons, in favour of parliamentary reform, was defeated but three Tipperary men voted for the bill. They were Prittie, Toler and Thomas Barton. As the passing of the bill would have meant the end of the boroughs it was opposed by O'Callaghan of Fethard, Moore of Clonmel and Pennefather of Cashel.

There was a general election held in 1806. Due to clerical manipulation the Catholic vote secured the election of Montague Mathew and Francis A. Prittie, the brother of the 1st Lord Dunalley, who had moved into the House of Lords. From this period on the Pritties, allied with the Mathew interest continued to be pro Catholic and more liberal in outlook.

---

[322] T. Power *Land, Politics & Society in 18th century Tipperary*
[323] Ibid.

The Pritties' liberal views may have been influenced by a tutor who was engaged to teach Francis Aldborough Prittie at Kilboy. He was Rev. Henry Fulton, the Church of Ireland curate to their parish, who was transported as a convicted United Irishman in 1798.[324]

When the 1st Lord Dunalley died in 1801 he was succeeded by his son Henry Sadleir Prittie who became the 2nd Lord Dunalley. Although married twice to Maria Trant and Emily Maude, the 2nd Lord had no children. He was very active in politics and worked with O'Connell to achieve Catholic Emancipation. The 2nd Lord Dunalley and Daniel O'Connell, the Liberator, were two of the first men to subscribe to having a monument erected to the Duke of Wellington, following the granting of Catholic Emancipation. The monument was to be erected 'in or near Dublin, commemorative of this the most glorious of his public services'. Henry Sadleir represented Carlow from 1797-1800. He supported the Union and his father was rewarded by being elevated to the Peerage. Henry Sadleir later represented Okehampton, Devon, as a Whig supporter from 1819-24.

Francis Aldborough Prittie was a very able man, whose son, Henry, by his second marriage, became the 3rd Lord Dunalley. Francis was an M.P. for Tipperary from 1806-12 and 1819-30. Prior to this he was M.P. for Doneraile in Cork in 1800 and for Carlow in 1801. His first wife was Martha or Maria Otway, the widow of George Hartpool[325] of Shrule Castle, Co. Laois, by whom he had a daughter.[326] His second wife was Elizabeth the daughter of the Hon. George Ponsonby, Lord Chancellor of Ireland. They had three sons and three daughters. The daughters were Mary, Hon. Catherine Charlotte and Hon. Frances Eliza. The last named married John

---

[324] This man's extraordinary story is told in *Renegade* by Marjorie Quarton.
[325] Barrington, the famous lawyer, wrote an account of the extraordinary life of George Harpole and his short marriage to Maria Otway. They were separated after less than eighteen months of marriage. She was Harpole's second wife. He had divorced his first wife, who stabbed him. He was insanely jealous of Maria and without proof of any infidelity on her part separated from her. He died of tuberculosis shortly afterwards. She married Prittie two years later but died in childbirth at the age of 23. For an extended notice of the Harpoles see pg. 211-213 of O'Nolan – *History of a People* by Art Kavanagh.
[326] Elizabeth Prittie married the Hon. Rev. Robert Maude

Bagwell of Marlfield in 1838 and her children inherited Marlfield. She died in 1901.

Francis Aldborough's second son, the Hon. George Ponsonby Prittie, married and had a family but only one of his daughters married and had a family. She was Florence who married W. Black from Scotland.

His third son, the Hon. Francis Sadleir Prittie of Glenview, Clonmel, became an Army Officer. He married an heiress, Mary Rose, and one of his daughters married Henry Irvine from Castle Irvine in Co. Fermanagh in 1862, and they had children.

Henry (b. 1807), the eldest son of Francis Aldborough, succeeded to the estates of the Pritties upon the death of his uncle, the 2nd Lord Dunalley, in 1854. He was a Deputy Lieutenant and High Sheriff of the county. He was married to Anne Maria the only daughter and heir of Cornelius O'Callaghan, Viscount Lismore.

Entrance Gate to Kilboy (courtesy I.A.A.)

His son, Henry O'Callaghan Prittie, a career Army Officer, succeeded to the title in 1885 as the 4th Baron. He was born in 1851 and was educated at Harrow and Trinity College, Cambridge. He was High Sheriff for Tipperary in 1883 and was Lieutenant for the county in 1905. He rose to the rank of Colonel in the 3rd Royal Irish Regiment. It was during his tenure that the successive Land Acts forced the gentry to sell their lands to the tenants. They were allowed to keep demesnes around their houses if they could prove that they could farm the lands productively.

Henry O'Callaghan Prittie was married to Mary, the daughter and heiress of Major General Farmer, and they had two sons and four daughters[327]. His eldest son, Henry Cornelius O'Callaghan Prittie, the 5th Baron, married Beatrix Graham, an heiress from Lanarkshire and they had two sons the eldest of whom was born in 1912. The 5th Baron was, like his father, an Army Officer and rose to the rank of Major in the Rifle Brigade. The 5th Baron's younger brother, Francis Reginald, a Captain in the Rifle Brigade, was killed in action in 1914.

Henry Cornelius O'Callaghan Prittie was also a distinguished author who wrote *Saddle & Steel* and *Khaki & Rifle Green*. He died in 1948.

His younger son, Terence Cornelius Farmer Prittie, was awarded an M.B.E. in 1946. Like his father he was an author. His book *South to Freedom* tells of his exploits as an escaped prisoner of war. Terence died in 1988 and left two sons, the eldest of whom, Oliver Allen, was twice married and has one son and three daughters.[328]

The eldest son, Henry Desmond Prittie, the 6th Baron, was born in 1912. He was educated at Stowe and R.M.C. Sandhurst. He served in World War II and afterwards in East Africa and the Far East. He retired in 1953 with the rank of Hon. Lieutenant Colonel. He was married to Mary Phillipa Carey the only daughter of Major Hon. Philip Carey. They had two sons and one daughter, the Hon. Mary Prittie who lives in Galway.[329]

---

[327] They were Maura, Kathleen, Mary and Irene who all died young.

[328] Dominic Terence (b. 1987), Jemma Victoria (b. 1975), Kinvara Louise (b. 1978) and Laura Zoe (b. 1989)

[329] The Hon. Mary is married and has one son Thomas Benjamin and three daughters, Flora Tasmine, Pollyanna Felicity and Lily Phillipa Joyce.

The younger son, the Hon. Michael Philip Prittie, educated at Stowe, now lives in Seattle in the U.S.A.

Henry Francis Cornelius Prittie, the 7th Baron, who was educated at Gordonstoun and Trinity College, Dublin, now lives in England. He is married to Sally Louise Vere and has one son, Joel Henry, and three daughters, Rebecca Louise, Hannah Beatrice and Rachel Sarah.

Ryan of Inch

While this short study deals with the Ryans of Inch only, it should be noted that Burkes Landed Gentry has notices of two families of Ryan in Tipperary, Ryans of Inch and Ryans of Ballymackeogh. The ancestor of the Ryans of Ballymackeogh, according to Burke, was William, whose son married a daughter of Colonel John Ewer in the later 1600s. These must be the same Ryans mentioned by the Earl of Cork who was seated at Lismore in the 1600s. He wrote in his diary that 'my cozen Wm. Ryan sent me a faier new yrish Harp which I sent to the Lord Keeper of England....'

No notice of an old Catholic Irish family would be complete without some macabre story being told concerning one of its members.

'Mr. Ryan was coming one night from Clonmel, on horseback accompanied by his servant. As they passed by Cashel they saw a light up in the Rock. Mr. Ryan determined to see what it was or what was going on, so he halted. He told the servant to come with him. The servant was afraid and refused to go but Mr. Ryan told him he would shoot him if he did not, so under pressure he agreed.

There was a huge woman in Cashel who made a practice of opening graves of aristocratic ladies after the burial, to rob them of their gold rings and other ornaments buried with them. When Mr. Ryan and his servant came to the door she struck him with a dead person's hand across the face. The terrified servant ran away. Mr. Ryan grappled with and overcame the woman. He took out his pistols, marched her to Cashel and gave her up to the authorities. She was hanged for the robberies, though, I suppose, the dead were not much concerned about the loss of the jewels.'[330]

A very strange case arose in connection with the estate of Daniel Ryan of Inch, the documented ancestor of the Ryans of Inch, who died in 1692. Pierce Purcell (of Loughmoe) had leased lands from John Ryan, who had inherited from his father Daniel. Purcell leased 'twenty messauges, thirty cottages, ten gardens, four orchards, 100 acres arable, 100 acres pasture and 100 acres meadow with their appurtenances, in the town and lands of Inchiefogurty'.

Purcell seems to have had sight of Daniel Ryan's will and on foot of that refused to pay the rents due. In the will, Daniel had left his estates to his wife Frances[331] for her lifetime. However the will also stated that if she got married again the estate would immediately pass to John Ryan, the eldest son. John contended that, in fact, she had married again, in secret, when he was away in England. He claimed she married a man called McCarthy and she had kept this a secret so that her claim to the estate would not be invalidated.

He went on to state that many witnesses knew she had been co-habiting with McCarthy[332] at Inch and in Dublin. Letters written to her had the name Mrs. Frances Ryan on the covers but the letters inside were to Mrs. Frances McCarthy. On his return from England, he had confronted her and she admitted to him she was married to McCarthy. McCarthy seems to have decided that he would have nothing more to do with Frances and she retracted her statement that she was married. John Ryan decided to bring a case against her but she declined to defend the case.

John said that Frances had married McCarthy in 1698. The Purcell side maintained that because the Ryans could not produce any witnesses to the marriage, no marriage had in fact taken place.

The matter was to be arbitrated on by Sir Stephen Rice and Sir Toby Butler.[333]

There is no record of what conclusion they arrived at but when Frances died in 1706 she mentioned only her son Joseph in her will.

---

[330] From the *Inch Papers*
[331] Frances was daughter of Patrick Ragget of Ballycormuck, Holycross, Co. Tipperary.
[332] He might have been a McCarthy of Spring House – comforting the widow!
[333] *Inch Papers*

Whatever the outcome, John Ryan was the recognised owner of the lands when he married in 1714. His wife was Mary, the daughter of Thomas Mathew[334] of Annfield.

What is most remarkable about the Ryans of Inch is that, by a quirk of fortune, they were able to survive the worst of the penal times, retain their lands and remain Catholic.[335]

There is not much known about the origins of the Ryans in Tipperary, except that sometime after the Norman invasion a small group arrived and settled in the western part of the county.[336]

Daniel Ryan of Inch was restored to his lands under the articles of Limerick or Galway (after 1690), as were Purcells in Loughmoe and Lord Dunboyne.

Following the death of his father, Daniel, in 1692, John Ryan inherited the lands in Inch parish, which had been purchased and assembled since 1668. These were further complemented by purchases in 1703. The total holding at that time was 3000 acres. John was highly regarded in Tipperary at this time. In 1705 he and James Butler were appointed commissioners for the plaintiffs in a case of thievery. This was a strange case, which had overtones of the Ryan versus Purcell case of the previous decade. A widow Shanahan married a man called Rawleigh and proceeded to take cattle, sheep, poultry and household goods away with her. She was prosecuted by her sons.

---

[334] See Mathew family in this book.

[335] After the proclamation of 1715, for the seizure of arms and horses belonging to Catholics, John Ryan was arrested and questioned, but released without charge. He was in fact imprisoned in Clonmel for several months and in a petition to the Privy Council he sought his release on the grounds that he was sickly and was no threat to the state. He offered security to the mayor of Clonmel for his future good behaviour.

[336] It is known that the Ryans of Idrone, in Carlow, a very strong and warlike sept, became the mortal enemies of Strongbow when they almost overcame his army in a battle near Tullow in 1171. Only for the action of a monk in Strongbow's service the Normans might have been completely overthrown. The monk killed O'Ryan, the leader of the attacking party with an arrow, and as was common practice in those days, the attackers withdrew when they suffered the loss of their leader. After that battle many of the O'Ryans left Carlow and headed west. It is thought that they settled in Tipperary. Art Kavanagh – *In the Shadow of Mount Leinster*

Having succeeded to the estates before 1700 John Ryan was unaffected by the penal legislation on succession and on his death in 1723 he left a single male heir, Daniel[337]. Daniel, who married Elizabeth, a daughter of Justin McCarthy of Spring House, had three sons, John, George and Denis and four daughters.[338] The two younger sons went abroad. George went to South America and Denis went into the military service in Austria.

When John inherited in 1767 there was no inquiry into his affairs. John, however, died without having a male heir and the estate passed to his brothers. A family arrangement was contrived so that George, in consideration of a payment to Denis,[339] inherited the entire estate.

John's will, on which all other Ryan wills seem to be based, is interesting in that he made it in 1774 but amended it somewhat in 1777 and 1778. He seems to have died shortly after that. In the will he left his wife £1000 and half the rents due for the year in which he died. He also left her all the household stuff, furniture ('my white knobbed bed which I would have remain in my house excepted'), her jewels, her watch and any plate he bought since his father's death. She was also to get one of his carriages and his draft horses and any two of his riding horses. He nominated George as his successor and stipulated that Denis was to receive £500. He left £10 to the poor of the parishes of Inch and Monroe. His stewart, Oliver Grace, was to be given a house and four acres. In a codicil to the will in 1777 he removed Oliver Grace from the will, as he had 'been well convinced of his bad behaviour towards me'. He did not nominate George as his executor 'as he is in foreign parts and out of this Kingdom and his return uncertain'.

The final will was made at Windsor and the only change was that he appointed Denis 'who is in the German service', as an executor.

When the penal laws on succession and inheritance were repealed in 1778 the Ryan estate was secure as a unit for the foreseeable future.

The Act of 1778, which gave an enormous measure of relief to the Catholics, was widely welcomed by the Catholics in Tipperary. The men

---

[337] By a strange quirk of fate Daniel married a daughter of Justin McCarthy of Spring House in 1737. Burke – *Landed Gentry*

[338] They were Margaret (m. Martin Harold of Cork), Mary (m. 1st Richard Harold and 2ndly James Nash), Frances (m. Walter Woulfe) and Elizabeth.

[339] An annuity of £100 per annum for life.

most associated with the carriage of the Act were Francis Mathew of Thomastown, Lord Clonmel (John Scott – a brother in law of Francis Mathew), Sir William Osborne and John Hely-Hutchinson. The main features of the Act were (1) the removal of the requirement that Catholic property had to be divided among the surviving sons. (2) Leases could now be given for more than 31 years. (3) The removal of the decree that a son who converted would get immediate possession making his parent a tenant for life only. The Act would only apply to people who took the oath of allegiance. In Tipperary county over 900 people took the oath. This number probably represented the vast majority of Catholic landowners in the county and included Archbishop Butler and many of his clergy. Denis and George Ryan took the oath.

In the last decade of the 18th century George Ryan played an active role in the promotion of Catholic Relief. There was a nation-wide movement, in the form of the Catholic Committee, in which Tipperary played a significant role. There were representatives from Carrick, Clonmel, Cashel, Nenagh and Thurles on the county committee. The county delegates were Laurence Smith, a merchant from Carrick, James Scully of Kilfeacle and John Lalor of Long Orchard.

A major Catholic Relief Act was passed in 1793, which gave very many concessions to the Catholics. The passage of the Act was marked by celebrations in Tipperary and by expressions of thanks from local delegates and towns.

When the entire country gave its vital support to O'Connell in his movement for Catholic Emancipation and for Repeal of the Union, Tipperary was very much to the fore in giving its financial support, which came mainly from the Catholics. In the Thurles area the Ryans of Inch and the Mahers of Turtulla were the most generous[340] and gave leadership by example.

George who inherited from his father John in the 1780s got married in 1783 to Mary Roche of Limerick[341] and they had four sons and two daughters. It was George who began the family tradition of trading internationally. He was in Lisbon in 1786, as we know from a letter

---

[340] Whelan in *Tipperary History & Society*
[341] He got a dowry of £5,000 from the Roches.

preserved in the Inch papers. The letter was written to him by a cousin, Justin McCarthy, of Spring House.

In 1785 George appointed James Fogarty to be his Seneschal or Stewart with the right to hold Courts Leets and Courts Baron in the Manor of Killnelongurty. These were minor law courts, which dealt with cases such as theft, trespass and default of payment of smaller fines.

The rents from the land in Inch grew significantly during the period from 1724 (£205) to 1818 (£19,700)[342]. This, combined with the Ryan commercial enterprise, ensured that the family retained considerable wealth for a long period.

George Ryan died in 1805 and was succeeded by his son George, who was the third son. His two older brothers, Daniel and Philip, both died about 1830 and neither married. Daniel was passed over as the successor because of his gambling. He was reported to have lost several townlands gambling in Dublin. They included lands bought by John Ryan from the Baron of Loughmoe and other townlands that he got with his wife Mary Mathew, namely Roskeen and Athshanbohy.[343] It is not known why Philip did not succeed. A fourth son, John Dennis, a career army officer, married an heiress, Elizabeth Lenigan of Castle Fogarty. His son Vivien inherited the Fogarty estates and took the surname of Ryan-Lenigan.

George was an able man and became a magistrate and a Deputy Lieutenant for the county. In 1811 he was involved in making sure that no blood was spilt in Thurles at the February fair. It would appear that the magistrates got wind of the word that a faction fight was to take place between the Caravats and the Shanavats.[344] George with Henry Langley

---

[342] T. Power in *Land, Politics and Society in 18th century Tipperary*.

[343] They were all redeemed by Stephen Grehan, his brother-in-law, of Rutland Square, Dublin. The Grehans held possession of the lands until the passing of the Land Purchase Act in 1885. Stephen was married to Margaret the eldest daughter of George Ryan. His second daughter, Elizabeth, m. Valentine Bennett of Thomastown House in Offaly. – *Burke's Irish Family Records*

[344] Faction fighting was fairly common in Tipperary at the time. In 1824 a Major Wilcocks gave evidence before a committee of the House of Commons. He mentioned a number of factions. In Owney and Arra the Ruskavallas fought the Coffees and the Dingens fought the Dawsons. The Ruskavallas were Murnanes. The Dingens were comprised of Kennedys, Ryans and Gleesons and took their name from a hill nearby. The Dawsons were comprised of Breens and Seymours, all from Duharrow, assisted by the Nenagh mob. The

took up weapons, which included two muskets, three fowling pieces, three swords and one ladle for melting lead.

At some stage during his lifetime George built a Catholic oratory beside his house at Inch. The Land Purchase Act was passed in 1885 and that meant the end of the way of life that the Ryans of Inch had enjoyed for two hundred years.

George, whose wife was Catherine, the daughter of Captain Edward Whyte of Co. Down, had four sons and two daughters. Two of his sons were unmarried. His second son married Florence Chester from Co. Louth. His two daughters married, Mary Frances to Power-Lalor of Long Orchard, and her sister to Whyte of Loughbrickland, Co. Down.

Mary Frances Power-Lalor was married in 1858 at the age of eighteen and she had two sons and five daughters. Despite having to cater for such a large household she found time to become deeply involved in charitable works. In 1879 she set up a Children's Fund. As a result of her appeal in all the major newspapers many thousand of American dollars were sent to Ireland enabling her to feed over 50,000 children who were threatened with starvation following the failure of the potato crop in 1879. Later in 1886 she organized the Distressed Ladies'Fund which succeeded in keeping many ladies of her own class above the poverty line. These were ladies whose annuities had disappeared when rents remained unpaid and estates were sold in the encumbered estates courts. She was also responsible for finding outlets for the lace and embroidery produced by some of those ladies.[345] She died in 1913.

George lived until 1884 and when he died he was succeeded by his son George Edward. George Edward was a J.P. in the Thurles area and he was High Sheriff of the county in 1878. His wife was the daughter of

---

cause of the tension between the Dingens and the Dawsons was that a woman named Seymour who was married to a Gleeson died. The Seymours wanted to bury her in their cemetery but the Gleesons did not. In the ensuing fight two men were killed. Another two factions were the Bootashees who were opposed by the Bogboys and the Tubbers. The Bootashees were O'Briens who lived in the area of Ballywilliam and Carrigtogher. They were called Bootashees because their leader wore leather boots and the rank and file wore leather straps around their legs. The Tubbers and Bogboys were Kennedys and Hogans who lived around Kilmore. Other groups were the Darrigs – Kellys – whose leader was red headed, and the Cumminses who lived around Toomevara.

[345] George Cunningham in *Moyne- Templtuohy, A Tipperary Parish*, Ed. By Wm. Hayes.

Sherlock of Stillorgan Castle, Co. Dublin. George, like many of the Inch Ryans, was educated at Stonyhurst. It fell to his lot to watch the passing of the way of life to which the Ryans had become accustomed since the time of Daniel Ryan in the late 1600s.

George Edward was married twice and the three children of his first marriage all died comparatively young and unmarried. His first wife died within four years of marriage (in 1878) and George Edward married again to Mary Power-Lalor of Blackrock, Co. Dublin. They had a son Richard Cecil and a daughter Mabel who died in her early twenties, unmarried.

George's (d.1884) other sons were Edward George, John[346] and Charles.[347] Edward George married an heiress, Florence Chester from Co. Louth, and had four sons and one daughter. His eldest son also called Edward George of Cartown Manor, Termonfeckin, Co. Louth, a Clongowes old boy, married Margarita McCurry from Belfast and he had one son and two daughters, one of whom, Veronica, lived in Stillorgan, Co. Dublin, in the mid 1900s.

The main branch continued through Richard Cecil. He was born in 1888 and educated at Stonyhurst. He joined the Royal Navy and served in the First World War. He retired as a Commander in 1929 but rejoined the forces to fight in World War II. He retired as Captain in 1945.

He married Kathleen Grehan of Banteer, Co. Cork and they had two sons, Richard Stephen and Arthur George. The latter, educated at Glenstal and Trinity College, Dublin, married Elizabeth Addison of Christchurch, New Zealand, and they have three sons and two daughters who were born in the 1960s.

Richard Stephen, who was educated at the Oratory and Trinity College in Dublin, joined the R.A.F. and served with distinction in World War II. He married Mary Wilford of Sussex and they have three daughters, Rosemary who married Michele Testa of Rome, Italy, Shelagh who married a Corsican, Joseph Gazano (they have a son Pierre) and Edwina who married Robert Dyson of Surrey.

---

[346] Died unmarried in 1884.

[347] A career Army Officer, Major Charles, who was educated at Stonyhurst, was the ancestor of a large number of descendants most of whom had very distinguished careers in the Army or, in the case of females, married Army officers.

Inch House has now passed out of the hands of the Ryan family.

Inch House in the mid 19th Century

Sadleir

One of the most extraordinary men to have ever emerged from Tipperary was John Sadleir. Described as 'the suicide banker' John was a financial wizard whose magic went sadly awry. He was the Nick Leeson of his time.

Clement Sadleir was married to Johanna, the sixth daughter of James Scully of Kilfeacle, in 1805.

Initially Johanna's hand was sought, not only by Sadleir, but also by a gentleman from County Limerick. James Scully himself favoured the Limerick suitor, but Johanna was more partial to Sadleir who, being a Tipperary man, was 'nearer to home'. James Scully gave a dowry of £2,500 with his daughter and promised a further £1000 in his will.

Clement and Johanna, who took up residence in Shronell House near Tipperary, had a family of five sons and two daughters. John was the fourth son. He was the man who made and lost a fortune in banking and eventually took his own life when his banking businesses collapsed in 1856.[348]

Banking may have been in his blood as James Scully, Sadleir's grandfather, established a bank in Tipperary town in 1803. Some years prior to this he had leased property from the Smith Barry estate and one of those houses became the location of the Scully Bank.

Legislation was passed in 1821, which allowed the establishment of Joint Stock Banks with more than six partners. This spelled the end of private banks and so Scully's bank was closed in 1827.

---

[348] Marnane: *Land and Violence – A History of West Tipperary from 1660* and O'Shea, *Prince of Swindlers*

MR. JOHN SADLEIR, M.P. FOR CARLOW.

John Sadleir, raised a Catholic by his Scully mother, had become a lawyer and in 1838 he founded the Tipperary Joint Stock Bank with James Scully, his uncle, as Chairman. He was educated at Clongowes College and succeeded an uncle in a prosperous solicitor's practice in Dublin. Sadleir and Scully opened the bank in the premises where the old Scully bank had operated and benefited immediately from the solid reputation that business had enjoyed.

The bank prospered and by 1845 there were nine branches in operation in Tipperary, Clonmel, Carrick-on-Suir, Nenagh, Roscrea, Thurles, Thomastown (Co. Kilkenny), Athy and Carlow. In 1842 the headquarters of the bank moved to Clonmel.

Following the death of James Scully in 1847, James Sadleir, John's brother, was installed as managing director of the Joint Stock Bank. James later became an M.P. for Tipperary. James lived with his wife and family at Clonacody, near Fethard.

John himself began to cast his net wider. He was elected M.P. for Carlow and moved to London. From his base there he began financing railway developments in countries as far afield as Sweden,[349] France and Italy. He was appointed chairman of the London and County Joint Stock Banking Company in 1848 and remained in that post until his death.

A.M. Sullivan described John at the zenith of his career in the following way: "The repute of his wealth, the extent of his influence, above all the worship of his success, was on every lip. Whatever he took in hand succeeded; whatever he touched turned to gold. He was, everyone said, one of your eminently practical politicians; no mere agitator, but a man of sagacity and prudence, whose name alone guaranteed the soundness of a scheme or the wisdom of a suggestion, He was a decided Liberal and an ardent Catholic and very soon made his mark among the Irish members."

He became more politically active as time progressed. When in 1851 the Whig government proposed legislation to undermine the Vatican's plan to reorganize the Catholic Church in England, Sadleir and William Keogh leaped to the defence of their religion and voted against the

---

[349] He was Chairman of the Royal Swedish Railway Company.

legislation, bringing their supporters with them. This was the start of an independent Irish opposition.[350] Sadleir was very involved in setting up the Catholic Defence Association of Great Britain and Ireland in the same year.

The following year John Sadleir founded his own newspaper in Dublin entitled *The Weekly Telegraph*.

After the general election of 1852 the M.P.s elected to represent tenant rights met in Dublin. Sadleir and Keogh joined them and they pledged to remain independent of the government, which didn't have a majority in the House.

When the Conservative government fell in December of that year they were replaced by a Liberal government. Under this administration Sadleir and Keogh were offered posts, which they accepted. Keogh was made Solicitor General of Ireland and Sadleir was made Lord of the Treasury.

In the election of 1855 John Sadleir lost his seat by a mere six votes. However in a by-election in Sligo in July he was elected M.P. Allegations of political misbehavior surfaced later when it was made known that Sadleir had used the pressure of the Joint Stock Bank in Carlow to influence some of the 208 electors in the constituency. He was forced to resign his seat.

His business affairs seemed to be prospering. In the course of the previous decade he had bought lands, under the Encumbered Estates Act, to the tune of some quarter of a million pound.[351] One of the estates he had purchased was the Cahir estate of the Earl of Glengall whose heir sold it to Sadleir for £68,000.

With the connivance of James, his brother, the Tipperary Bank gave the impression of being a flourishing business. They paid a dividend of six per cent, a point or two higher than their competitors. English shareholders had been encouraged to put their assets in the bank. False bookkeeping showed reserves of £17,000. But behind the outward show there was deceit and criminal intent.

His need for money compelled him to forge shares in some of the companies with which he was involved such as the Royal Swedish Railway

---

[350] The party became known as 'the Pope's brass band' and 'the Irish Brigade'.
[351] Marnane: *Land and Violence – A History of West Tipperary from 1660*

Company. He was forced to borrow from the Tipperary Bank at an increasing rate.

On the 13th February 1856 the London agents of the Tipperary Bank refused to honour drafts of the Tipperary bank. By Saturday the 16th February John Sadleir knew the game was up. He wrote a letter of grief and remorse to his cousin Robert Keating M.P. and on the following morning his body was found on Hampstead Heath. A silver cream jug and a half consumed bottle of poison were found beside the body.

When the whole story was unraveled it transpired that John Sadleir's own overdraft had climbed to £250,000. The Royal Swedish Railway Company had been defrauded of £300,000 by forging shares and the Bank of Ireland lost £122,000

This is a copy of the letter he sent to Robert Keating." To what infamy I have come step-by-step – heaping crime upon crime – and now I find myself the author of numberless crimes of a diabolical character and the cause of ruin and misery and disgrace to thousands – ay, to tens of thousands. Oh how I feel for those on whom all this ruin must fall! I could bear all punishments but I could never bear to witness the sufferings of those on whom I have brought such ruin. It must be better that I should not live. No one has been privy to my crimes-they sprung from my own cursed brain alone. I have swindled and deceived without the knowledge of any one."

Then after some directions as to his affairs he concluded his letter.

"Oh, that I had never quitted Ireland! Oh, that l had resisted the first attempts to launch me into speculations. If I had had less talents of a worthless kind and more firmness I might have remained, as I once was, honest and truthful-and I would have lived to see my dear father and mother in their old age. I weep and weep now, but what can that avail?"

The losses arising from the crash of Sadleir's Bank amounted to some £400,000. The depositors of the Tipperary branch lost £70,000. It took a long time to unravel the affairs of the bank. At the end of the day the depositors got back forty per cent of what they had deposited.[352] A large number of Scullys lost considerable amounts.

---

[352] These were mainly small farmers, clerks and tradesmen who had been tricked into depositing their money in the bank with the promise of high interest rates.

The Nation (Dublin) described Sadleir at the time of his death as a sallow faced man 'wrinkled with multifarious intrigue, cold, callous and cunning'. A bachelor he had few expensive habits except for a small stud of horses he kept at Watford to hunt with the Gunnersbury hounds. The character of Mr. Merdle in Dickens's *Little Dorrit* was, according to the author, shaped out of 'that precious rascality' John Sadleir.[353]

James Sadleir, the manager, was forced to flee from Ireland. An M.P., he was expelled from the House of Commons in 1857. He lived the rest of his life in Zurich supported by his wife's family. He was murdered there in 1881.

There appears to have been two separate families of Sadleir in Tipperary. Thomas Sadleir, a Colonel in Cromwell's Army was the ancestor of the Sadleirs of Sopwell Hall and Castletown in Tipperary. At various times in the 1650s Colonel Sadleir was governor of Wexford and of Galway. While he was in Galway he was given the task of looking after the priests who were in prisons in Ireland. He received £100 from the government to move them to Inishboffin and build cabins there for them. The Colonel was allotted lands in Tipperary in lieu of his pay. He probably bought up debentures too, as did his fellow officers. By the end of the 17th century he had over 5,000 acres of land.

His great grandson, Francis Sadleir of Sopwell Hall, had no son and he cut off the entail to the family lands, as he had no liking for his cousin Thomas of Castletown. When he died in 1797 his estates were divided between his two daughters who were married to the son of the 1st Lord Ashtown (a Trench of Galway) and Henry Prittie of Kilboy.

This family was represented thereafter by the family of Castletown.

The other Sadleir family in Tipperary was descended from John Sadleir, an adventurer, who did not come to Ireland until the 1660s, when his lands had been secured under the Act of Settlement. According to accounts of this family in Marnane's *Land & Violence in West Tipperary* this Sadleir family was from Stratford-on-Avon and was related to the Shakespeare family. They were business people. Shakespeare's children were called after their godparents Hamnet and Judith Sadler.

---

[353] *The Dictionary of National Biography.*

Sopwell Hall (courtesy I.A.A.)

According to Prendergast in the Cromwellian Settlement of Ireland a John Sadler received 100 acres of land in Offaly in the barony of Garrycastle where the Irish owner, Mrs. Mary Coughlan, refused to be ejected. Prendergast does not elaborate on the outcome but if that John Sadler is the same man as the Tipperary John Sadleir then it would seem that he was compensated in some way for his loss in Offaly by being given lands in Tipperary. The only other Sadleir mentioned in Prendergast is Colonel Thomas of the Sopwell Hall dynasty.

Clement Sadleir was the third son of John Sadleir of Ballintemple who was married to Grace the daughter of William Chadwick of Ballinard. They had seven sons but only three of them produced sons from whom descended the Sadleirs of more modern times. They were Clement of Shronell, Nicholas of Golden Garden and Sadeir's Wells and Richard of Holycross and Scalaheen.

Clement of Shronell had a son William who seems to have died in the early 1790s, and it was his son, Clement, who married Johanna Scully as noted above. John 'the Banker' was the great grandson of Clement of

Shronell. James, the brother of John 'the Banker', was the last of that particular line and he was killed, as we have seen, in 1881 in Switzerland.

The descendants of Nicholas Sadleir of Golden Garden were his son Richard who died in 1823, his grandson Richard (d.1834), and his great grandson Richard of Sadleir's Wells who died in 1877.[354]

It was the Scalaheen branch that survived into modern times, the last of the family, Marshal, of Brookville, dying in 1964. Marshal was the fifth generation descended from Richard, the brother of Clement of Shronell.

Clement Sadleir, the ancestor of the Shronell family, and great grandfather of John 'the Banker', was a middleman who rented about 700 acres from the Damer estate. The lease was renewed in 1791 by William, Clement's son and in 1820 the leases were again renewed for three lives, from Lady Caroline Damer, by Clement, the father of John 'the Banker'.

The lives of the various Sadleirs before and after that of John 'the Banker' do not appear to have been in any way extraordinary and none of them appear to have been politically active or overly ambitious.

---

[354] The Sadleirs had many other sons and daughters but only the eldest sons are mentioned in the abbreviated family tree used for this article.

Scully

William Scully from Ballynaclough, near Golden in Co. Tipperary, was an extraordinary man by any standards. He was the man who instigated the Battle of Ballycohey, which occurred on August 14th 1868.

He was a brother of Vincent Scully of Castle Park, Cashel, who owned almost 6000 acres of land. William himself owned over 1300 acres and another relative, Francis, was M.P. for Tipperary before, during and after the Famine. Vincent Scully was an M.P. for Cork from 1852 when he was elected in a by-election. The Scullys were an old respected Catholic family and seem to have originated from Mantlehill and Kilfeacle where they built a Catholic Chapel.

The Scullys have been described as comprising part of the Catholic Gentry, which included the Butlers of Cahir and Kilcash, the McCarthys of Springhouse, the Mandevilles of Ballydine, the Ryans of Inch, the Mathews of Thurles and the Fogartys of Castlefogarty.[355]

William Scully was an adventurous man who had emigrated to America in his youth and made a large fortune during the Civil War there.[356] When he came back to Ireland he began to invest in land.

He was no stranger to conflict and confrontation. In 1849 he was tried in the Clonmel Assizes for shooting two sons of a tenant named Bergin. He was acquitted. Shortly after that he went to America.

---

[355] K. Whelan in *Tipperary History & Society* pg. 216

[356] He made his money in land speculation. In 1850-51 he bought over 30,000 acres for less than a dollar an acre from veterans of the Mexican War. Most of the capital was borrowed from his brother Thomas. He sold less than 4000 acres in 1857 for almost $40,000 – Marnane A *History of West Tipperary from 1660*

On his return he resumed his old ways and in 1865 he was again before the courts. On this occasion he was charged with wounding a woman. It seems he broke into the house of a tenant called Teahen, at night, in order to serve notice to quit or indeed to seize the 110-acre property, as the lease had expired. In the resulting commotion he injured Mrs. Teahen. In the Kilkenny Assizes he was found guilty of wounding and sentenced to twelve months hard labour. He never served the sentence, as the landlord class was reluctant to press for the incarceration of one of its own kind.

In 1866 lands became available at Ballycohey[357] (about 510 acres in all) and he bought the estate from Charles Grey, the Earl of Derby's agent for £12,000[358]

He made up his mind that he was going to clear the land of tenants and turn the estate into a ranch for cattle raising. At this time there were thirty tenants on the land with holdings ranging from fifty acres down to one. In order to accomplish this he drew up a set of conditions, which he knew would be unacceptable to the tenants. All the rents were increased. Rent was to be paid quarterly in advance. Tenants were to quit their holdings at one month's notice, which would be handed to them or posted on their farms. Tenants were to pay all poor rates and any other taxes and there would be no compensation should they be ordered to quit, not even for crops in the ground.

In the summer of 1868 Scully waited in Dobbyn's Hotel in Tipperary for his tenants to come to pay the rents and sign the new contracts. He was armed and under police protection. Unlike most landlords Scully was a hands-on person. His tenants came. They paid the rent but no person signed the new contract.

On August 11th 1868 Sheehy duly organised his agent, Darby Gorman, to accompany him on his mission of serving notices on the tenants. They were met by a big hostile crowd, that prevented him from serving any notices, and he was obliged to retreat and go back to Tipperary.

Three days later on the 14th he set out again with Gorman, Meagher who was a herdsman, and some policemen to serve the notices by force.

---

[357] About six miles north of Tipperary.

[358] These lands were part of the old Damer estate and were leased by relatives of William Scully. When the lease expired it was put up for sale by the 3rd Lord Portarlington who had inherited the Damer estate.

Again they were met by the same large hostile crowd and were compelled to retreat towards the railway station at Limerick Junction.

On the way Scully noticed that the house of Pat O'Dwyer seemed to be unprotected and he resolved to serve a notice on the tenants there. He rushed the house with Gorman, Maher, and a policeman called Morrow. They were met by a hail of bullets. Gorman and Morrow fell to the ground. Morrow was killed instantly and Gorman, though he recovered was never again able to speak. Scully and Meagher were wounded but were able to get back to the shelter of the gatepost outside. From there Scully began firing on the house with his shotgun and revolver. He was joined by the head constable and sub constable Culleton. Though wounded Scully resolved to rush the house again. He was joined by the two policemen. As they entered the house they were fired upon again and Culleton was shot and wounded. Scully was wounded yet again. The defending party escaped through a hole in the thatch and was never apprehended. It was said that they escaped to America. Scully escaped death because he was wearing a coat of mail under his clothes.

The shocking news of the events at Ballycohey stunned everyone, including the landlords of Tipperary. The story was reported in many newspapers and questions were asked in the House of Parliament.

Undeterred by his notoriety Scully sought to organise the serving of notices once more but the magistrates forbade either bailiffs or police to accompany him.

Stephen Moore of Moorsfort stepped in at this stage and offered to buy the land from Scully. Realising that he would never be able to achieve his ambition of turning the estate into a ranch Scully sold the lands.

This amazing man concentrated his energies on his American lands after the Ballycohey disaster. His incomes from his various holdings in both Ireland and America returned over £12,000 annually. He continued to buy land in America and by 1888 his holdings in the four states of Illinois, Kansas, Nebraska and Missouri totaled almost a quarter of a million acres of land. This made him the most extensive landowner in America. He entrusted the management of his American properties to his illegitimate son John, who was born in 1849.

He still owned over 3,000 acres of land in Ireland in 1875, half of which was in Co. Tipperary.

William Scully married his first wife, a Sweetman of Dublin, in 1851 and they had three daughters. She died in 1861. He married again in 1876[359] and had three sons and a daughter from this union. He had homes in London and Washington D.C. where he eventually settled down in the last decade of the century. He became an American citizen in 1900. At about this time he transferred his Irish property to his son Thomas.

He died in 1906, in his London home, at the age of eighty-five. In his will he left all his property to his wife and disinherited his daughters by his first marriage.

The remarkable Scully family descended from a Jeremiah Scully who was born in 1645 in either Longford or Offaly. He settled with his brother Roger near Cashel after the restoration of Charles II. Jeremiah married a daughter of Roger Ryan of Kilnemanagh and they had nine sons and two daughters. The second son, Roger of Kilfeacle, was the ancestor of the Scullys of Kilfeacle and Mantle Hill.

Roger, in 1734, married Mary, a daughter of Gilbert Maher of Tullamaine Castle and they had seven sons and ten daughters. In this article we will be dealing with the descendants of his eldest son, James, only.[360]

James married Catherine, a daughter of Denis Lyons of Croom House, Limerick in 1760[361] and they had six sons and six daughters. Five of the daughters were married, one of them to a Frenchman, Jean Bernard Pasquet of Bordeaux. The others married Sausse, Keating, Mahon and Sadleir.[362]

James Scully was a diarist and for the years 1775 to 1790 he recorded that the business and financial affairs in the country at large were deteriorating. There were poor prices for stock and a low demand for beef in the years 1775, 1777 and 1782. In 1776 there was very bad weather, which led to a scarcity of hay and loss of livestock. In 1784 there was poor

---

[359] This lady is simply called Chynoweth in Burkes Landed Gentry.

[360] His other sons were Edmund of Cashel, Jeremiah of Silverfort, William of Dually, Timothy, Roger and Patrick of Carrick-on-Suir. Most of them married and had families some of whom became Army Officers. The females married into such families as the Ryans, Meaghers, Moores and Colles.

[361] He received a dowry of £500 from the Lyons family.

[362] James was able to pay a dowry of £2,000 when his daughter Anne married Thomas Mahon in 1791.

demand for cattle at fairs and to cap it all there were bank failures in Cork in 1779 and 1784. But when matters improved after 1790 his diary entries were more optimistic – in 1790 he wrote ' a great prospect of a good season next year for butter, beef, sheep and wool', and in 1791 'land seems high in demand now owing to two good seasons'.

Entrance Gate to a Scully Mansion (completely gone) at Golden

While not politically active he was very much to the fore in promoting the Catholic cause. In the last decade of the 18th century there was a nation-wide movement, in the form of the Catholic Committee, in which Tipperary played a significant role. There were representatives from Carrick, Clonmel, Cashel, Nenagh and Thurles on the county committee. The county delegates were Laurence Smith, a merchant from Carrick, James Scully of Kilfeacle and John Lalor of Long Orchard.

James had the honour and the distinction of being the first Catholic in the county to be chosen as a Justice of the Peace, following the passage of the 1793 Catholic Relief bill. He was also made a magistrate at the behest of John Bagwell M.P.

In 1798 James Scully of Kilfeacle described in his diary that 16th July was a busy night for what he termed "Defenders". He referred to a report of Defenders attacking Tipperary town on that night and how three days later three of the leaders were hanged and beheaded at Cashel. He made other references in his diary to the growing boldness of the Defenders. On 23rd March about ten of them arrived at his house in Kilfeacle and demanded arms. They were given a gun, a case of pistols and a sword. Scully reported them behaving in a very civil manner and departing without fuss. However they came again a month later at about one o'clock in the morning but were refused arms this time. They then smashed some windows and fired one shot. Scully explained that there was no return fire because he was not prepared.[363]

Clement Sadleir was married to Johanna, the sixth daughter of James Scully of Kilfeacle, in 1805. Initially Johanna's hand was sought not only by Sadleir but also by a gentleman from County Limerick. Scully himself favoured the Limerick man but Johanna was more partial to Sadleir who was 'nearer to home'. Sadleir received £2,500 of a dowry with a promise of a further £1000 on James Scully's death.

Clement and Johanna had a family of five sons and two daughters. John was the fourth son. He was the man who made and lost a fortune in banking and eventually took his own life when his banking businesses collapsed in 1856.[364]

Banking may have been in his blood as James Scully, Sadleir's grandfather established a bank in Tipperary town in 1803. Some years prior to this he had leased property from the Smith Barry estate and one of those houses became the location of the Bank. James was joined in the enterprise

---

[363] In a totally unrelated report he wrote about a major fire in Tipperary town in April when one hundred and thirteen houses near the church were burned. He mentioned that 'many poor people were greatly distressed'. Marnane in *A history of West Tipperary from 1660*
[364] Ibid.

by his third son, James. When James senior died, Denys his second son became a partner.[365]

There is a story told about how James overcame a run on his bank by sitting outside on the street surrounded by butter firkins which were apparently filled with golden guineas and ready to meet every demand. By this show of confidence in his ability to pay he restored the faith of his customers.[366]

Sometime around 1810 James Scully, who was the head tenant of the Mathew estate of Thomastown, bought land to the value of £33,200 from them and thus became one of the landed gentry of Tipperary.

Mantlehill, a large Georgian residence, was built by James Scully around 1815 and this became the main family residence from then on. When the Clanwilliam (Meade)[367] estate was being sold James Scully bought out his own tenancy and that of others for the sum of £19,380. James, a J.P., died in 1816 and his wife died two years later.

Of his family of seven sons, James, the third son, of Shanballymore and Tipperary, was the man who outlived his siblings.

James of Shanballymore was a very prominent Catholic in Tipperary and when he died in 1847 his Death Notice recognised his achievements. It mentioned that he was the only surviving son of James Scully of Kilfeacle House and that he was the co-founder, with his father of the Joint Stock Bank. It noted that he was a Grand Juror for the county and after 1829 (Catholic Emancipation) he was a Peace Commissioner and a senior Magistrate. It went on to say 'As long as the name of the late James Scully is remembered it will be associated with all those recollections of generosity, high-mindedness, independence and sterling principle which through his life marked his character.'[368]

---

[365] The eldest son Roger may have been an invalid. He is seldom mentioned. He died unmarried in 1797 at the age of 25. His fourth son, William was an M.D. in Torquay. He married Margaret Roe of Rockwell. They had no family.

[366] Marnane in *A history of West Tipperary from 1660*

[367] Sir John Meade was made Earl of Clanwilliam in 1766. He had estates in Cork, Kilkenny and Down (in the right of his wife) as well as Tipperary. He was an absentee.

[368] James of Shanballymore had three sons – James of Shanballymore, a J.P. who was married twice and who died in 1878 leaving a family, John a Resident Magistrate and a Captain in the 80th Regiment and Francis an M.P. for Tipperary from 1847 to 1857.

After the death of James in 1847, James Sadleir, his nephew, became the managing director of the Bank in Tipperary. James Sadleir's brother John (who eventually broke the Bank) had gone to London to make his fortune. In the general election of that year John Sadleir got himself elected as M.P. for Carlow. His cousin Robert Keating was elected as an M.P. for Waterford County as a Repealer. Francis Scully was also elected for Tipperary on the same ticket. In 1852 they were joined by James Sadleir for Tipperary and Vincent Scully for Cork County. All five men, who were in Westminster together, were grandsons of James Scully senior of Kilfeacle.

Edmund Scully of Tipperary town, the 5th son of James of Kilfeacle, reminded the reluctant repeal M.P. for Tipperary, Thomas Wyse, a member of the Catholic Association, that ' a member for our county is obliged to act in the house (of commons) to please the people with a forward determined bold tone on all questions regarding Ireland'[369] Edmund, a Justice of the Peace, was a member of the Relief Committee of Middlethird barony which was convened in January 1847, to discuss how monies were to be allocated so that work could be provided for the poor. The meeting was chaired by Sir John Judkin Fitzgerald[370] and others attending were William Despard and Colonel Palliser, both also J.P.s, and Protestant and Catholic clergy. Edmund, though married, died without having any family in 1839.

Denys, the second son of James of Kilfeacle, inherited most of his property and resided at Kilfeacle and Mantle Hill. Denys was a Barrister-at-Law who is best remembered for his book *Statement of the Penal Laws*. He was also the father of the amazing man, William Scully, whose career has already been detailed above. Denys, too, was a shareholder in the Bank in Tipperary, when he replaced his father on the board after that man's death in 1816. Denys himself died in 1830. He was married twice and both his wives were English women. His first wife died in 1806 and his second wife outlived him, dying in 1843. His first wife had no children but he had five sons and three daughters, two of whom became nuns. The other daughter married a Spanish Grandee, Prince Antonio Publicola Santa Croce.

---

[369] Wyse Papers N.L.I.
[370] Sir John, of Lisheen, was the son of the infamous Sir Thomas Judkin Fitzgerald, Sheriff of the county in 1798, whose cruelty and high-handedness led to his being indicted.

His eldest son James was murdered in 1842. These are the details surrounding the incident: At about 5 o'clock on the afternoon of Saturday 26th November, 1842, James Scully, who was thirty three and unmarried, left Kilfeacle House with his youngest brother William (of Ballycohey notoriety) in order to shoot some duck on a nearby pond. Within a short time William returned home because his feet became wet or perhaps because his gun had jammed (both reasons are mentioned in newspaper accounts). When his brother failed to return home, William became alarmed and notified the police at Bansha. The previous April, the Scully home had been fired into and James had been slightly wounded in the face. In 1835, James Scully had returned to Kilfeacle from a period spent out of Ireland and began to manage the family property. Some of his actions ran counter to the wishes of a number of his tenants, especially his dealings with the Griffith family. Ever since the attack of April, James Scully had taken precautions, so naturally when he failed to return home that November evening in 1842 the alarm was raised. A search was made of the area near the pond but, as it was dark, Scully's body was not found for some hours. He had been shot and his face and head battered possibly with the stock of his gun.[371]

Following the murder there was a meeting of the magistrates who wrote to Dublin requesting the introduction of sterner measures of law enforcement. A £2,000 reward was offered for information, half of which was contributed by the Scully family but to no avail. Three people were arrested including a chief suspect called Griffith, but they were never charged.

According to some accounts James Scully of Golden, was murdered because of the high-handed way he treated his tenants. He had evicted a woman about to give birth. The child was born on a dunghill as the woman looked at the flames consuming her home. Scully was educated in England and spent a long time there. He was castigated by a Catholic priest for his bearing and hauteur which was offensive and anti national.[372]

---

[371] Marnane in *A history of West Tipperary from 1660*
[372] The Nation 8th April 1843

With the death of James Scully, his brother, Vincent, was the senior member of the family and he gave evidence to refute speculation that competition for land was the cause of his brother's death.

Vincent was also a shareholder in the ill-fated Tipperary Joint-Stock bank, though not at all involved in the management. He seems to have had misgivings about the enterprise as he decided to dispose of his shares in 1856. Unfortunately for Vincent his paperwork had not been completed by the time the crash occurred so that he was held responsible along with the other shareholders.

On the fateful day in February 1856 when it became clear that the Bank had a problem people congregated in Tipperary trying to get their money from the bank. James Scully of Shanballymore, a shareholder and brother of Francis Scully M.P., went to the bank and personally guaranteed about £2,000 worth of deposit receipts in an effort to restore credibility.

As a result of the crash Vincent Scully lost about £8,000. The family of James Scully of Shanballymore (Sadleir's uncle) who held shares inherited from their father lost a huge amount of money. James, the eldest son, lost £20,000.

Apart from James and William, Vincent had two other brothers. They were Rodolph and Thomas Joseph. Rodolph married the daughter of a sculptor called John Graham Lough and they had four sons, the youngest of whom, Thomas Vincent (a Barrister born in 1857), married his first cousin, Rosa, a daughter of Vincent. Thomas Joseph died unmarried in 1857.

Vincent an M.P. for Cork 1852-57 and 1865-69 had a home in Merrion Square in addition to Mantle Hill. He married Susanna Grogan, a sister of Sir Edward Grogan of Dublin in 1841. They had one son, Vincent and three daughters, one of whom became a nun, Rosa mentioned above, and Catherine who died unmarried. Vincent senior died in 1871.

His son Vincent, a graduate of Christ Church, Oxford, became a J.P. and a Deputy Lieutenant for the county (a very prestigious post). He married a Waterford lady Emma Barron, and he had two surviving sons and three daughters. The sons were Denis Vincent and Vincent Marcus, while the girls were named Katherine, Manella and Louise.

War and Humanity– The Story of Patrick Grubb (North Africa 1941), based on an account written by Alexander Grubb.

The war in North Africa is unique in that is was the only time that a genuine attempt was made to abide by the Hague Convention as far as prisoners were concerned. Essentially this proposed the proper care of prisoners and where possible to have repatriation exchanges of the wounded. North Africa was a unique theatre. It was largely an uninhabited desert and where there was habitation, the native Arab population portrayed a kind of " neutral indifference" to the protagonists. Therefore this theatre was amenable to the implementation of the 1900 agreement's central philosophy: "to serve the interests of humanity and civilization".

Patrick Grubb (the author's grandfather), joined his father's regiment, the Kings Own Third Hussars in 1938. A family tradition was established because the Hussars were based in Fermoy and Cahir during the 1890s. His father, Raymond, had just retired as commanding officer of the regiment when Patrick joined.

Along with the officers and men of his regiment, he left the UK for Egypt on 22nd August 1940. They saw their first action in Mersa Matrah, fighting as the Seventh Armoured Brigade under General O' Connor. On the 9th of September they began their push against the Italians, covering a distance of almost 500 miles. This resulted in the capture 130,000 prisoners, 400 tanks and 1,290 guns. The Third Hussars in Buk Buk killed 52 Italians and captured 42,000. They finally cut off the Italians in the first week of February 1941, South of Benghazi at Breda Fomm. Following this rout Churchill withdrew most of O'Connor's army for redeployed action in Greece.

233

"Soon after we began to notice the arrival on the scene of German aircraft" (probably ME103s), but even at that point they did not "think that a major attack was imminent". What they didn't realise was that the inefficient Italians were now reinforced by the infamous Afrika Korps, led by Erwin Rommel. Also, they were completely ignorant as to the extent of the superior German force that was amassing against them. German panzers completely outgunned and out armoured the British forces, which were now mainly equipped with Italian M13 medium tanks and Lancia trucks salvaged from the rout at Breda Fomm. Following a series of sustained attacks they "began a near headlong retreat", finishing for Patrick Grubb, on the morning of April 7th near the aerodrome just East of Derna. There the column was suddenly cut off by German forces which had taken the hard way around the mountainous Jebel Akhdar, exactly as the British had done with the Italians in the opposite direction a few months previously.

Patrick recounts that "almost immediately machine gun bullets tore through the windscreen of the Lancia truck" in which he was a front seat passenger. Hit in the upper body through one lung, he fell out of the cab. His Sergeant, Murfin, was unable to haul him back in, himself being then hit in the arm. Instead he fell into a drain ditch at the side of the road and lay there for the whole day, "mostly in a state of unconsciousness". The fighting in the immediate area moved back and forth, the main part of the German unit having pressed on into Derna where they ran straight into General O'Connor and General Neame. A fellow officer, Lt. Heseltine, in the course of the action saw a wounded or dead officer by the road, and following a quick examination of him, presumed him dead. (Heseltine didn't realise his error until 1995 when he and Grubb corresponded).

It was not until evening that the area had been secured by the German forces and a passing patrol found Patrick Grubb to be still alive. He was immediately taken to a captured Australian dressing station where some emergency surgery was performed. Next day, he and other wounded were taken to the aerodrome to be loaded on board Italian transport aircraft. Immediately after being loaded the aerodrome was attacked by the RAF and the Italians abandoned everyone until the next morning. (Many of the wounded died overnight.)

Following this the wounded were flown to Benghazi, now over two hundred miles behind the lines. In the recent action a senior German officer had also been wounded in the lung and the head of the German medical service, Professor Giesel, had flown the 400 miles from Tripoli to attend to this man. Seeing Patrick Grubb's condition, he had him put on his aircraft and took him back to Tripoli. Meanwhile Patrick Grubb had been reported dead by his regiment and so it would remain for several weeks. The Professor operated on his wound and he gradually became stronger. Speaking some German, having been on military exchange before the war, he was able to persuade one of the ward orderlies, Gunter Swanthaler, to send a telegram to his parents who lived in neutral Ireland.

It was then determined that he would have to go to a clinic in Germany and he was put along with others on a ship to Naples. When the German officer in charge went to make the rail transport arrangements, the wounded prisoners were seized by the Italian authorities, eventually ending up in a military hospital in Piacentza. It was noted by my Grandfather that in "no way was he badly treated". The food served to them was of a higher quality than what the Italian ranks got themselves. Also following an agreement with the Red Cross from both sides, he was given a certain amount of pay that enabled him to get cigarettes and even clothes from the local village. Also to help them was a smartly uniformed Italian Captain, who had spent a year in London and was "surprisingly pro-British".

After several more operations, Patrick Grubb and the rest of the wounded prisoners were placed under the auspices of the Vatican and the Swiss Red Cross. Later they were sent by rail to Bari in Southern Italy and put on a hospital ship which took them to Izmir in Turkey. There they were exchanged for a similar number of Italian prisoners and sent back through the Suez Canal and around the Cape eventually arriving back in the UK in the autumn of 1941 – where Patrick served out the remainder of the war as a training instructor.

Unfortunately, Professor Giesel was not to survive and correspondences between his wife and Grubb's family in Ireland, following the war, demonstrated the very harsh conditions that faced the survivors.

This is a remarkable story of survival, dependent entirely on a level of goodwill exhibited by both sets of combatants in the spirit of the Hague Convention.

Sadleir, 88, 141, 197, 198, 199, 202,
   203, 215, 217, 218, 219, 220, 221,
   226, 228, 230, 232
   Clement, 215, 228
   Col. Thomas, 220
   Francis, 220
   James, 217
   John, 66, 215, 217, 218, 219, 230
   Marshal, 222
   Nicholas, 222
   Richard, 222
Salle
   Anne, 138
Sandhurst, 39, 120, 204
Sandy
   Captain, 103
Sankey, 109
Santa Croce., 230
Sausse, 226
Scalaheen, 221, 222
Scotland, 203
Scott, 38, 64, 143, 146, 210
   Sir Walter, 188
Scully, 22, 105, 146, 200, 210, 215, 217,
   221, 223, 224, 225, 226, 228, 229,
   231, 232
   Chynoweth, 226
   Denys, 229, 230
   Edmund, 230
   Francis, 230
   Francis M.P., 232
   James, 227, 228
   James son of Denys, 231
   Johanna, 228
   Roger, 226
   Vincent, 232
   William, 226
Seattle, 205
Seymour, 212
Shakespeare, 220
Shanahan, 208
Shanavats, 211

Shanbally, 18, 19, 160, 161, 162, 165,
   166
Shanballymore, 229, 232
Shanghai, 37
Shanrahan, 19, 167
Shaw, 16, 26, 35, 102
Sheehy, 17, 18, 19, 22, 62, 150, 155,
   163, 164, 224
   Fr. Nicholas, 16
Shelly, 146
Sherlock, 213
Sherwill, 154
Shetland Islands, 90
Shinrone, 74
Shronell, 80, 81, 84, 215, 221, 222
Sinclair, 37
Sladen, 37
Slattery, 17
Slieveardagh, 111, 113, 114, 115, 182,
   187, 188, 189
Sligo, 137, 218
Smith, 22, 66, 80, 86, 105, 153, 200,
   210, 215, 227, 228
Smithwick, 70, 201
Smyth, 146
Somerset, 26, 79, 194
Somme, 41
Sommerton, 156, 157
Sopwell Hall, 220
Sorrento, 166
South Africa, 38, 97, 107, 192
St. George, 190
Staples, 34
Steel
   Anthony, 158
Steer, 38
Stillorgan Castle, 213
Stirling, 36
Stonyhurst, 213
Stourbridge, 196
Stowe, 158, 204, 205
Strabane, 37
Stradbally, 122

Chateau